ATLAS
OF THE
MIDDLE EAST

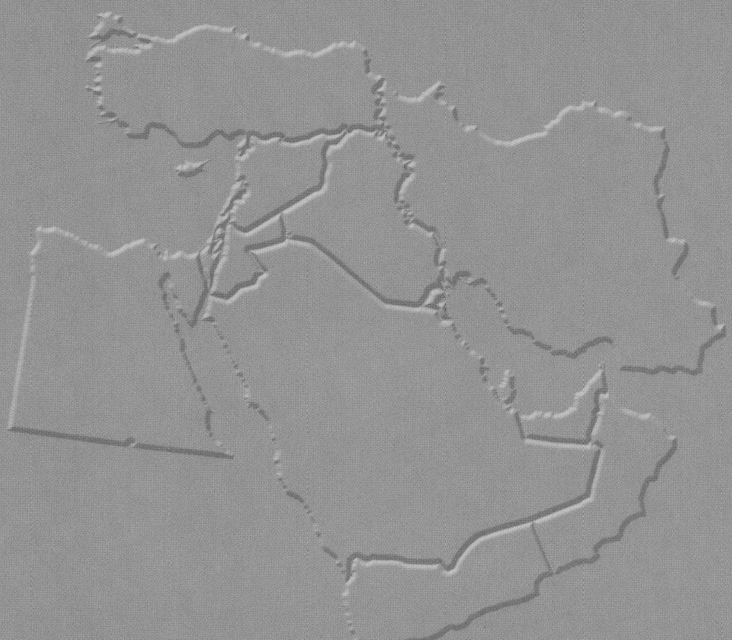

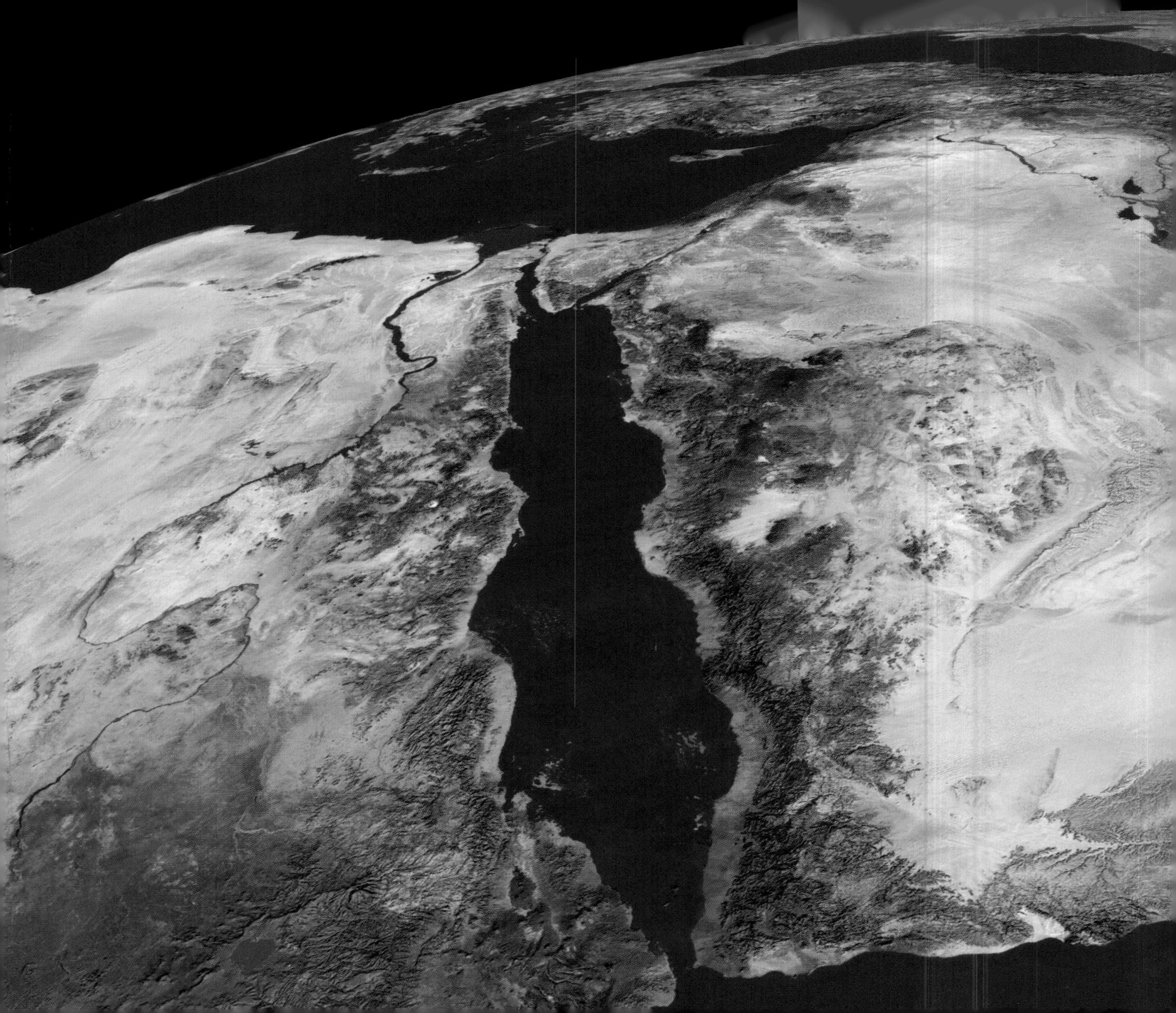

ATLAS OF THE MIDDLE EAST

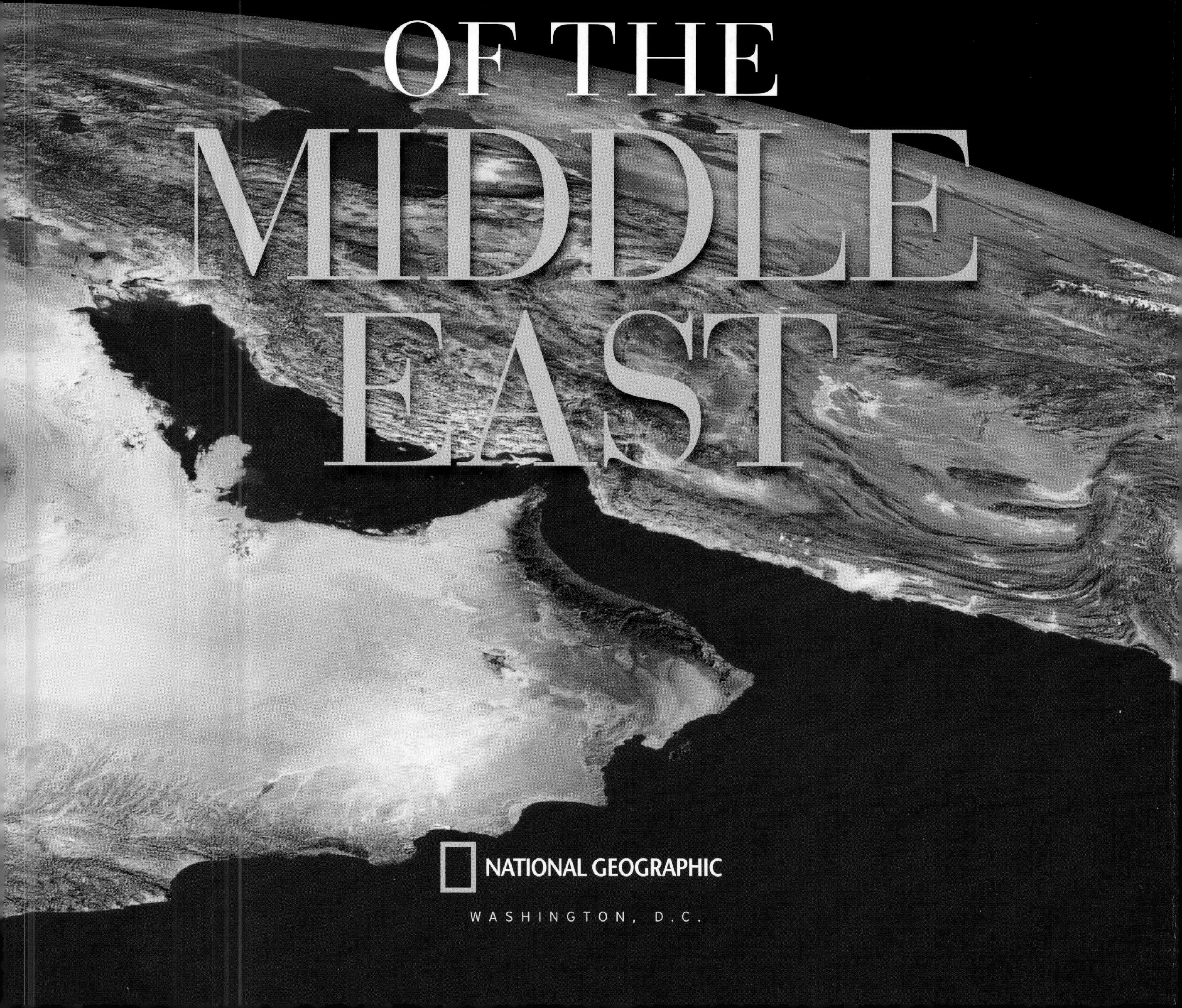

NATIONAL GEOGRAPHIC
WASHINGTON, D.C.

OPPOSITE: Morning breaks in Istanbul, Turkey, lifting the veil of night from the dome and slender minarets of the Blue Mosque. Built by Sultan Ahmed I (1590-1617), the 17th-century mosque gets its name from the richly colored tiles that adorn its interior.

Shifting Sands

BY JOHN M. FAHEY, JR.

SILENT WITNESS to 5,000 years of history, the Sphinx keeps watch near Chephren's Pyramid at Giza, Egypt.

FIXING THE MIDDLE EAST WITH INK ON PAPER is like reviewing a play in the middle of the second act. So volatile is the region, so unpredictable its continuing drama, that we can only set the stage and name the players. The ending—what will ultimately happen to political borders, resources, governments, and peoples—is yet to be written. The only current certainty is that events here will profoundly affect the rest of the world. In these pivotal times, we have designed this atlas of the Middle East to help you fit the pieces into place as the drama unfolds.

A dramatic role is not new for the Middle East, which sits at the crossroads of three continents—Africa, Europe, and Asia. Civilization itself is rooted in its river valleys—the Jordan, Euphrates, and Nile. The three great monotheistic faiths—Judaism, Christianity, and Islam—call it the Holy Land. And 65 percent of the world's oil reserves come from the Middle East, giving it political clout far beyond that of its individual states.

No other area on Earth provokes such fury and fervor, or cradles so many human aspirations, as the Middle East. No other has riveted our attention to its affairs almost daily for more than half a century, ever since the United Nations adopted a plan calling for the partition of Palestine into two states. The hostility engendered between Israelis and Palestinians continues to this day, periodically erupting to turn the Jewish state into a virtual fortress and calcifying intolerance in both camps. The fate of Iraq, once an oil-prosperous and progressive nation, is as lethal an issue and may reverberate as powerfully in the coming decade.

For struggling Middle Eastern governments as well as the West, radical Islamic movements have brought increasing apprehension, even dread, to an already uncertain future. These

Islamists are split into two factions—nationalists, whose goal has been the overthrow of what they consider corrupt and "heretical" regimes, and globalists such as the shadowy leaders of al-Qaeda, whose goal is to hijack both Islam and the Arab world into a jihad against modernity and its most formidable practitioner, the United States. The globalists have been routed from Afghanistan and many are in hiding, but they keep the world awake at night.

Another continuing challenge for the nations of the Middle East is to become full partners in the global economic community without sacrificing cultural values. Iran, for example, wavers between its reformist politicians and conservative mullahs. Saudi Arabia's royal family simultaneously attempts to satisfy Western obligations and keep the loyalty of its masses. Turkey metaphorically straddles its own geography, embracing both European ideals and its Islamic heritage.

Beyond the political turmoil, the Middle East faces a deep, long-term demographic crisis. Its population nearly quadrupled from 81 million in 1950 to an estimated 309 million at the beginning of the 21st century. Almost half of its people are 18 or younger. But in the Middle East, feeding these burgeoning numbers is a struggle; most of the largely desert region's meager freshwater resources are rivers and aquifers that cross international boundaries and provoke quarrels. For decades agriculture has endured drought, soil degradation, erosion, and pollution. Millions of people have fled the land into cities—Cairo, Beirut, Damascus, Tehran—whose infrastructures, schools, and social institutions are overwhelmed, and whose economies cannot begin to provide meaningful jobs. Even in the region's oil-producing states, the population explosion has severely diluted per capita oil revenues, which are less than a quarter of what they were in 1980.

STRETCHING to the horizon, the main oil pipeline of Saudi Arabia carries the lifeblood of the kingdom's economy.

Many Middle Easterners feel under siege, yet today's flood of global communications, difficult to censor, has given them new perspectives on the larger world as well as their own place within it. The Torah, the Bible, and the Koran may still speak to their hearts, but the Internet, satellite television, and videos now link them to a torrent of facts and opinions that cut across religious, cultural, and national lines. Even the gap between opportunities for men and women is diminishing as the region takes stock of its needs.

An 11th-century Shiite poet, lamenting the savagery of the Crusades, concluded that the world was not divided between Christians, Jews, and Muslims, but between people who believe and people who think. The task of the Middle East today is to determine how to do both well. The task of this atlas is to help you make sense of this tumultuous region's past, the challenges of its present, and the possibilities of its future.

A Land Caught in a Vortex

By Priit J. Vesilind

Gilbert Hovey Grosvenor, the venerable Editor of National Geographic magazine from 1903 to 1954, grew up in the vibrant, culturally unsettling city of Constantinople, today's Istanbul. They were the declining years of the Ottoman Empire, and young Grosvenor in the former capital city was bombarded with the Babel of tongues and cultures. "His nurse was an Armenian," wrote Maynard Owen Williams, chief of the magazine's Foreign Editorial Staff. "Kurdish porters toiled up the cobbled paths carrying provisions to his home. Albanians, Bulgarians and Greeks were his classmates."

Williams might well have added Arabs, Lebanese, Jews, Persians, Azeri, and Englishmen to the mix. "East is East and West is West," wrote Rudyard Kipling, "and never the twain shall meet." He was wrong. The twain met in the Middle East, a region that has served as a cultural stew and commercial suq for some three thousand years.

The Middle East is a land of nuance and subtlety: The obvious will always have a caveat; the clear-cut often takes on softer edges. The nomenclature itself is problematic. Before the New World was known or considered part of recognized civilization, geographers used terminology that was logical to people living in the huge world-island of Eurasia. "East" was the eastern shores of that world-island, "West" was its western parts. In between were the Urals to the north, and the lands of the eastern Mediterranean to the south, today's Middle East.

DURING A pilgrimage to Mecca, or hajj, Muslims visit the Sacred Mosque and circle the Kaaba, Islam's holiest shrine.

The region is known as the Middle East in the English language because to Europeans the "Far East" was India, China, and Japan; the nations of the eastern Mediterranean, beyond Greece, were considered midway there. The term Orient simply means East in Latin. "Levant," meaning the coastal shelf of the eastern Mediterranean, was from the Italian word, *levanti*, the "rising" of the sun. "Near East" was used to speak of the Ottoman Empire of the 14th to 20th centuries, which extended as far north as the European Balkans.

The people of the Middle East have never seen themselves as halfway to anything, but

rather in the center of it all. Jewish, Christian, and Muslim believers alike place the Garden of Eden and the fields of Cain on the Harran Plain near the Turkish-Syrian border. Nearly 5,000 years ago, in the fertile valleys of the Tigris and Euphrates Rivers, in today's Iraq, people called Sumerians first harvested a surplus of grain, enabling others among them to develop skills other than food production. Thus the first civilization begat its artisans, craftsmen, and merchants, and learned to build cities, conduct commerce, and record history on clay tablets.

From here, the tools and techniques of civilization spread in a Fertile Crescent from Anatolia, today's Turkey, through Syria and into Egypt. While Europeans still lived in rough huts in the forest, the Middle East threw up elaborate empires such as Mesopotamia, Babylonia, Assyria, and Persia. It raised gilded cities with temples and terraces, irrigation systems and highways. It produced legal codes, calendars, coinage, and postal systems, allowed the rise of bureaucrats, scribes, and scholars. It was already ancient 300 years before the birth of Christ.

The definition of "Middle East" is surely not unanimous among scholars,

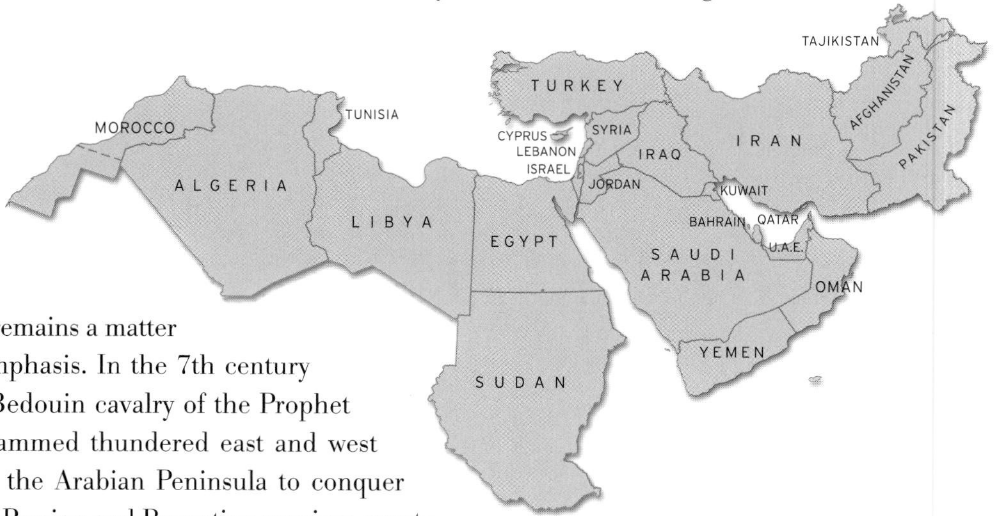

and remains a matter of emphasis. In the 7th century the Bedouin cavalry of the Prophet Mohammed thundered east and west from the Arabian Peninsula to conquer both Persian and Byzantine empires, creating an Arab Empire from southern France to India. Today the single unifying factor of the Middle East remains Islam, with its Arab roots. Half of the population speaks Arabic, and more than 90 percent of Middle Easterners are followers of the Prophet. Thus, while the geographic "middle east" only extends from Egypt to Iran, and Turkey to Yemen (opposite), the cultural Middle East (above) stretches across Moorish North Africa to Morocco.

THE BROADER definition of the Middle East is used in a cultural sense to describe lands in southwest Asia and northeast Africa that are predominantly Islamic. The remaining states in north Africa and Afghanistan and Pakistan are among these.

This atlas concentrates on the geographic Middle East, the nations and political entities that occupy the crucible of cultures between three continents. It is divided into three main sections: Nations, Regional Themes, and History. The Nations section devotes a full two-page spread to every nation-state and political unit. The format allows us to focus in unprecedented large scale on small political entities such as Qatar, Kuwait, Bahrain, and the United Arab Emirates. Israel, for example, a thin north-south sliver of land no larger than the northern peninsula of Michigan, is printed sideways across both pages to reveal critical details such as the farmland surrounding the Sea of Galilee. An entirely separate spread telescopes in on the Israeli-occupied Palestinian territories, showing the stricken villages of the Gaza Strip.

City maps of Baghdad, Jerusalem, Cairo, Damascus, Beirut, and Tehran take us into the streets, place us on intimate terms with the urban landscape as current events unfold. Because the region has been so dynamic, we have carefully re-researched changes in place names, using diacritical marks to show how they are pronounced in their native languages. We have added roads and settlements, the locations of oil fields and pipelines.

The Regional Themes section begins with a remarkable satellite composite image of the entire physical area, revealing the twisted mountain chains and desert expanses whose desolation has pushed populations into urban centers. The Black and Caspian Seas, the Mediterranean, the Persian Gulf, and the Red Sea are the highways that marine commerce, from Phoenician galleys to Arab dhows, followed to the marketplaces of the near world. Conversely, they provide easy access to visitors and invaders alike, and they also serve as natural insulation between ethnic and cultural groups.

THE FOCUS of the territory depicted on the map above is what is more commonly termed the "Middle East." The pages of maps and graphs that follow, reflect this treatment.

Following the mosaic are maps that begin to layer the political and physical maps with deeper insight. Using a variety of graphs, pie charts, and brilliant photographs, each page-spread tackles a different issue. Two show the region's most critical resources: oil and freshwater reserves. Others demonstrate the blessings and limiting effects of climate. Another reveals the population explosion that's made the Middle East the world's fastest-growing area. Some outline ethnic distribution, the spread of religion, the paths and extent of the *aliyah*, the ingathering, the Jewish migration to Israel. Finally, they come to grips with the uncertain economic future by outlining such indicators as fertility, life expectancy, and poverty rates. Other maps and spreads explore economic factors such as imports, exports, and gross per capita domestic products.

The History section highlights the remains of ancient empires and grand civilizations, including World Heritage Sites. Time-lapse maps show the regional conflicts and origin of today's nation-states. Finally, a four-page time line illustrates the dynamic, often terrifying modern history of the Middle East, from 1900 through the current crises in Israel and Iraq.

We kept these sections on hold until the last possible print deadline, in order to include fresh information. In the months and years ahead we hope this volume will serve as your companion to understanding.

90°
180°
150°
120°
90°
60°
30°
Longitude West of Greenwich
A R C T I C
ARCTIC CIRCLE
60°
NORTH AMERICA
NORTH
NORTH
30°
PACIFIC
TROPIC OF CANCER
ATLANTIC
OCEAN
OCEAN
A
0°
EQUATOR
SOUTH AMERICA
SOUTH
TROPIC OF CAPRICORN
ATLANTIC
30°
SOUTH PACIFIC
OCEAN
OCEAN
60°
A N T A R
90°
180°
150°
120°
90°
60°
30°

30° 60° 90° 120° 150° 180° 90°
Longitude East of Greenwich
OCEAN
ARCTIC CIRCLE
60°
EUROPE
ASIA
NORTH PACIFIC OCEAN
30°
GEORGIA
AZERB.
Caspian Sea
BULG.
Black Sea
TURKMEN.
GREECE
TURKEY
Mediterranean Sea
CYPRUS
SYRIA
LEB.
ISRAEL
IRAQ
IRAN
AFGHAN.
PAKISTAN
JORDAN
KUWAIT
BAHRAIN
QATAR
LIBYA
EGYPT
SAUDI ARABIA
UNITED ARAB EMIRATES
OMAN
Red Sea
YEMEN
Gulf of Aden
ARABIAN SEA
SUDAN
AFRICA
TROPIC OF CANCER
PHILIPPINE SEA
SOUTH CHINA SEA
EQUATOR
0°
INDIAN OCEAN
AUSTRALIA
TROPIC OF CAPRICORN
30°
ANTARCTIC CIRCLE
60°
ANTARCTICA
Winkel Tripel Projection
SCALE 1:96,361,000
1 CENTIMETER = 963 KILOMETERS; 1 INCH = 1521 MILES AT THE EQUATOR
0 500 1000 1500 2000 2500
KILOMETERS
0 500 1000 1500 2000 2500
STATUTE MILES
30° 60° 90° 120° 150° 180° 90°

The Middle East in The World

NATIONS

LEFT TO RIGHT: Iraqi soldiers training in Baghdad following the 1990 invasion of Kuwait; The flags of Turkey (white on red), and the self-declared Turkish Republic of Northern Cyprus (red on white), hanging outside the headquarters of the National Unity Party in northern Cyprus; PLO leader Yasser Arafat, Jordan's King Hussein, U.S. President Bill Clinton, and Israeli Prime Minister Benjamin Netanyahu during a peace summit at the White House in October, 1996; An off-duty Israeli soldier and two Orthodox Jews using public telephones in Jerusalem; The Blue Mosque in Istanbul, Turkey; Palestinian youths take cover behind a sheet of corrugated iron during a clash with police in the Gaza Strip.

POLICE

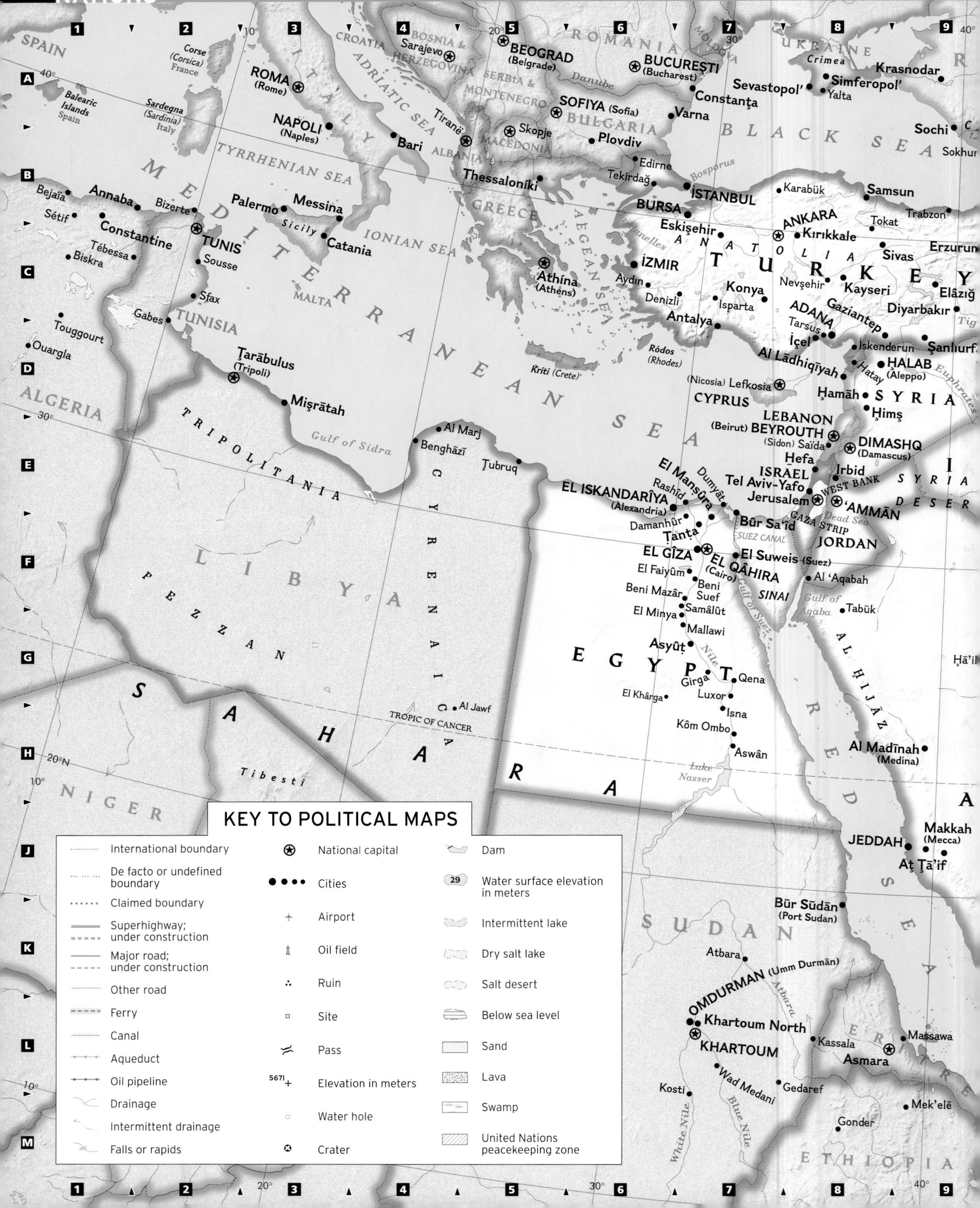
SPAIN
Corse (Corsica) France
Balearic Islands Spain
Sardegna (Sardinia) Italy
ROMA (Rome)
NAPOLI (Naples)
Bari
ITALY
CROATIA
BOSNIA & HERZEGOVINA
Sarajevo
ADRIATIC SEA
BEOGRAD (Belgrade)
SERBIA & MONTENEGRO
ROMANIA
BUCUREŞTI (Bucharest)
Danube
MOLDOVA
UKRAINE
Crimea
Sevastopol'
Simferopol'
Yalta
Krasnodar
Constanţa
Varna
SOFIYA (Sofia)
BULGARIA
Skopje
MACEDONIA
Tiranë
ALBANIA
Plovdiv
BLACK SEA
Sochi
Sokhumi
Edirne
Tekirdağ
Bosporus
İSTANBUL
Karabük
Samsun
Trabzon
TYRRHENIAN SEA
Thessaloníki
GREECE
BURSA
Eskişehir
ANKARA
Kırıkkale
Tokat
Sivas
Erzurum
MEDITERRANEAN SEA
Bejaïa
Annaba
Bizerte
Palermo
Messina
Sicily
Catania
IONIAN SEA
Sétif
Constantine
TUNIS
Tébessa
Biskra
Sousse
Sfax
MALTA
Gabes
TUNISIA
Touggourt
Ouargla
ALGERIA
Athína (Athens)
AEGEAN SEA
Dardanelles
İZMIR
Aydın
Denizli
ANATOLIA
TURKEY
Konya
Isparta
Nevşehir
Kayseri
Elâzığ
Diyarbakır
Gaziantep
ADANA
Tarsus
İçel
Antalya
İskenderun
Şanlıurfa
Hatay
HALAB (Aleppo)
Euphrates
Ródos (Rhodes)
Kríti (Crete)
Al Lādhiqīyah
Ţarābulus (Tripoli)
Mişrātah
Gulf of Sidra
(Nicosia) Lefkosia
CYPRUS
Ḩamāh
Ḩimş
SYRIA
LEBANON
(Beirut) BEYROUTH
(Sidon) Saïda
DIMASHQ (Damascus)
Hefa
ISRAEL
Tel Aviv-Yafo
Irbid
WEST BANK
Jerusalem
'AMMĀN
Dead Sea
GAZA STRIP
JORDAN
SYRIAN DESERT
Al Marj
Benghāzī
Ţubruq
TRIPOLITANIA
CYRENAICA
LIBYA
FEZZAN
El Manşûra
Dumyât
Rashîd
EL ISKANDARÎYA (Alexandria)
Damanhûr
Ţanţa
Bûr Sa'îd
SUEZ CANAL
EL GÎZA
EL QÂHIRA (Cairo)
El Suweis (Suez)
El Faiyûm
Beni Suef
Beni Mazâr
SINAI
Al 'Aqabah
Gulf of Aqaba
Tabūk
El Minya
Samâlût
Mallawi
Gulf of Suez
Asyûţ
Nile
EGYPT
Girga
Qena
El Khârga
Luxor
Isna
Kôm Ombo
Aswân
Lake Nasser
AL HIJAZ
Ḩā'il
RED SEA
Al Madīnah (Medina)
SAHARA
Al Jawf
TROPIC OF CANCER
Tibesti
NIGER
JEDDAH
Makkah (Mecca)
Aţ Ţā'if
Būr Sūdān (Port Sudan)
SUDAN
Atbara
OMDURMAN (Umm Durmān)
Khartoum North
KHARTOUM
Kassala
Massawa
ERITREA
Asmara
Wad Medani
Gedaref
Kosti
White Nile
Blue Nile
Mek'elē
Gonder
ETHIOPIA
KEY TO POLITICAL MAPS
International boundary
De facto or undefined boundary
Claimed boundary
Superhighway; under construction
Major road; under construction
Other road
Ferry
Canal
Aqueduct
Oil pipeline
Drainage
Intermittent drainage
Falls or rapids
National capital
Cities
Airport
Oil field
Ruin
Site
Pass
5671 Elevation in meters
Water hole
Crater
Dam
29 Water surface elevation in meters
Intermittent lake
Dry salt lake
Salt desert
Below sea level
Sand
Lava
Swamp
United Nations peacekeeping zone

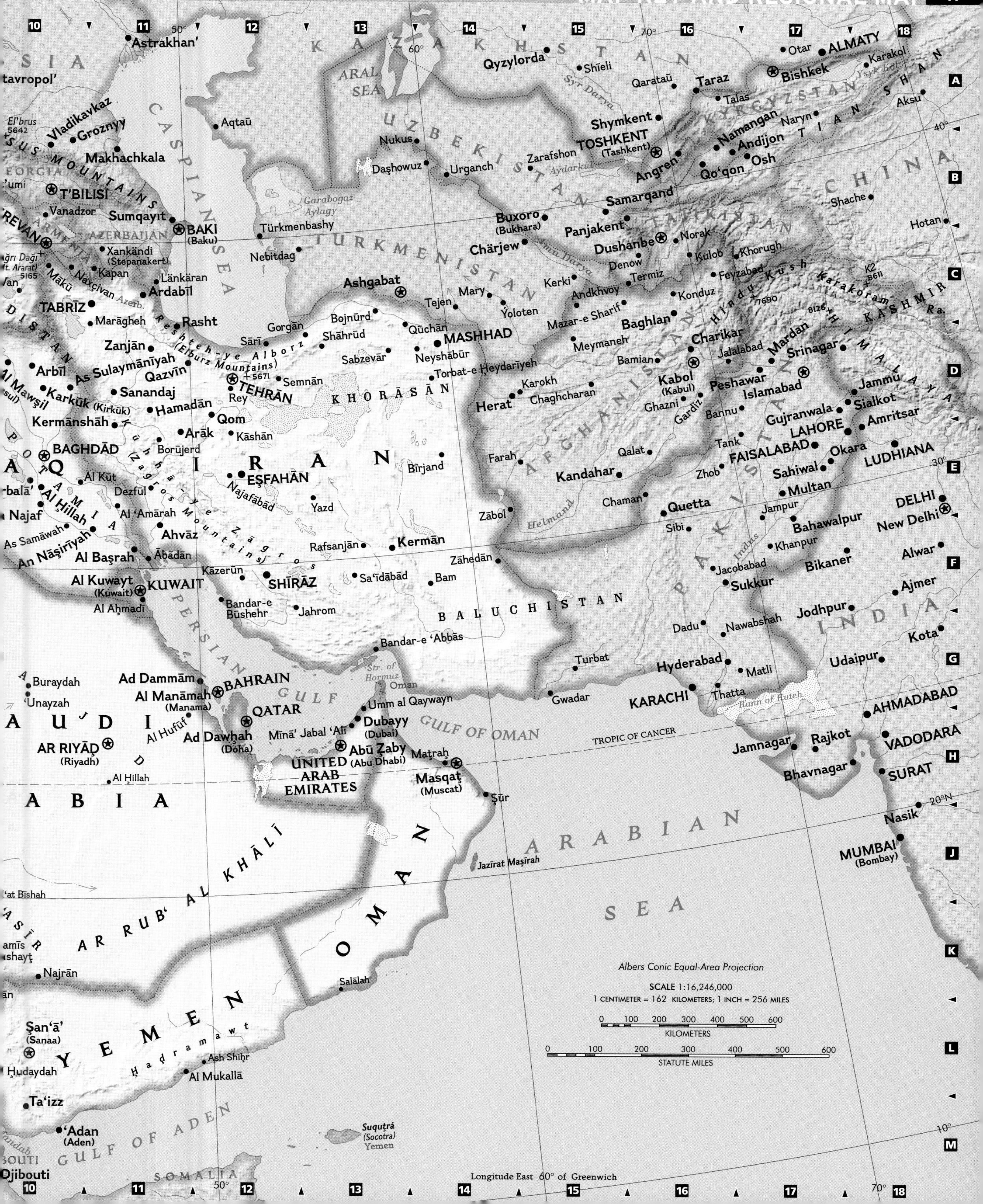

10
11
12
13
14
15
16
17
18
Astrakhan'
K A Z A K H S T A N
ARAL SEA
Qyzylorda
Shīeli
Otar
ALMATY
Karakol
Ysyk Köl
Bishkek
Taraz
Qarataū
Talas
Syr Darya
K Y R G Y Z S T A N
T I A N S H A N
Aksu
tavropol'
C A S P I A N S E A
Aqtaū
El'brus 5642
Vladikavkaz
Groznyy
Makhachkala
U Z B E K I S T A N
Nukus
Dashowuz
Urganch
Zarafshon
Aydarkul
TOSHKENT (Tashkent)
Shymkent
Namangan
Andijon
Naryn
Angren
Qo'qon
Osh
C H I N A
Shache
Hotan
T'BILISI
Vanadzor
Sumqayit
BAKI (Baku)
AZERBAIJAN
ARMENIA
Garabogaz Aylagy
Türkmenbashy
Buxoro (Bukhara)
Samarqand
Panjakent
TAJIKISTAN
Dushanbe
Norak
T U R K M E N I S T A N
Chärjew
Amu Darya
Nebitdag
Xankändi (Stepanakert)
Kapan
Länkäran
Ardabīl
Naxçivan
Azerb.
Mākū
Ashgabat
Tejen
Mary
Yoloten
Kerki
Andkhvoy
Termiz
Denow
Kulob
Khorugh
Feyzabad
Konduz
H i n d u K u s h
7690
K2 8611
K a r a k o r a m R a.
K A S H M I R
TABRĪZ
Marāgheh
Rasht
Gorgān
Bojnūrd
Shāhrūd
Qūchān
MASHHAD
Mazar-e Sharif
Baghlan
Charikar
Jalalabad
Mardan
Srinagar
8126
H I M A L A Y A
Zanjān
Reshteh-ye Alborz (Elburz Mountains)
Sārī
Sabzevār
Neyshābūr
Meymaneh
Bamian
Arbīl
As Sulaymānīyah
Qazvīn
+5671
TEHRĀN
Semnān
Torbat-e Heydarīyeh
Kabol (Kabul)
Peshawar
Islamabad
Jammu
Karkūk (Kirkūk)
Sanandaj
Rey
K H O R Ā S Ā N
Karokh
Chaghcharan
Herat
Ghazni
Gardīz
Bannu
Sialkot
Gujranwala
Amritsar
Kermānshāh
Hamadān
Qom
Kāshān
Arāk
LAHORE
BAGHDĀD
Borūjerd
I R A N
Bīrjand
Farah
Qalat
A F G H A N I S T A N
Tank
FAISALABAD
Okara
LUDHIANA
Al Kūt
Dezfūl
EŞFAHĀN
Najafābād
Kandahar
Zhob
Sahiwal
Multan
Najaf
Al Ḩillah
Al 'Amārah
Yazd
Chaman
Quetta
Jampur
DELHI
New Delhi
As Samāwah
An Nāşirīyah
Ahvāz
Kūhhā-ye Zāgros (Zagros Mountains)
Zābol
Helmand
Sibi
Bahawalpur
Al Başrah
Ābādān
Rafsanjān
Kermān
Zāhedān
Khanpur
Indus
Alwar
Al Kuwayt (Kuwait)
KUWAIT
Kāzerūn
SHĪRĀZ
Sa'īdābād
Bam
Jacobabad
Sukkur
Bikaner
Ajmer
Al Aḩmadī
Bandar-e Būshehr
Jahrom
B A L U C H I S T A N
P A K I S T A N
Dadu
Nawabshah
Jodhpur
I N D I A
Kota
P E R S I A N G U L F
Bandar-e 'Abbās
Turbat
Hyderabad
Matli
Udaipur
Buraydah
Ad Dammām
BAHRAIN
Str. of Hormuz
Oman
Gwadar
KARACHI
Thatta
Rann of Kutch
AHMADABAD
'Unayzah
Al Manāmah (Manama)
QATAR
Umm al Qaywayn
S A U D I A R A B I A
Al Hufūf
Ad Dawḩah (Doha)
Mīnā' Jabal 'Alī
Dubayy (Dubai)
GULF OF OMAN
TROPIC OF CANCER
Jamnagar
Rajkot
VADODARA
AR RIYĀḌ (Riyadh)
Abū Ẓaby (Abu Dhabi)
UNITED ARAB EMIRATES
Maţraḩ
Masqaţ (Muscat)
Bhavnagar
SURAT
Al Ḩillah
Şūr
A R A B I A N S E A
Nasik
MUMBAI (Bombay)
AR RUB' AL KHĀLĪ
O M A N
Jazīrat Maşīrah
'at Bīshah
'ASĪR
amīs
shayţ
Najrān
Şalālah
Albers Conic Equal-Area Projection
SCALE 1:16,246,000
1 CENTIMETER = 162 KILOMETERS; 1 INCH = 256 MILES
0 100 200 300 400 500 600
KILOMETERS
0 100 200 300 400 500 600
STATUTE MILES
Şan'ā' (Sanaa)
Y E M E N
Ḩ a ḑ r a m a w t
Ash Shiḩr
Al Mukallā
Ḩudaydah
Ta'izz
'Adan (Aden)
GULF OF ADEN
Suquţrá (Socotra) Yemen
Djibouti
SOMALIA
Longitude East 60° of Greenwich
50°
60°
70°
40°
30°
20°N
10°
A
B
C
D
E
F
G
H
J
K
L
M

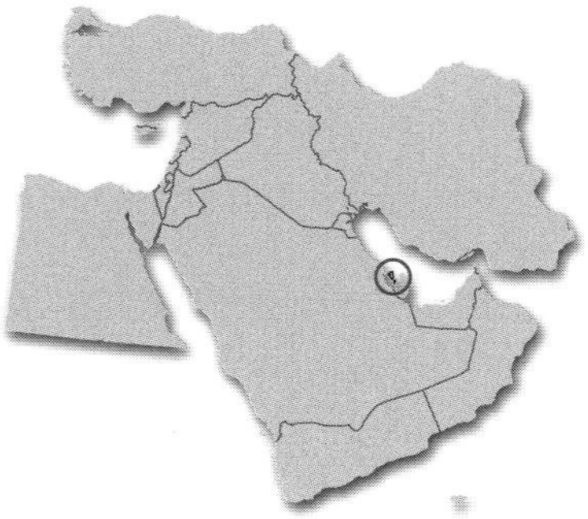

Bahrain

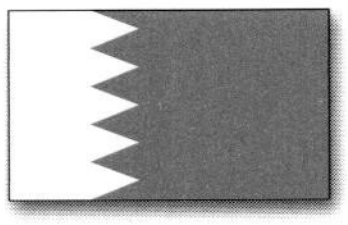

KINGDOM OF BAHRAIN

AREA	665 sq km (257 sq mi)
POPULATION	700,000
CAPITAL	Al Manāmah (Manama) 150,000
RELIGION	(percent of population): Muslim 82% (mostly Shiite), Christian 9%, other 9%
LANGUAGE	Arabic (official), English, Persian, Urdu
LITERACY	88.5%
LIFE EXPECTANCY	74 years
TROOPS	Active: 11,000
GDP PER CAPITA	$13,000
CRUDE OIL RESERVES	100,000,000 barrels
ECONOMY	IND: petroleum processing and refining, aluminum smelting, offshore banking, ship repairing; tourism. AGR: fruit, vegetables; poultry, dairy products; shrimp, fish. EXP: petroleum and petroleum products, aluminum, textiles.
AREA COMPARISON	Bahrain encompasses 0.0083% of the 48 contiguous United States.

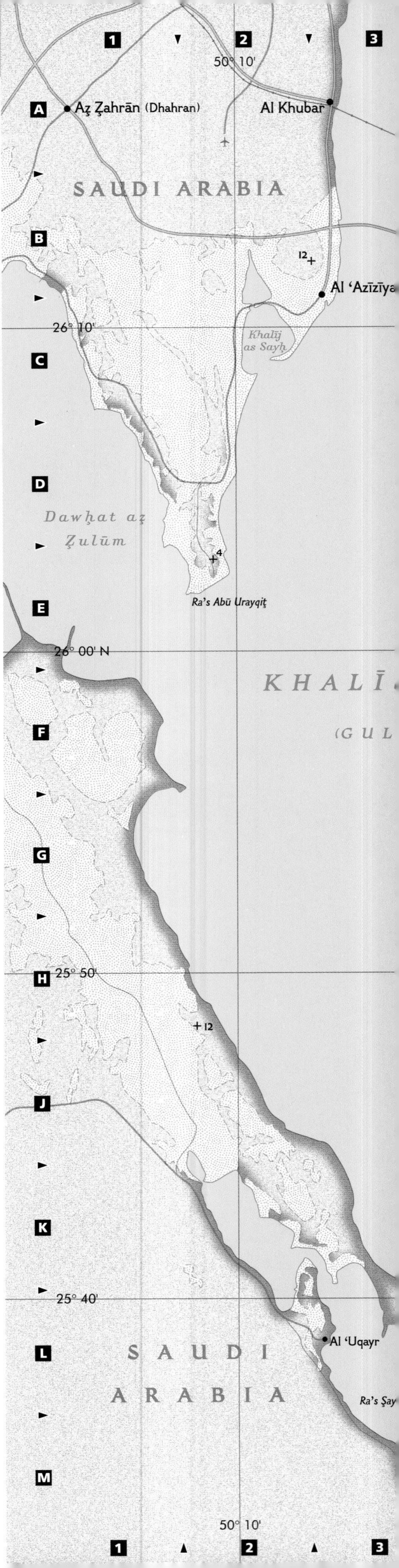

PERSIAN GULF
KHALĪJ AL BAHRAYN
(GULF OF BAHRAIN)
BAHRAIN
HAWAR ISLANDS
Bahrain and Qatar nearly went to war over these disputed islands in 1986. In March 2001, the International Court of Justice, located in The Hague, awarded the Hawar Islands to Bahrain.
QATAR
Al Manāmah (Manama)
Al Muḩarraq
Jazīrat al Muḩarraq
Ad Dayr
Samāhīj
Qalālī
Al Busaytīn
'Arid
Al Ḩadd
Ra's al Qal'ah
Bārbār
Karbābād
Karranah
Ad Dirāz
Al Budayyi'
Banī Jamrah
Al Muḩammadīyah
Jiddah
KING FAHD CAUSEWAY
Al Qurayyah
Sār
Jidd Ḩafş
Al Muşallá
Al Jufayr
Dawḩat al Qudaybīyah
Khawr al Qulay'ah
Khawr al Kāb
Salmābād
Jazīrat an Nabī Şāliḩ
Madīnat 'Īsá
Al Qaryah
Sitrah
Qaşşār al Qulay'ah
Wādiyān
Marqūbān
Al Jasrah
Umm an Na'sān
Al Hamalah
Lawzī Lake
Ar Rifā' ash Shamālī
An Nuwaydirāt
Al Ma'āmīr
Juzar ad Dar
Dumistān
Ar Rifā' al Gharbī
Ar Rifā' ash Sharqī
Ḩālat Umm al Bayḑ
Jazīrat Ya'şūf
Al Mālikīyah
Madīnat Ḩamad
Dawḩat al Fārisīyah
'Awālī
Şadad
Ra's Abū Jarjūr
'Askar
Az Zallāq
Jabal ad Dukhān
Ra's Ḩayyān
Al Wasmīyah
Al Makhrūq
Jaww
Al 'Adā'im
Al 'Amar
Ad Dūr
Ash Shabak
Al Ghaynah
Ra's al Jazā'ir
Mamlaḩat al Mamţalah
Abū al 'Awsaj
Ra's al Qurayn
Al Mamţalah
Ar Rumaythah
Qarn Ibrāhīm
Umm Jidr aş Şummān
Ra's al Mamţalah
Ra's al Jusayrah
Ḩadd al Jamal
Ḩadd al Bahrain
Ra's al Barr
Jazīrat Mashtān
Al Mu'tariḑ
Ra's Umm Ḩīsh
Rabaḑ al Gharbīyah
Rabaḑ ash Sharqīyah
Jazīrat 'Ajīrah
Jazīrat Ḩawār
Suwād ash Shamālīyah
Umm Kharūrah
Suwād al Janūbīyah
Ra's Abrūq
Ḩadd ad Dīb
Dawḩat al Ḩuşayn
Jazīrat Zakhnūnīyah
Jazīrat Janān Qatar
Transverse Mercator Projection
SCALE 1: 327,000
1 CENTIMETER = 3.3 KILOMETERS; 1 INCH = 5.2 MILES
KILOMETERS
STATUTE MILES
Longitude East 50° 30' of Greenwich
50° 20'
50° 30'
50° 40'
50° 50'
26° 10'
26° 00' N
25° 50'
25° 40'

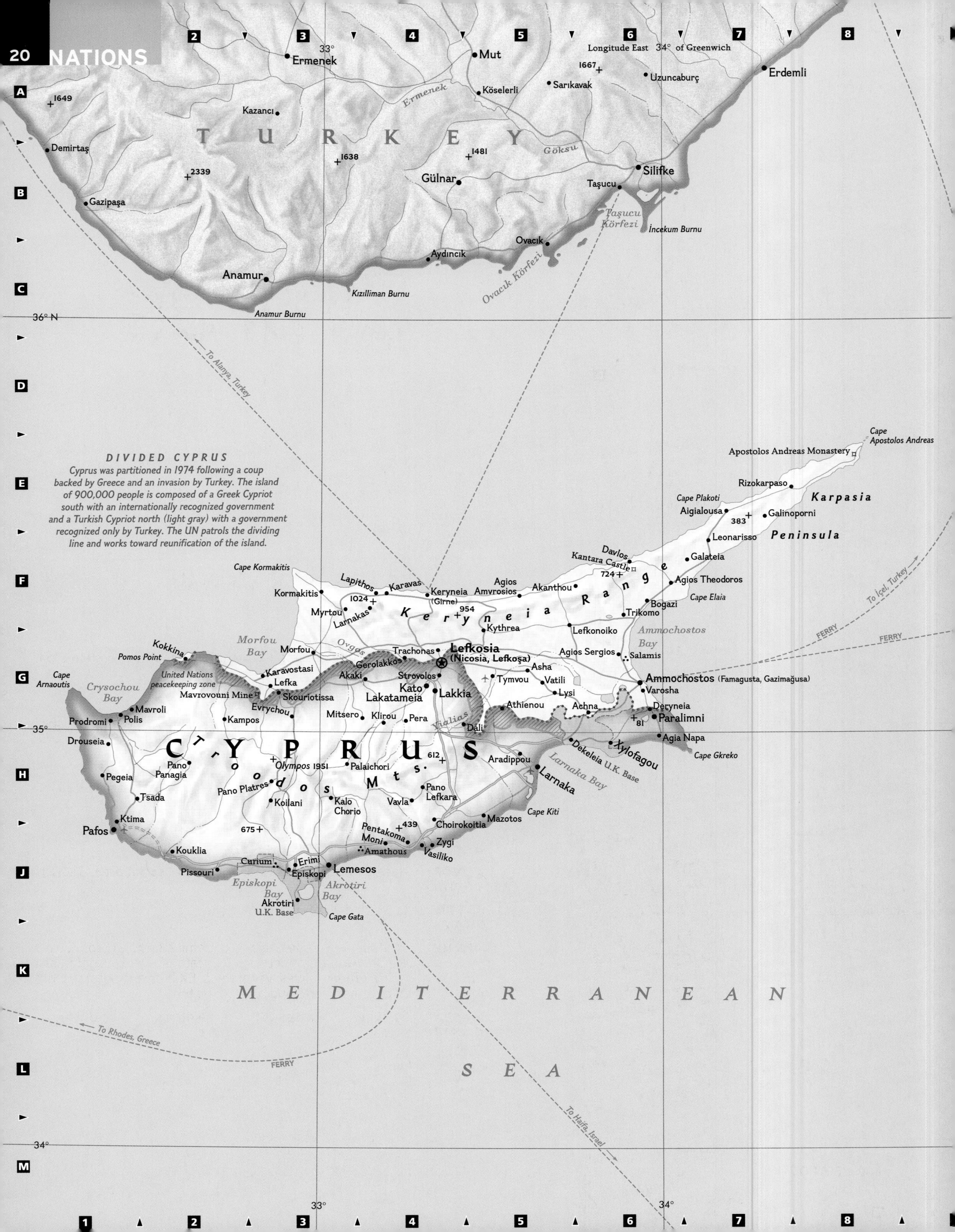

Longitude East 34° of Greenwich
33°
36° N
35°
34°
T U R K E Y
Ermenek
Mut
Erdemli
Köselerli
Sarıkavak
Uzuncaburç
Kazancı
Demirtaş
Gazipaşa
Gülnar
Silifke
Taşucu
Taşucu Körfezi
İncekum Burnu
Ovacık
Aydıncık
Anamur
Kızılliman Burnu
Anamur Burnu
Ovacık Körfezi
Göksu
To Alanya, Turkey
DIVIDED CYPRUS
Cyprus was partitioned in 1974 following a coup backed by Greece and an invasion by Turkey. The island of 900,000 people is composed of a Greek Cypriot south with an internationally recognized government and a Turkish Cypriot north (light gray) with a government recognized only by Turkey. The UN patrols the dividing line and works toward reunification of the island.
Cape Apostolos Andreas
Apostolos Andreas Monastery
Rizokarpaso
Karpasia Peninsula
Cape Plakoti
Aigialousa
Galinoporni
Leonarisso
Davlos
Kantara Castle
Galateia
Agios Theodoros
Cape Elaia
Bogazi
Trikomo
Kyrenia Range
Cape Kormakitis
Kormakitis
Lapithos
Karavas
Keryneia (Girne)
Agios Amvrosios
Akanthou
Myrtou
Larnakas
Kythrea
Lefkonoiko
Ammochostos Bay
Salamis
To İçel, Turkey
FERRY
Morfou Bay
Morfou
Ovgos
Trachonas
Lefkosia (Nicosia, Lefkoşa)
Agios Sergios
Kokkina
Pomos Point
Cape Arnaoutis
Crysochou Bay
United Nations peacekeeping zone
Karavostasi
Lefka
Mavrovouni Mine
Skouriotissa
Gerolakkos
Akaki
Strovolos
Kato Lakatameia
Lakkia
Asha
Tymvou
Vatili
Lysi
Ammochostos (Famagusta, Gazimağusa)
Varosha
Mavroli
Polis
Prodromi
Evrychou
Kampos
Mitsero
Klirou
Pera
Athienou
Achna
Deryneia
Paralimni
Vialias
Dali
Drouseia
CYPRUS
Troodos Mts.
Olympos 1951
Palaichori
Aradippou
Agia Napa
Cape Gkreko
Xylofagou
Dekeleia U.K. Base
Larnaka Bay
Larnaka
Pano Panagia
Pegeia
Pano Platres
Koilani
Kalo Chorio
Vavla
Pano Lefkara
Tsada
Ktima
Pafos
Mazotos
Cape Kiti
Choirokoitia
Pentakomo
Moni
Amathous
Zygi
Vasiliko
Kouklia
Curium
Erimi
Episkopi
Lemesos
Pissouri
Episkopi Bay
Akrotiri Bay
Akrotiri U.K. Base
Cape Gata
MEDITERRANEAN SEA
To Rhodes, Greece
To Haifa, Israel

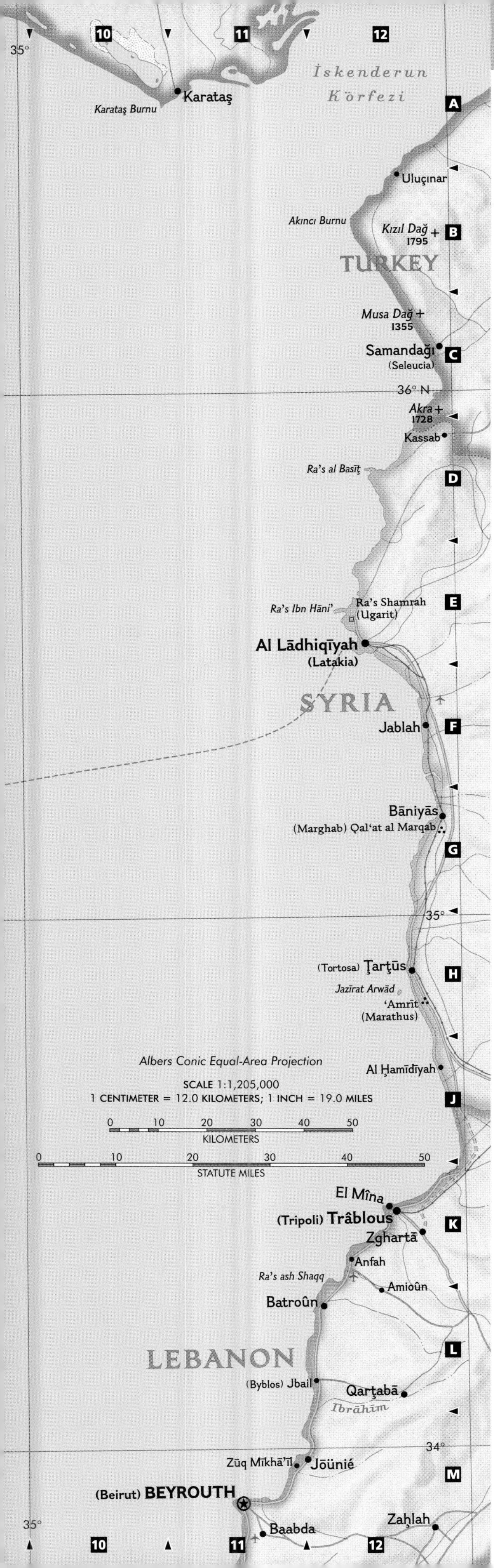

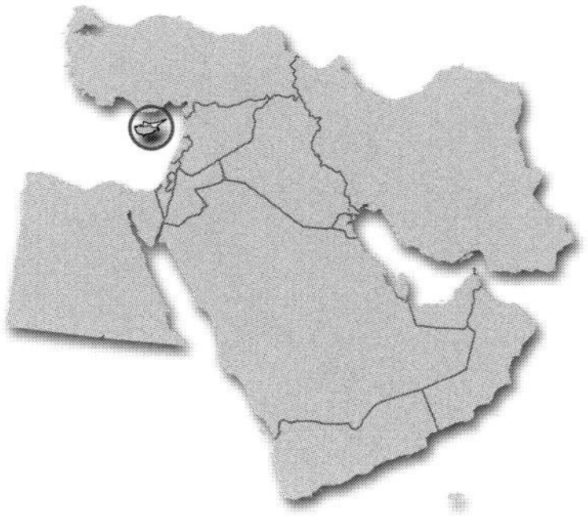

Cyprus

REPUBLIC OF CYPRUS

AREA	9,251 sq km (3,572 sq mi) includes Turkish-occupied region
POPULATION	900,000
CAPITAL	Lefkosia (Nicosia, Lefkoşa) 199,000
RELIGION	(percent of population): Greek Orthodox 78%, Muslim 18%, Maronite, Armenian Apostolic, and other 4%
LANGUAGE	Greek (official), Turkish (official), English
LITERACY	97%
LIFE EXPECTANCY	77 years
TROOPS	Active: 10,000; Reserves: 10,000
GDP PER CAPITA	Greek Cypriot Area: $15,000; Turkish Cypriot area: $7,000
CRUDE OIL RESERVES	None or negligible
ECONOMY	IND: food, beverages, textiles, chemicals, metal products, tourism, wood products. AGR: potatoes, citrus, vegetables, barley, grapes, olives, vegetables. EXP: citrus, potatoes, grapes, wine, cement, clothing and shoes, textiles.
AREA COMPARISON	Cyprus encompasses 0.11% of the 48 contiguous United States.

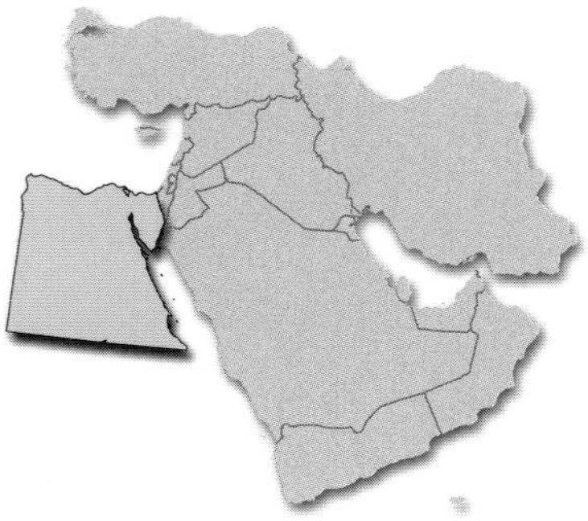

Egypt

ARAB REPUBLIC OF EGYPT

AREA	1,001,449 sq km (386,662 sq mi)
POPULATION	71,200,000
CAPITAL	El Qâhira (Cairo) 9,586,000
RELIGION	(percent of population): Muslim 89% (mostly Sunni), Christian 11% (mostly Coptic)
LANGUAGE	Arabic (official), English and French widely understood by educated classes
LITERACY	51.4%
LIFE EXPECTANCY	66 years
TROOPS	Active: 443,000; Reserves: 254,000
GDP PER CAPITA	$3,700
CRUDE OIL RESERVES	2,900,000,000 barrels
ECONOMY	IND: textiles, food processing, tourism, chemicals, hydrocarbons, construction, cement, metals. AGR: cotton, rice, corn, wheat, beans, fruit, vegetables; cattle, water buffalo, sheep, goats. EXP: crude oil and petroleum products, cotton, textiles, metal products, chemicals.
AREA COMPARISON	Egypt encompasses 12.5% of the 48 contiguous United States.

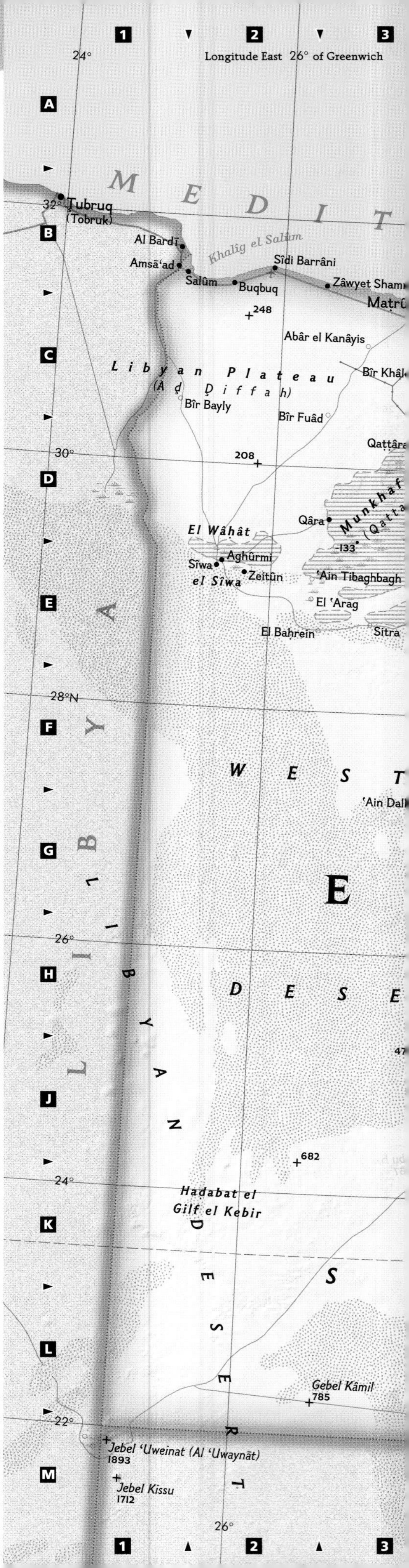

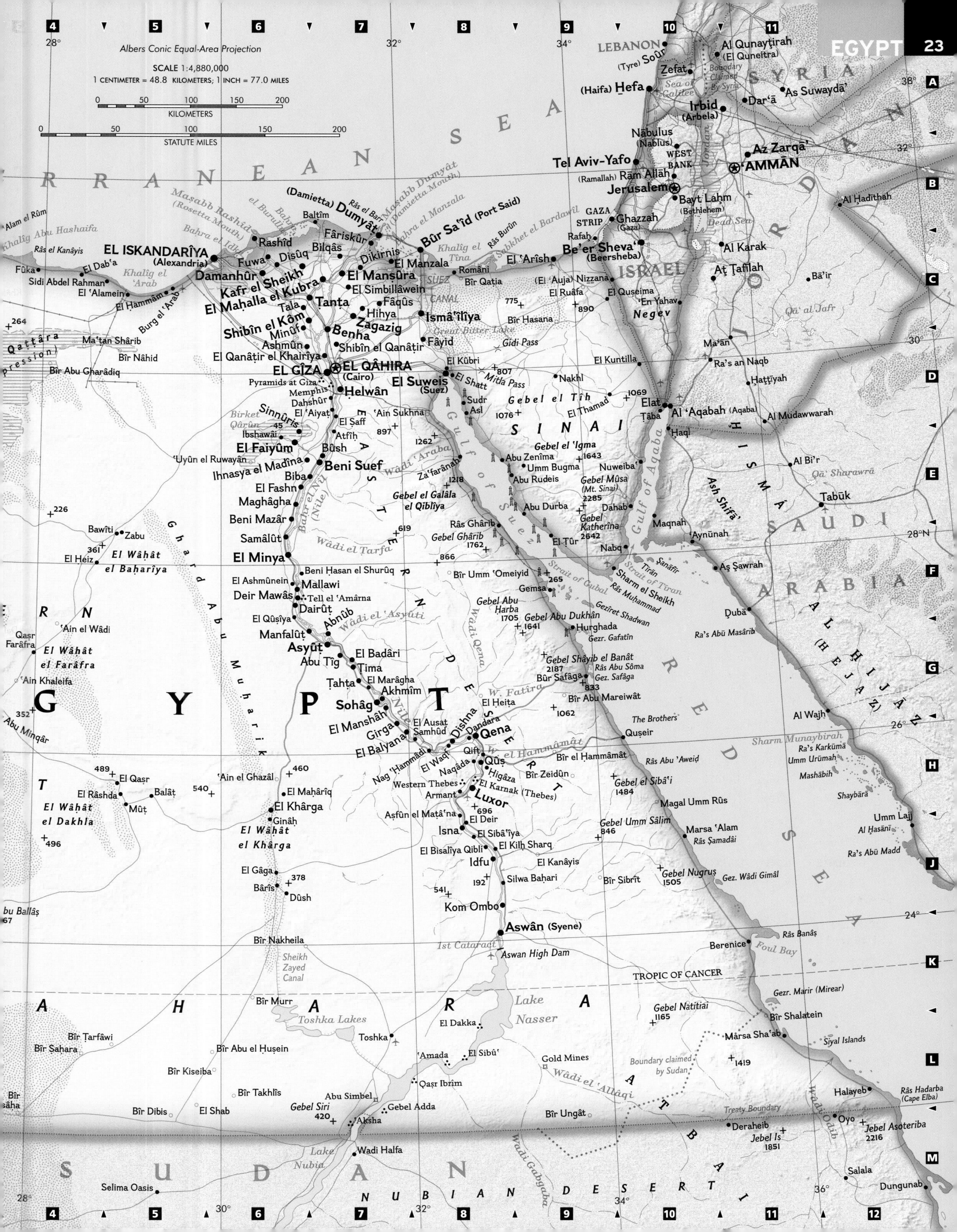
Albers Conic Equal-Area Projection
SCALE 1:4,880,000
1 CENTIMETER = 48.8 KILOMETERS; 1 INCH = 77.0 MILES
KILOMETERS
STATUTE MILES
LEBANON
(Tyre) Soûr
Al Qunayţirah (El Quneitra)
Zefat
Boundary Claimed By Syria
Sea of Galilee
S Y R I A
(Haifa) Hefa
As Suwaydā'
Dar'ā
Irbid (Arbela)
Nābulus (Nablus)
WEST BANK
Az Zarqā'
AMMĀN
Tel Aviv-Yafo
(Ramallah) Rām Allāh
Jerusalem
Bayt Laḩm (Bethlehem)
Al Ḩadīthah
GAZA STRIP
Ghazzah (Gaza)
Dead Sea
Rafah
Be'er Sheva' (Beersheba)
Al Karak
ISRAEL
Aţ Ţafīlah
Bā'ir
(El 'Auja) Nizzana
El Ruâfa
El Quseima
'En Yahav
Negev
Qā' al Jafr
J O R D A N
M E D I T E R R A N E A N S E A
Maşabb Rashîd (Rosetta Mouth)
Maşabb Dumyât (Damietta Mouth)
(Damietta) Dumyât
Râs el Bar
Baltîm
Bahra el Manzala
Bûr Sa'îd (Port Said)
Râs Burûn
Sabkhet el Bardawîl
'Alam el Rûm
Khalîg Abu Hashaifa
Râs el Kanâyis
EL ISKANDARÎYA (Alexandria)
Rashîd
Disûq
Bilqâs
Fâriskûr
Dikirnis
El Manzala
Khalîg el Tîna
Români
Bîr Qatia
El 'Arîsh
Fûka
El Dab'a
Sidi Abdel Rahman
El 'Alamein
El Ḩammâm
Burg el 'Arab
Khalîg el 'Arab
Damanhûr
Fuwa
Kafr el Sheikh
El Mahalla el Kubra
El Manşûra
El Simbillâwein
SUEZ CANAL
Tanta
Fâqûs
Tala
Hihya
Ismâ'ilîya
Shibîn el Kôm
Minûf
Zagazig
Benha
Great Bitter Lake
Fâyid
Gidi Pass
Bîr Hasana
Qattâra Depression
Ma'tan Shârib
Bîr Nâhid
Ashmûn
Shibîn el Qanâţir
El Qanâţir el Khairîya
Bîr Abu Gharâdiq
EL GÎZA
EL QÂHIRA (Cairo)
El Kûbri
Mitla Pass
Nakhl
El Kuntilla
Ma'ān
Ra's an Naqb
Ḩaţţīyah
Pyramids at Giza
Memphis
Helwân
El Suweis (Suez)
El Shatt
Dahshûr
El 'Aiyat
'Ain Sukhna
Sudr
Asl
Gebel el Tîh
El Thamad
Elat
Ţāba
Al 'Aqabah (Aqaba)
Ḩaql
Al Mudawwarah
Birket Qârûn
Sinnûris
El Şaff
Ibshawâi
Atfîh
S I N A I
El Faiyûm
Bûsh
Gebel el 'Igma
'Uyûn el Ruwayân
Beni Suef
Wâdi 'Araba
Abu Zenîma
Umm Bugma
Nuweiba'
Al Bi'r
Ihnasya el Madîna
Za'farâna
Abu Rudeis
Gebel Mûsa (Mt. Sinai)
Qā' Sharawrā
Biba
El Fashn
Gulf of Suez
Gulf of Aqaba
Ash Shifā'
Tabūk
Maghâgha
Gebel el Galâla el Qiblîya
Abu Durba
Dahab
Beni Mazâr
Bahr el Nîl (Nile)
Gebel Katherîna
Maqnah
Bawîti
Zabu
Râs Ghârib
El Tûr
'Aynūnah
Samâlût
Gebel Ghârib
Nabq
SAUDI ARABIA
El Wâhât el Baharîya
El Heiz
Wâdi el Tarfa
El Minya
Tîrân
Şanâfîr
Aş Şawrah
Beni Hasan el Shurûq
Bîr Umm 'Omeiyid
Strait of Gubal
Strait of Tiran
Sharm el Sheikh
Râs Muhammad
El Ashmûnein
Mallawi
Gemsa
Deir Mawâs
Tell el 'Amârna
Gebel Abu Harba
Ghard Abu Muharik
Dairût
Wadi Qena
Gezîret Shadwan
Duba
El Qûşîya
Abnûb
Wâdi el 'Asyûti
Gebel Abu Dukhân
Hurghada
'Ain el Wâdi
Manfalût
Gezr. Gafatîn
Ra's Abū Masārib
Qasr Farâfra
El Wâhât el Farâfra
Asyût
Abu Tîg
El Badâri
Gebel Shâyib el Banât
Tima
Râs Abu Sôma
'Ain Khaleifa
Tahta
El Marâgha
Bûr Safâga
Gez. Safâga
Akhmîm
Bîr Abu Mareiwât
E G Y P T
Sohâg
W. Fatîra
El Heiţa
Al Hijāz (Hejaz)
Abu Minqâr
El Manshâh
El Ausat
Dishna
Dandara
The Brothers
Al Wajh
Girga
Samhûd
Qena
Quşeir
El Balyana
Qift
Wâdi el Hammâmât
Bîr el Hammâmât
Râs Abu 'Aweiḑ
Sharm Munaybirah
Ra's Karkūmā
Umm Urūmah
Mashābih
El Qasr
El Rashda
Balât
Mût
El Wâhât el Dakhla
'Ain el Ghazâl
El Mahârîq
Nag' Hammâdi
El Waqf
Naqâda
Qûş
Higâza
Bîr Zeidûn
Western Thebes
El Karnak (Thebes)
Gebel el Sibâ'i
Shaybārā
El Khârga
Armant
Luxor
Magal Umm Rûs
Ginâh
El Wâhât el Khârga
Aşfûn el Matâ'na
El Deir
Gebel Umm Sâlim
Umm Lajj
Isna
El Sibâ'îya
Marsa 'Alam
Râs Şamadâi
Al Ḩasānī
El Bisalîya Qibli
El Kilh Sharq
Ra's Abū Madd
El Kanâyis
El Gâga
Idfu
Silwa Bahari
Bîr Sibrît
Gebel Nugruş
Gez. Wâdi Gimâl
Bâris
Dûsh
bu Ballâş
Kom Ombo
Aswân (Syene)
R E D S E A
Râs Banâş
Bîr Nakheila
1st Cataract
Berenice
Foul Bay
Aswan High Dam
Sheikh Zayed Canal
TROPIC OF CANCER
Gezr. Marir (Mirear)
S A H A R A
Bîr Murr
Lake Nasser
Gebel Natitiai
Toshka Lakes
El Dakka
Bîr Shalatein
Bîr Tarfâwi
Toshka
Marsa Sha'ab
Siyal Islands
Bîr Şahara
Bîr Abu el Husein
'Amada
El Sibû'
Gold Mines
Boundary claimed by Sudan
Bîr Kiseiba
Qaşr Ibrîm
Wâdi el 'Allâqi
Bîr Takhlîs
Abu Simbel
Halayeb
Râs Hadarba (Cape Elba)
Bîr Şâha
Bîr Dibis
El Shab
Gebel Siri
Gebel Adda
Bîr Ungât
Treaty Boundary
Oyo
'Aksha
Deraheib
Jebel Asoteriba
Jebel Is
Wadi Halfa
Lake Nubia
Wâdi Gabgaba
Wadi Odib
S U D A N
Salala
Dungunab
Selima Oasis
N U B I A N D E S E R T
A T B A I

Longitude East 52° of Greenwich
Lambert Conformal Conic Projection
SCALE 1:6,728,000
1 CENTIMETER = 67.3 KILOMETERS; 1 INCH = 106.2 MILES
KILOMETERS
STATUTE MILES
AZERBAIJAN
ARMENIA
NAXÇIVAN (Azerbaijan)
TURKEY
BAKI (Baku)
Qazimämmäd
Äli Bayramlı
Salyan
Xankändi
Füzuli
Naxçıvan
Kapan
Bilăsuvar
Masallı
Länkäran
Astara
Ästārā
Türkmenbashy
Cheleken
CASPIAN SEA
-28
TURKME
GARAGUM CANAL
Büzmeyin
Ashgabat
Köpetdag
Gyzyletrek
Esenguly
Bandar-e Torkaman
Gonbad-e Kāvūs
Bojnūrd
Chaman Bid
Qūchān
Gorgān
Behshahr
Sārī
Shāhrūd
Mashhad
Neyshābūr
Sabzevār
TABRĪZ
Ardabīl
Khovy
Salmās
Marand
Ahar
Orūmīyeh (Urmia)
Daryācheh-ye Orūmīyeh (Lake Urmia)
Marāgheh
Bonāb
Mīāndoāb
Mahābād
Mīāneh
Rasht
Lāhījān
Bandar-e Anzalī
Kargānrūd
Zanjān
Mehrābād
KURDISTAN
Rawandoz
As Sulaymānīyah
Karkūk (Kirkuk)
Saqqez
Bāneh
Marīvān
Sanandaj
Qazvīn
Tākestān
Karaj
TEHRĀN
Tajrīsh
Rey
Kūh-e Damāvand
Semnān
Dāmghān
RESHTEH-YE ALBORZ (ELBURZ MTS.)
5671
Hamadān (Ecbatana)
Tūysarkān
Kermānshāh
Qaşr-e Shīrīn
Khānaqīn
Ba'qūbah
BAGHDĀD
Sāveh
Qom (Qum)
Daryācheh-ye Namak
Dasht-e Kavīr (Salt Desert)
KHORĀSĀN
Torbat-e Ḩeydarīyeh
Kāshmar
Kavīr-e Namak
Gonābād
Bejestān
Arāk
Malāyer
Borūjerd
Nahāvand
Khorramābād
Ārān
Kāshān
Golpāyegān
Naţanz
Kūh-e Karkas 3896
Khunsar
Ardestān
Anārak
Jandaq
Khvor
Ţabas
Ferdows
Qāyen
Bīrjand
IRAN
Khomeynīshahr
Najafābād
EŞFAHĀN (Isfahan)
Nā'īn
Posht-e Bādām
Dasht-e Lūt
KŪHHĀ-YE ZĀGROS (ZAGROS MOUNTAINS)
Dezfūl
Shūshtar
Masjed Soleymān
Ahvāz
Shahr-e Kord
Zard Kūh 4548
Qomsheh
Yazd
Ardakān
Mehrīz
Shīr Kūh 4075
Kermānshāhān
Rāvar
Namakzār-e Shahdād
IRAQ
Babylon
Al Kūt
Ad Dīwānīyah
Al 'Amārah
Al Furāt (Euphrates)
Dijlah (Tigris)
An Nāşirīyah
Al Qurnah
Al Başrah (Basra)
Az Zubayr
Khorramshahr
Ābādān
Khosrowābād
Al Fāw
Umm Qaşr
Bandar-e Māh Shahr
Behbehān
Kūh-e Dīnār 4276
Ābādeh
Abarkūh
Deh Bīd
Rafsanjān
Kermān
Māhān
Persepolis
Marv Dasht
SHĪRĀZ
Kāzerūn
Sa'īdābād (Sīrjān)
Kūh-e Hazārān 4420
Bam
Kūh-e Jabāl Bārez 3692
Jīroft
KUWAIT
United Nations peacekeeping zone
Jazīrat Būbīyān
Al Jahrā'
Al Kuwayt (Kuwait)
Al Aḩmadī
Khārk
Bandar-e Būshehr
Borāzjān
Daryācheh-ye Bakhtegān
Neyrīz
Eşţahbānāt
Fasā
Dārāb
Jahrom
Fīrūzābād
Ḩafar al Bāţin
Al Khīrān
Ra's al Mish'āb
King Khalid Military City
Al Warī'ah
Kangan
Ţāherī
Deyyer
Lār
Bandar-e 'Abbās
Ḩājjīābād
Ţārom
Dowlatābād
Kahnūj
Rudan
Minab
Hāmūn-e Jaz Mūrīān
SAUDI ARABIA
PERSIAN GULF
Ra's az Zawr
Abū 'Alī
Al Jubayl
Al Wannān
Nāy Band
Gāvbandī
Bandar-e Maqām
Lāvān (Sheykh Sho'eyb)
Bandar-e Chārak
Qeys
Bandar-e Lengeh
Qeshm
Hormoz
Str. of Hormuz
Ra's Musandam
Oman
Al Qaţīf
Ad Dammām
Al Manāmah (Manama)
BAHRAIN
Ar Ru'ays
Al Khawr
QATAR
Ad Dawḩah (Doha)
Al Hufūf
AR RIYĀḐ (Riyadh)
Ad Dahnā'
Forūr
Tunb Is. Iran
Sīrrī Iran
Ra's al Khaymah
Ash Shāriqah
'Ajmān
Al Fujayrah
Dubayy (Dubai)
UNITED ARAB EMIRATES
(Abu Dhabi) Abū Z̧aby
GULF OF OMAN
Jāsk
Sīrīk
Kangān
Sūrak
Remeshk
Angohrān

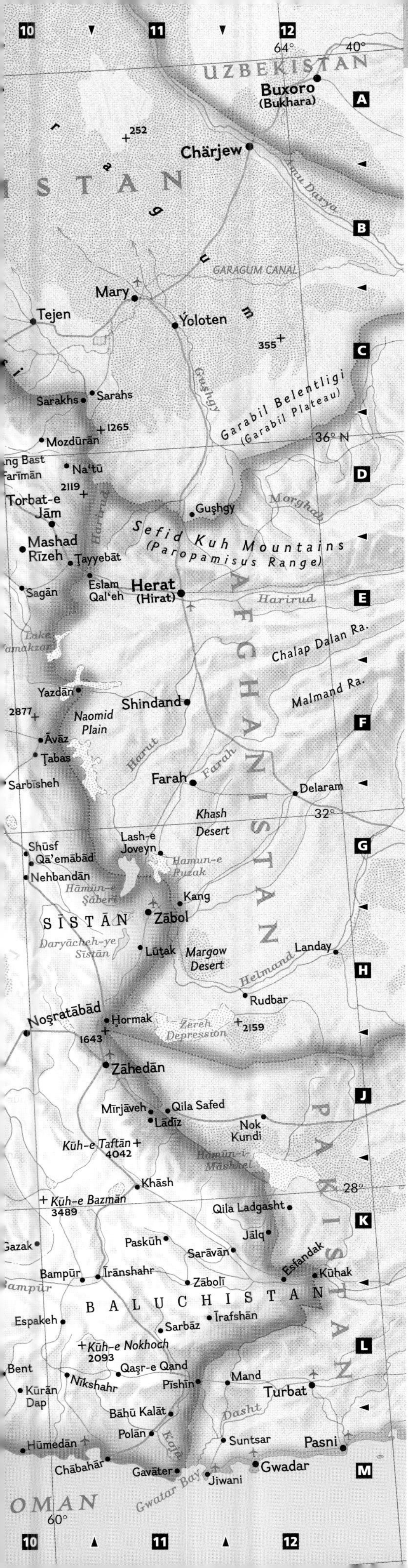

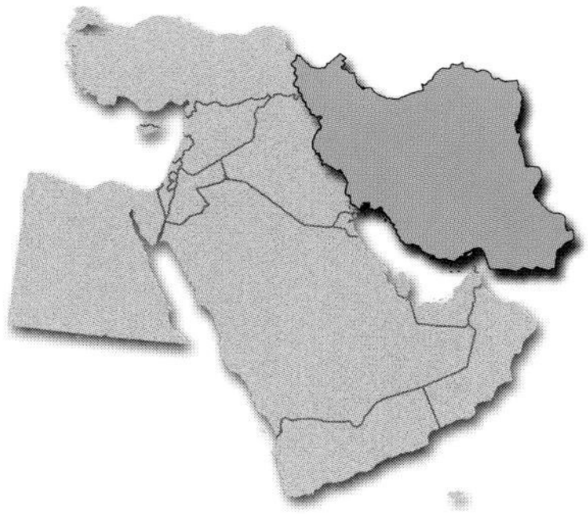

Iran

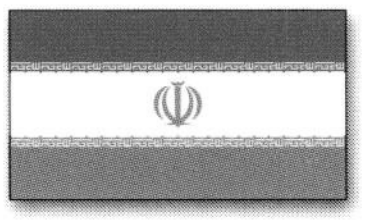

ISLAMIC REPUBLIC OF IRAN

AREA	1,648,000 sq km (636,296 sq mi)
POPULATION	65,600,000
CAPITAL	Tehrān 7,038,000
RELIGION	(percent of population): Muslim 99% (mostly Shiite, Sunni 10%), other 1% (Zoroastrian, Jewish, Christian, Baha'i)
LANGUAGE	Persian and Persian dialects 58%, Turkic and Turkic dialects 26%, Kurdish 9%, Luri 2%, Baluchi, Arabic, Turkish, other 2%
LITERACY	72.1%
LIFE EXPECTANCY	69 years
TROOPS	Active: 513,000; Reserves: 350,000
GDP PER CAPITA	$6,400
CRUDE OIL RESERVES	89,700,000,000 barrels
ECONOMY	IND: petroleum, petrochemicals, textiles, cement and other construction materials, food processing, metal fabricating, armaments. AGR: wheat, rice, other grains, sugar beets, fruits, nuts, cotton; dairy products, wool; caviar. EXP: petroleum 85%, carpets, fruits and nuts, iron and steel, chemicals.
AREA COMPARISON	Iran encompasses 20.6% of the 48 contiguous United States.

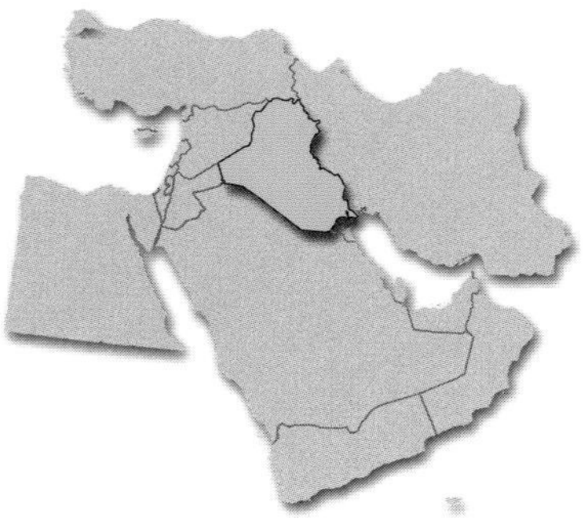

Iraq

REPUBLIC OF IRAQ

AREA 437,072 sq km (168,754 sq mi)

POPULATION 23,600,000

CAPITAL Baghdād 4,958,000

RELIGION (percent of population): Muslim 95% (mostly Shiite, Sunni 35%), Christian 5%

LANGUAGE Arabic, Kurdish (official in Kurdish area), Assyrian, Armenian

LITERACY 58%

LIFE EXPECTANCY 58 years

TROOPS Active: 389,000; Reserves: 650,000

GDP PER CAPITA $2,500

CRUDE OIL RESERVES 112,500,000,000 barrels

ECONOMY IND: petroleum, chemicals, textiles, construction materials, food processing. AGR: wheat, barley, rice, vegetables, dates, cotton; cattle, sheep. EXP: crude oil.

AREA COMPARISON Iraq encompasses 5.4% of the 48 contiguous United States.

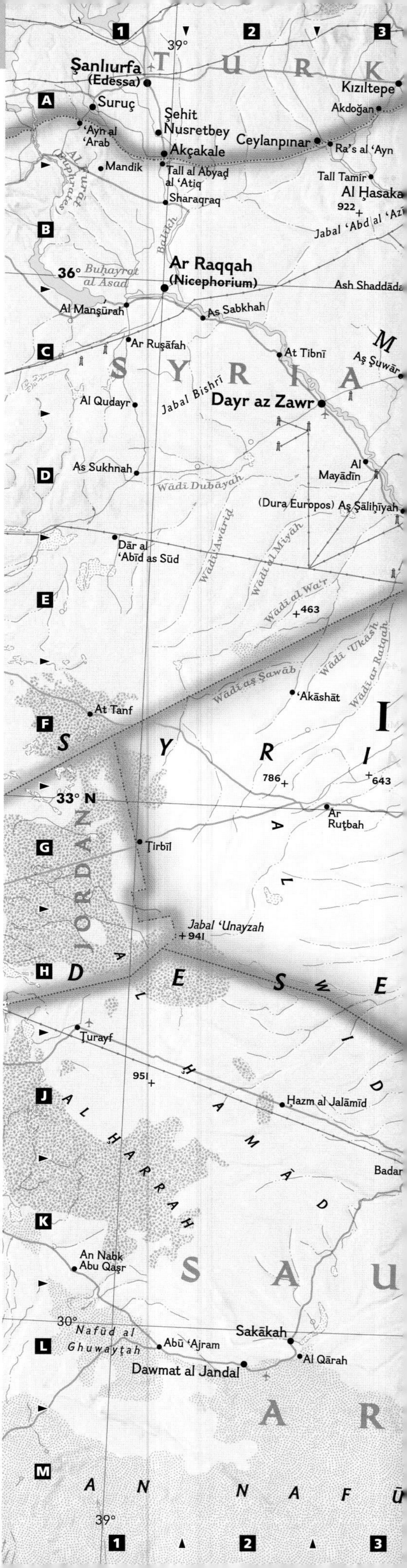

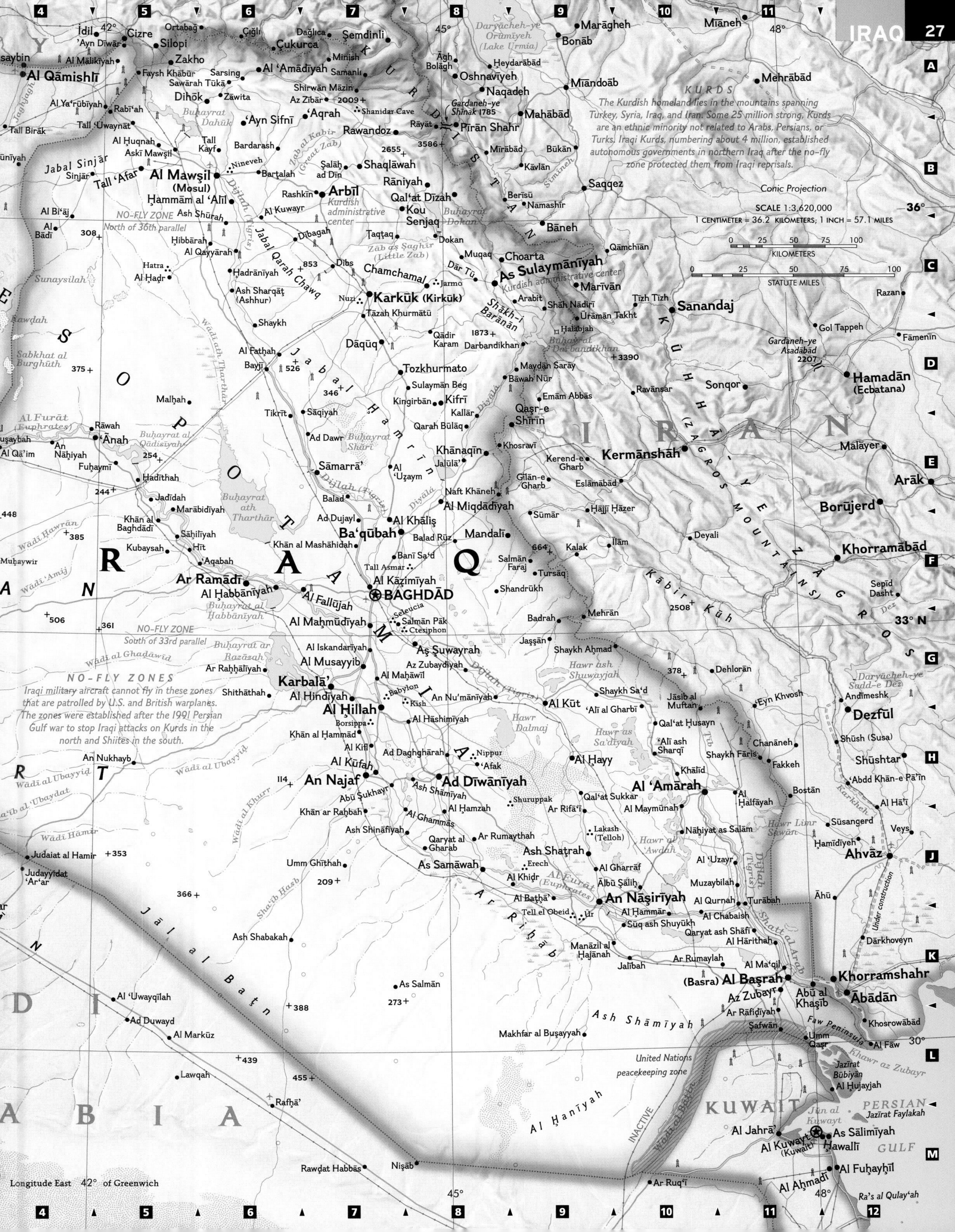
KURDS
The Kurdish homeland lies in the mountains spanning Turkey, Syria, Iraq, and Iran. Some 25 million strong, Kurds are an ethnic minority not related to Arabs, Persians, or Turks. Iraqi Kurds, numbering about 4 million, established autonomous governments in northern Iraq after the no-fly zone protected them from Iraqi reprisals.
Conic Projection
SCALE 1:3,620,000
1 CENTIMETER = 36.2 KILOMETERS; 1 INCH = 57.1 MILES
KILOMETERS
STATUTE MILES
NO-FLY ZONES
Iraqi military aircraft cannot fly in these zones that are patrolled by U.S. and British warplanes. The zones were established after the 1991 Persian Gulf war to stop Iraqi attacks on Kurds in the north and Shiites in the south.
NO-FLY ZONE
North of 36th parallel
NO-FLY ZONE
South of 33rd parallel
IRAQ
IRAN
KUWAIT
MESOPOTAMIA
KURDISTAN
ZAGROS MOUNTAINS
BAGHDĀD
Al Mawşil (Mosul)
Arbīl
Kurdish administrative center
As Sulaymānīyah
Kurdish administrative center
Karkūk (Kirkūk)
Ba'qūbah
Ar Ramādī
Al Fallūjah
Karbalā'
Al Ḩillah
An Najaf
Ad Dīwānīyah
Al Kūt
Al 'Amārah
An Nāşirīyah
As Samāwah
(Basra) Al Başrah
Al Kuwayt (Kuwait)
Khorramshahr
Ābādān
Kermānshāh
Hamadān (Ecbatana)
Sanandaj
Dezfūl
Ahvāz
Dijlah (Tigris)
Al Furāt (Euphrates)
Shaţţ al 'Arab
Buḩayrat ath Tharthār
Buḩayrat al Ḩabbānīyah
Persian Gulf
United Nations peacekeeping zone
INACTIVE
Under construction
Jāl al Baţn
Ash Shāmīyah
Al Ḩanīyah
Longitude East 42° of Greenwich
45°
48°
36°
33° N
30°

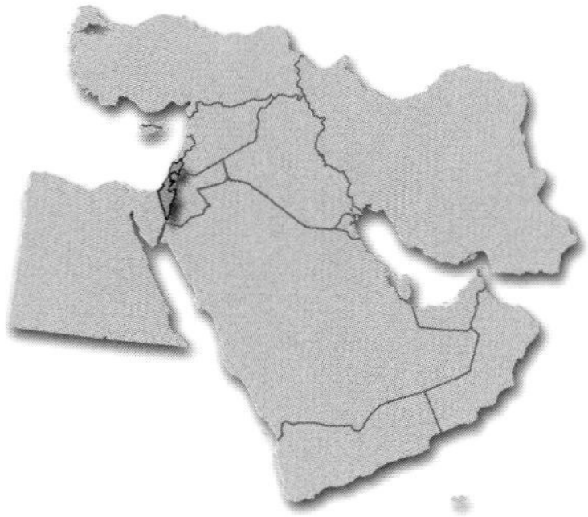

Israel

STATE OF ISRAEL

AREA	20,770 sq km (8,019 sq mi)
POPULATION	6,600,000
CAPITAL	Jerusalem 661,000
RELIGION	(percent of population): Jewish 81%, Muslim 15% (mostly Sunni), Christian 2%, other 2%
LANGUAGE	Hebrew (official), Arabic used officially for Arab minority, English most commonly used foreign language
LITERACY	95%
LIFE EXPECTANCY	78 years
TROOPS	Active: 163,500; Reserves 425,000

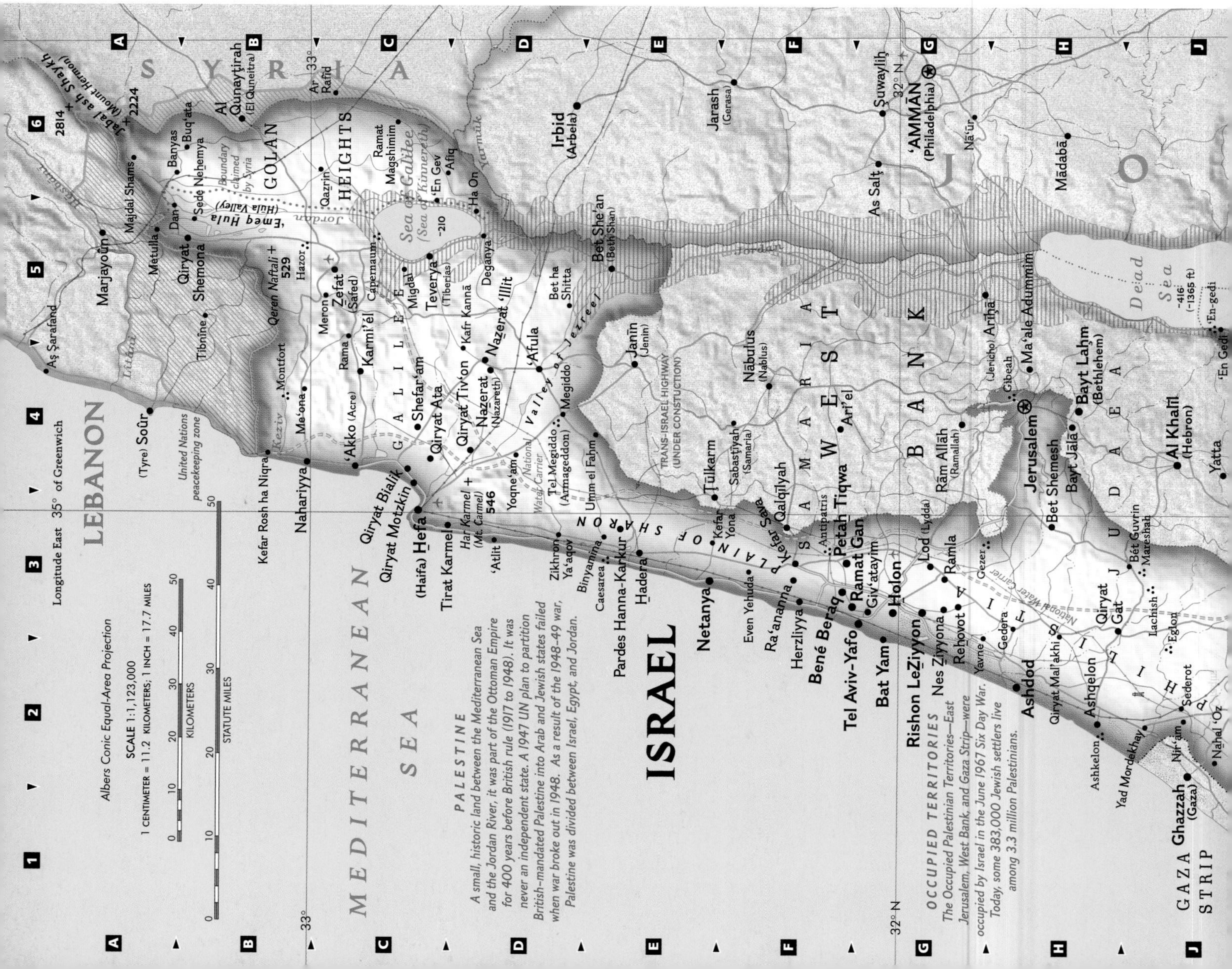
SYRIA
LEBANON
MEDITERRANEAN SEA
ISRAEL
GOLAN HEIGHTS
GALILEE
WEST BANK
SAMARIA
JUDAEA
GAZA STRIP
JORDAN
Dead Sea
Sea of Galilee
Jerusalem
Tel Aviv-Yafo
Hefa (Haifa)
'AMMĀN (Philadelphia)
Longitude East 35° of Greenwich
Albers Conic Equal-Area Projection
SCALE 1:1,123,000
1 CENTIMETER = 11.2 KILOMETERS; 1 INCH = 17.7 MILES
KILOMETERS
STATUTE MILES
United Nations peacekeeping zone
PALESTINE
A small, historic land between the Mediterranean Sea and the Jordan River, it was part of the Ottoman Empire for 400 years before British rule (1917 to 1948). It was never an independent state. A 1947 UN plan to partition British-mandated Palestine into Arab and Jewish states failed when war broke out in 1948. As a result of the 1948-49 war, Palestine was divided between Israel, Egypt, and Jordan.
OCCUPIED TERRITORIES
The Occupied Palestinian Territories—East Jerusalem, West Bank, and Gaza Strip—were occupied by Israel in the June 1967 Six Day War. Today, some 383,000 Jewish settlers live among 3.3 million Palestinians.

GDP PER CAPITA $20,000

CRUDE OIL RESERVES None or negligible

ECONOMY IND: high-technology projects (including aviation, communications, computer-aided design and manufactures, medical electronics), wood and paper products, potash and phosphates, food, beverages, and tobacco, caustic soda, cement, diamond cutting. AGR: citrus, vegetables, cotton; beef, poultry, dairy products. EXP: machinery and equipment, software, cut diamonds, agricultural products, chemicals, textiles and apparel.

AREA COMPARISON Israel encompasses 0.26% of the 48 contiguous United States.

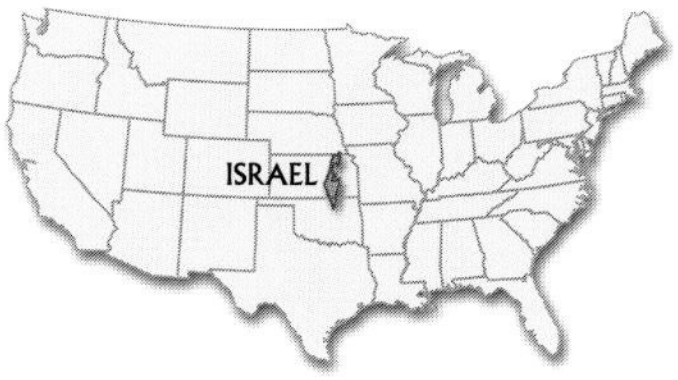

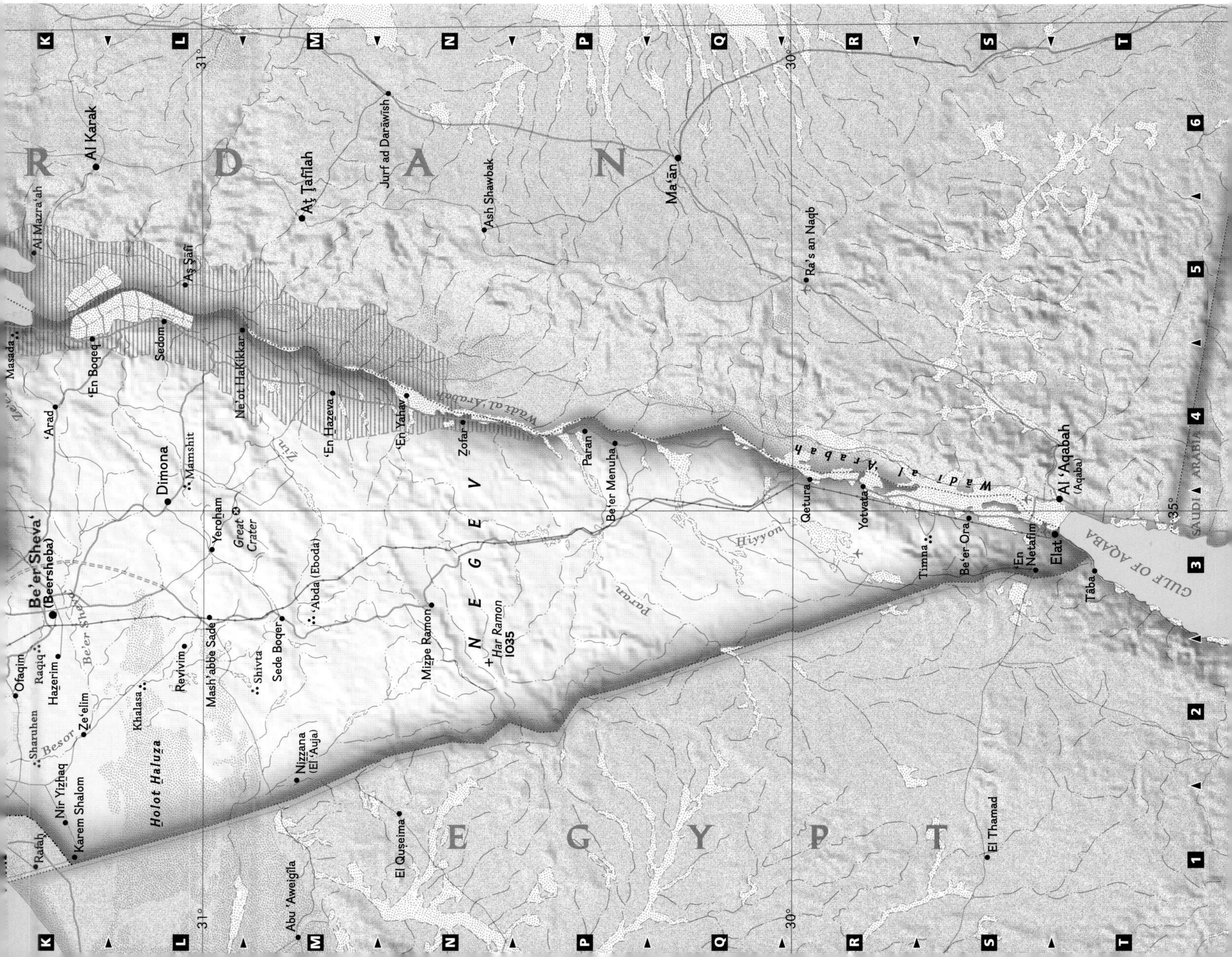

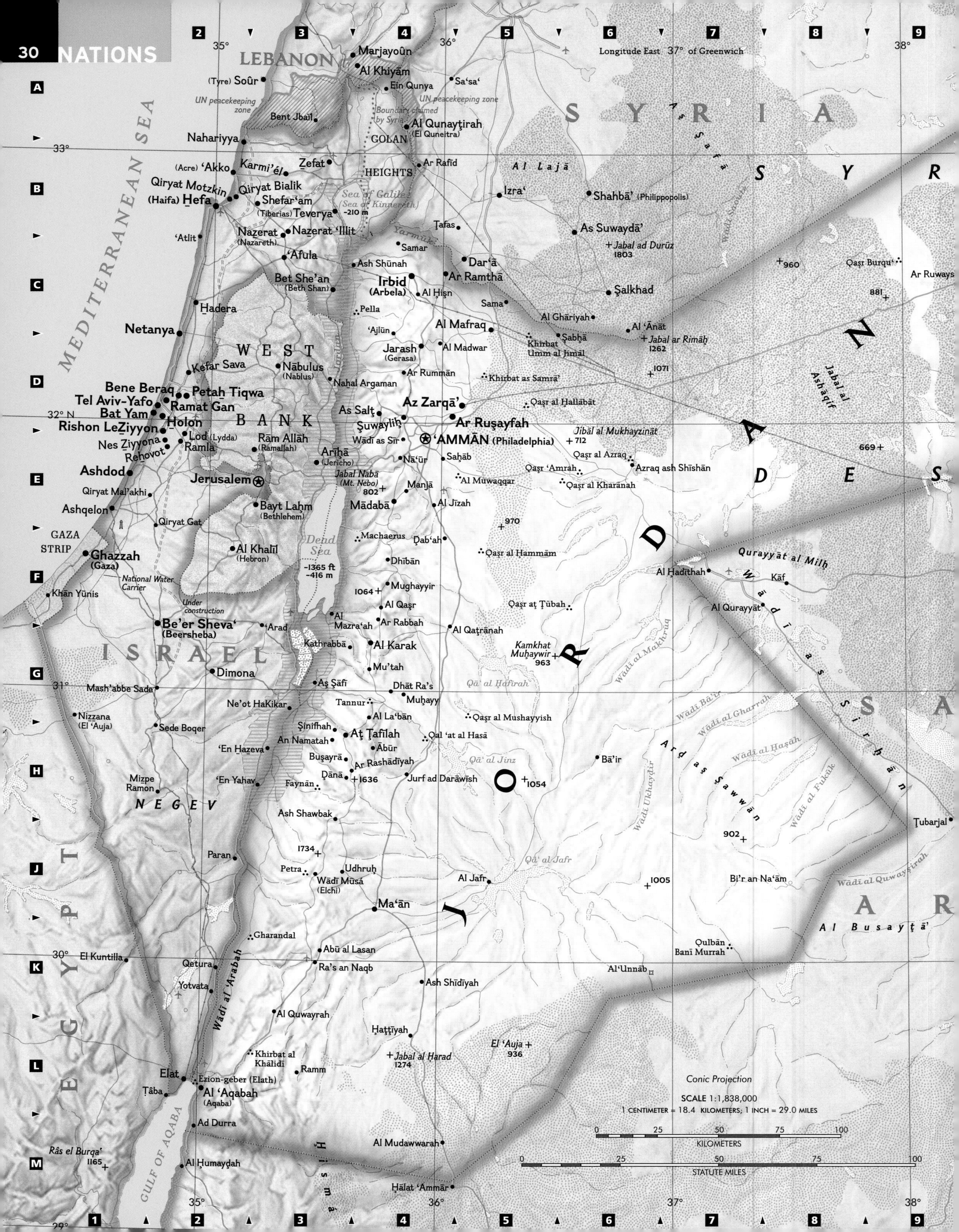

Longitude East 37° of Greenwich
35°
36°
38°
33°
32° N
31°
30°
29°
37°
LEBANON
Marjayoûn
Al Khiyām
(Tyre) Soûr
Ein Qunya
Sa'sa'
UN peacekeeping zone
UN peacekeeping zone
Boundary claimed by Syria
Bent Jbaïl
Al Qunayţirah (El Quneitra)
GOLAN HEIGHTS
Nahariyya
SYRIA
Aş Şafā
(Acre) 'Akko
Karmi'él
Zefat
Ar Rafīd
Al Lajā
SYR
Qiryat Motzkin
Qiryat Bialik
(Haifa) Hefa
Shefar'am
Sea of Galilee (Sea of Kinnereth)
-210 m
Izra'
Shahbā' (Philippopolis)
(Tiberias) Teverya
'Atlit
Nazerat
(Nazareth)
Nazerat 'Illit
Ţafas
Yarmūk
As Suwaydā'
Jabal ad Durūz 1803
Samar
'Afula
Ash Shūnah
Dar'ā
960
Qaşr Burqu'
Ar Ruways
MEDITERRANEAN SEA
Bet She'an (Beth Shan)
Irbid (Arbela)
Ar Ramthā
Al Ḩişn
Şalkhad
881
Hadera
Pella
Sama
Al Ghāriyah
Netanya
'Ajlūn
Al Mafraq
Al 'Ānāt
Jabal ar Rimāḩ 1262
Jarash (Gerasa)
Al Madwar
Şabḩā
Khirbat Umm al Jimāl
WEST BANK
Kefar Sava
Nābulus (Nablus)
Ar Rummān
Khirbat as Samrā'
1071
Jabal al Ashāqif
Nahal Argaman
Bene Beraq
Petah Tiqwa
Tel Aviv-Yafo
Ramat Gan
Bat Yam
Holon
Rishon LeZiyyon
Az Zarqā'
Qaşr al Ḩallābāt
As Salţ
Şuwayliḩ
Ar Ruşayfah
Wādī as Sīr
'AMMĀN (Philadelphia)
Jibāl al Mukhayzināt
712
669
Nes Ziyyona
Lod (Lydda)
Ramla
Rehovot
Rām Allāh (Ramallah)
Arīḩā (Jericho)
Na'ūr
Saḩāb
Qaşr al Azraq
Azraq ash Shīshān
Ashdod
Jabal Nabā (Mt. Nebo) 802
Qaşr 'Amrah
Jerusalem
Manjā
Al Muwaqqar
Qaşr al Kharānah
Qiryat Mal'akhi
Mādabā
Al Jīzah
Ashqelon
Bayt Laḩm (Bethlehem)
Qiryat Gat
970
GAZA STRIP
Machaerus
Dab'ah
Dead Sea
Al Khalīl (Hebron)
Qaşr al Ḩammām
Ghazzah (Gaza)
Dhībān
-1365 ft -416 m
National Water Carrier
Qurayyāt al Milḩ
Al Ḩadīthah
Kāf
Khān Yūnis
1064
Mughayyir
Under construction
Al Qaşr
Qaşr aţ Ţūbah
Al Qurayyāt
Be'er Sheva' (Beersheba)
'Arad
Al Mazra'ah
Ar Rabbah
Al Qaţrānah
Kathrabbā
Al Karak
Kamkhat Muḩaywir 963
ISRAEL
Dimona
Mu'tah
Wādī al Makhrūq
Mash'abbe Sade
Aş Şāfī
Dhāt Ra's
Qā' al Ḩafīrah
Ne'ot HaKikar
Tannur
Muḩayy
Nizzana (El 'Auja)
Al La'bān
Qaşr al Mushayyish
Wādī Bā'ir
Wādī al Gharrah
Sede Boqer
Şinifḩah
Aţ Ţafīlah
An Namatah
Qal 'at al Hasā
'En Hazeva
'Ābūr
Qā' al Jinz
Bā'ir
Wādī al Ḩaşāh
Buşayrā
Ar Rashādīyah
Ardaş Şawwān
Mizpe Ramon
'En Yahav
Dānā
1636
Jurf ad Darāwīsh
1054
Faynān
Wādī al Fukūk
Wādī Sirḩān
NEGEV
Wādī Ukhayḑir
Ash Shawbak
Ţubarjal
902
1734
Paran
Qā' al Jafr
Petra
Udhruḩ
Wādī Mūsā (Elchi)
Al Jafr
1005
Bi'r an Na'ām
Wādī al Quwayşirah
Ma'ān
JORDAN
SAUDI ARABIA
Al Busayţā'
EGYPT
Gharandal
Qulbān Banī Murrah
El Kuntilla
Abū al Lasan
Qetura
Ra's an Naqb
Al'Unnāb
Yotvata
Ash Shidīyah
Wādī al 'Arabah
Al Quwayrah
Hattīyah
Khirbat al Khālidī
Jabal al Ḩarad 1274
El 'Auja 936
Elat
Ramm
Ezion-geber (Elath)
Conic Projection
Ţâba
Al 'Aqabah (Aqaba)
SCALE 1:1,838,000
1 CENTIMETER = 18.4 KILOMETERS; 1 INCH = 29.0 MILES
Ad Durra
0 25 50 75 100
KILOMETERS
Al Mudawwarah
Râs el Burqa' 1165
Al Ḩumayḑah
0 25 50 75 100
STATUTE MILES
GULF OF AQABA
Ḩismá
Ḩālat 'Ammār
A B C D E F G H J K L M
1 2 3 4 5 6 7 8 9

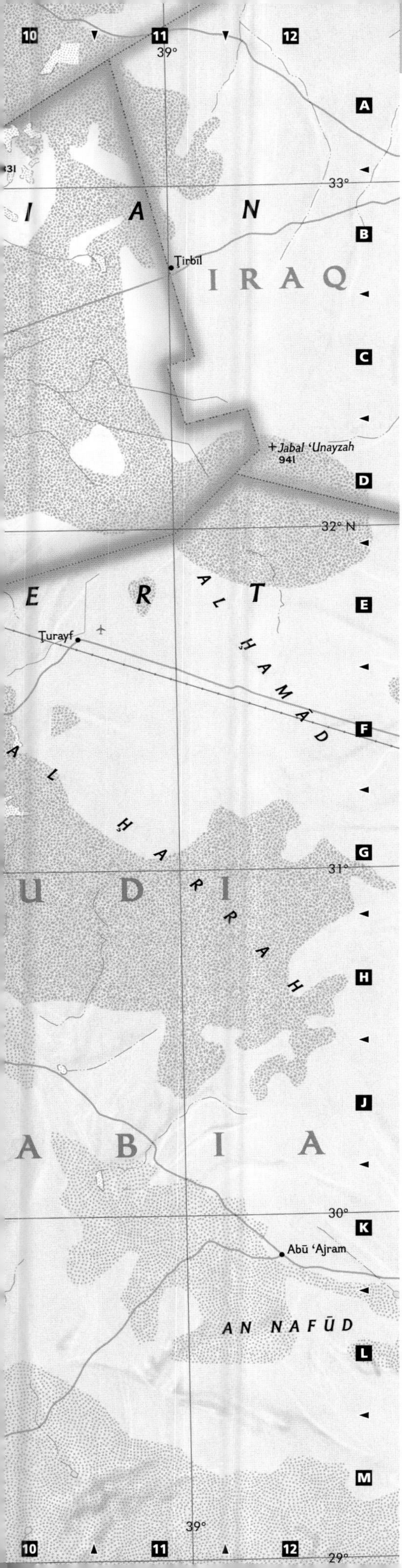

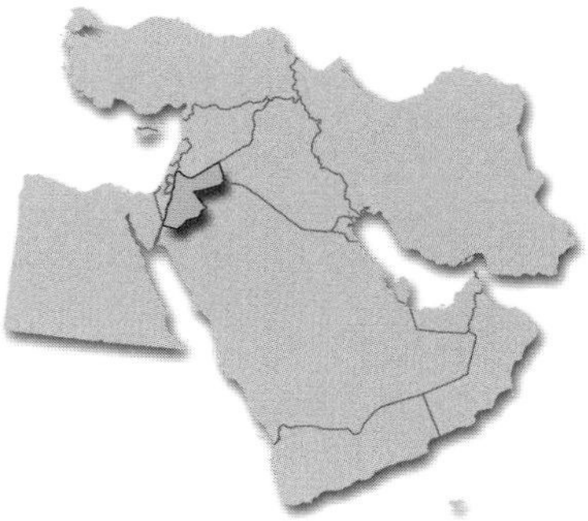

Jordan

HASHEMITE KINGDOM OF JORDAN

AREA	92,300 sq km (35,637 sq mi)
POPULATION	5,300,000
CAPITAL	'Ammān (Philadelphia) 1,181,000
RELIGION	(percent of population): Muslim 96% (mostly Sunni), Christian 4%
LANGUAGE	Arabic (official), English widely understood among upper and middle classes
LITERACY	86.6%
LIFE EXPECTANCY	70 years
TROOPS	Active: 100,200; Reserves: 35,000
GDP PER CAPITA	$4,200
CRUDE OIL RESERVES	None or negligible
ECONOMY	IND: phosphate mining, petroleum refining, cement, potash, light manufacturing, tourism. AGR: wheat, barley, citrus, tomatoes, melons, olives; sheep, goats, poultry. EXP: phosphates, fertilizers, potash, agricultural products, manufactures, pharmaceuticals.
AREA COMPARISON	Jordan encompasses 1.15% of the 48 contiguous United States.

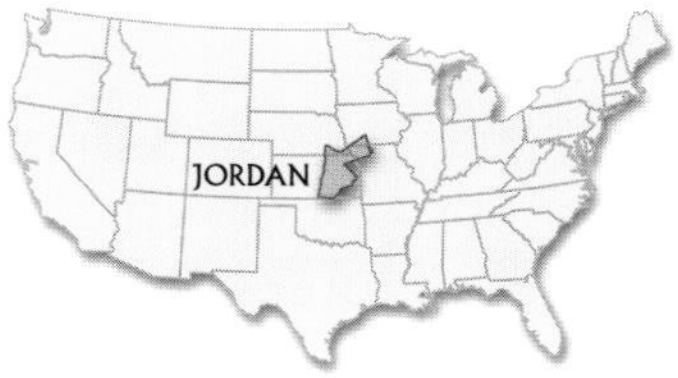

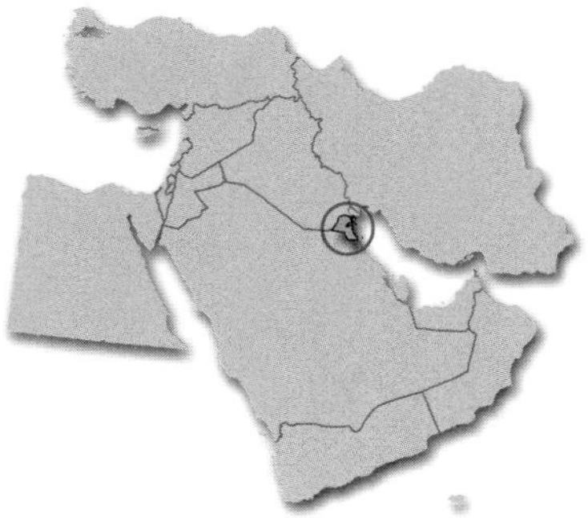

Kuwait

STATE OF KUWAIT

AREA 17,820 sq km (6,880 sq mi)

POPULATION 2,300,000

CAPITAL Al Kuwayt (Kuwait) 888,000

RELIGION (percent of population): Muslim 85% (mostly Sunni, Shiite 25%), other 15% (Christian, Hindu)

LANGUAGE Arabic (official), English widely spoken

LITERACY 78.6%

LIFE EXPECTANCY 76 years

TROOPS Active: 15,500; Reserves: 23,700

GDP PER CAPITA $15,100

CRUDE OIL RESERVES 96,500,000,000 barrels

ECONOMY IND: petroleum, petrochemicals, desalination, food processing, construction materials. AGR: practically no crops; fish. EXP: oil and refined products, fertilizers.

AREA COMPARISON Kuwait encompasses 0.22% of the 48 contiguous United States.

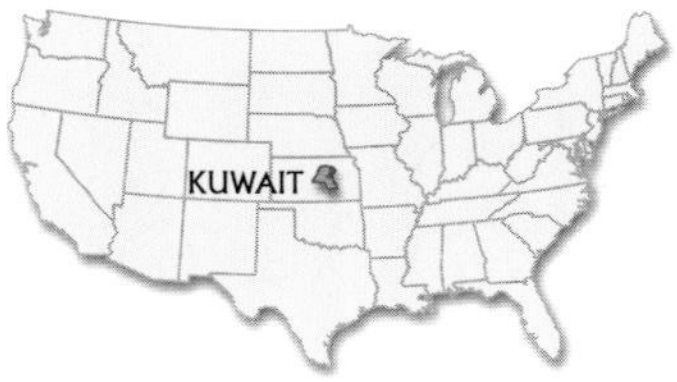

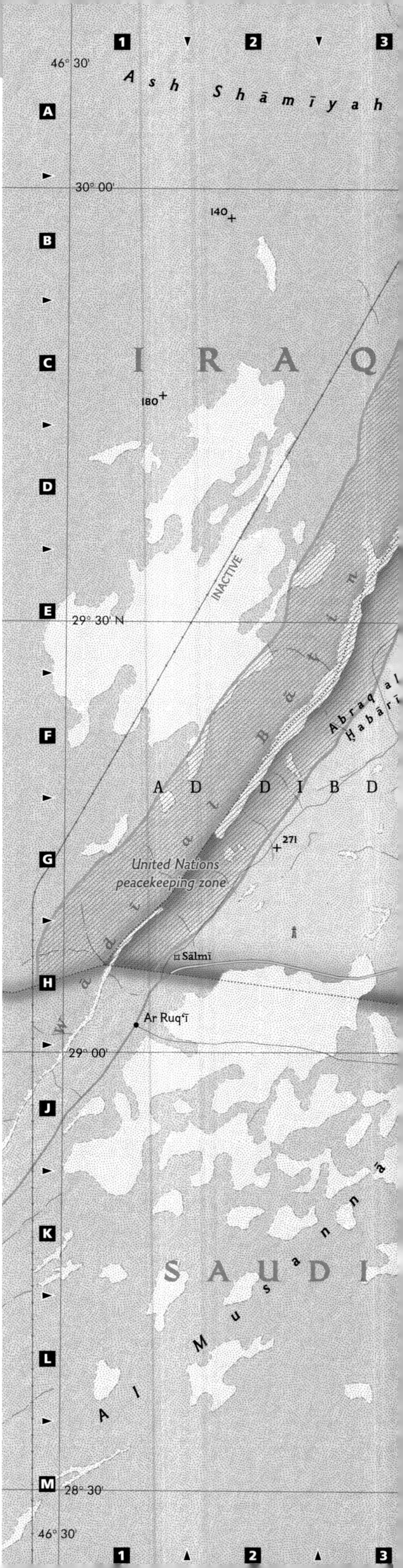

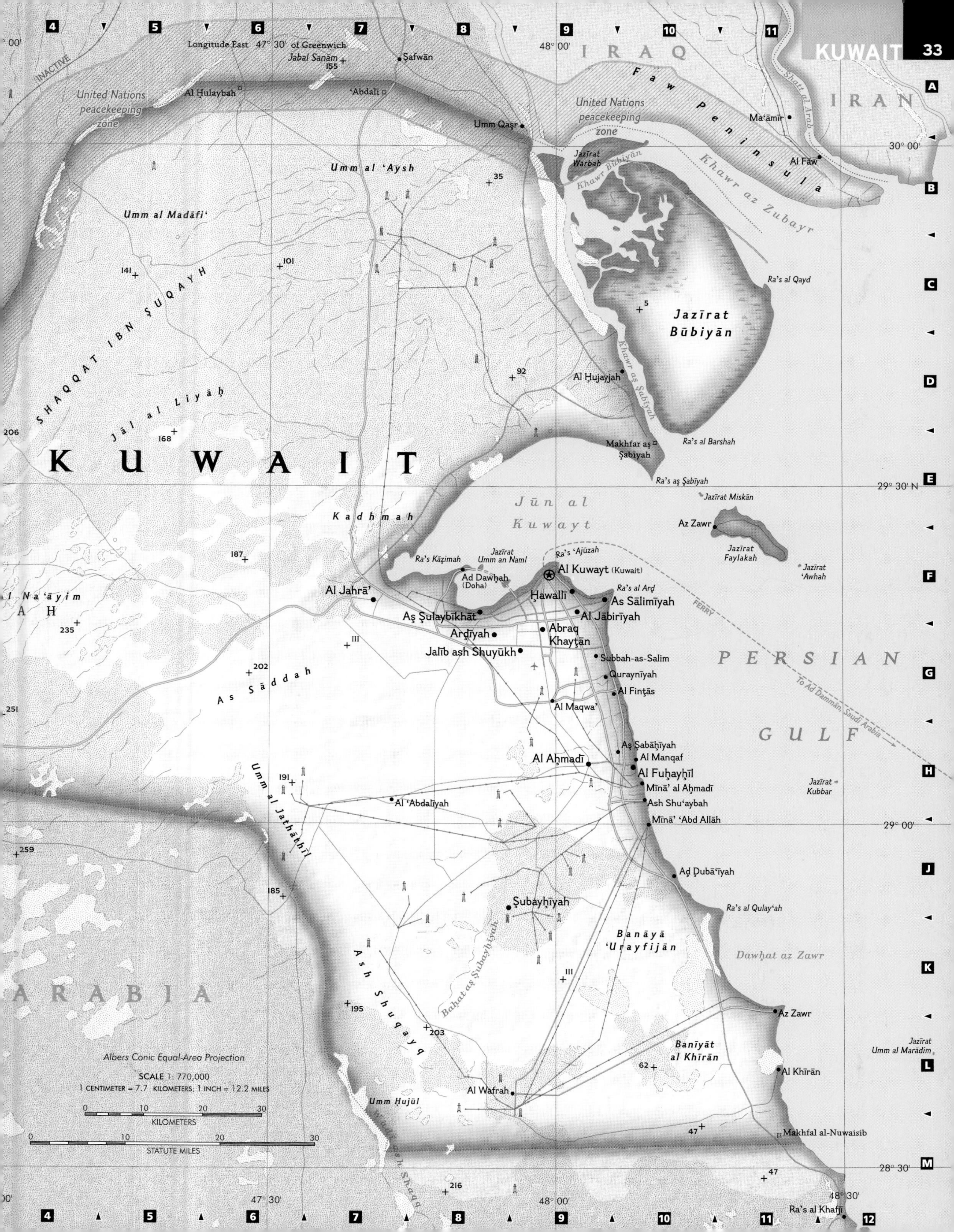
IRAQ
IRAN
Faw Peninsula
Shatt al Arab
Ma'āmir
Al Fāw
Khawr az Zubayr
Khawr Būbiyān
Jazīrat Warbah
United Nations peacekeeping zone
INACTIVE
Longitude East 47° 30' of Greenwich
Jabal Sanām 155
Şafwān
Al Hulaybah
'Abdalī
Umm Qaşr
Umm al 'Aysh
Umm al Madāfi'
SHAQQAT IBN ŞUQAYH
Jāl al Liyāh
KUWAIT
Jazīrat Būbiyān
Ra's al Qayd
Khawr aş Şabīyah
Al Hujayjah
Makhfar aş Şabīyah
Ra's al Barshah
Ra's aş Şabīyah
Jazīrat Miskān
Jūn al Kuwayt
Az Zawr
Jazīrat Faylakah
Jazīrat 'Awhah
Kadhmah
Ra's Kāzimah
Jazīrat Umm an Naml
Ra's 'Ajūzah
Al Kuwayt (Kuwait)
Ad Dawhah (Doha)
Ra's al Arḑ
Al Jahrā'
Hawallī
As Sālimīyah
Aş Şulaybīkhāt
Al Jābirīyah
Arḑīyah
Abraq Khayţān
Jalīb ash Shuyūkh
Subbah-as-Salim
Quraynīyah
Al Finţās
Al Maqwa'
FERRY
To Ad Dammān, Saudi Arabia
PERSIAN GULF
As Sāddah
Aş Şabāḩīyah
Al Manqaf
Al Aḩmadī
Al Fuḩayḩīl
Mīnā' al Aḩmadī
Ash Shu'aybah
Mīnā' 'Abd Allāh
Jazīrat Kubbar
Umm al Jathāthīl
Al 'Abdalīyah
Aḑ Ḑubā'īyah
Ra's al Qulay'ah
Şubayḩīyah
Banāyā 'Urayfijān
Dawḩat az Zawr
Baţn aş Şubayḩīyah
Ash Shuqayq
ARABIA
Az Zawr
Jazīrat Umm al Marādim
Banīyāt al Khīrān
Al Khīrān
Al Wafrah
Umm Hujūl
Wādī ash Shaqq
Makhfal al-Nuwaisib
Ra's al Khafjī
30° 00'
29° 30' N
29° 00'
28° 30'
48° 00'
47° 30'
48° 30'
Albers Conic Equal-Area Projection
SCALE 1: 770,000
1 CENTIMETER = 7.7 KILOMETERS; 1 INCH = 12.2 MILES
KILOMETERS
STATUTE MILES

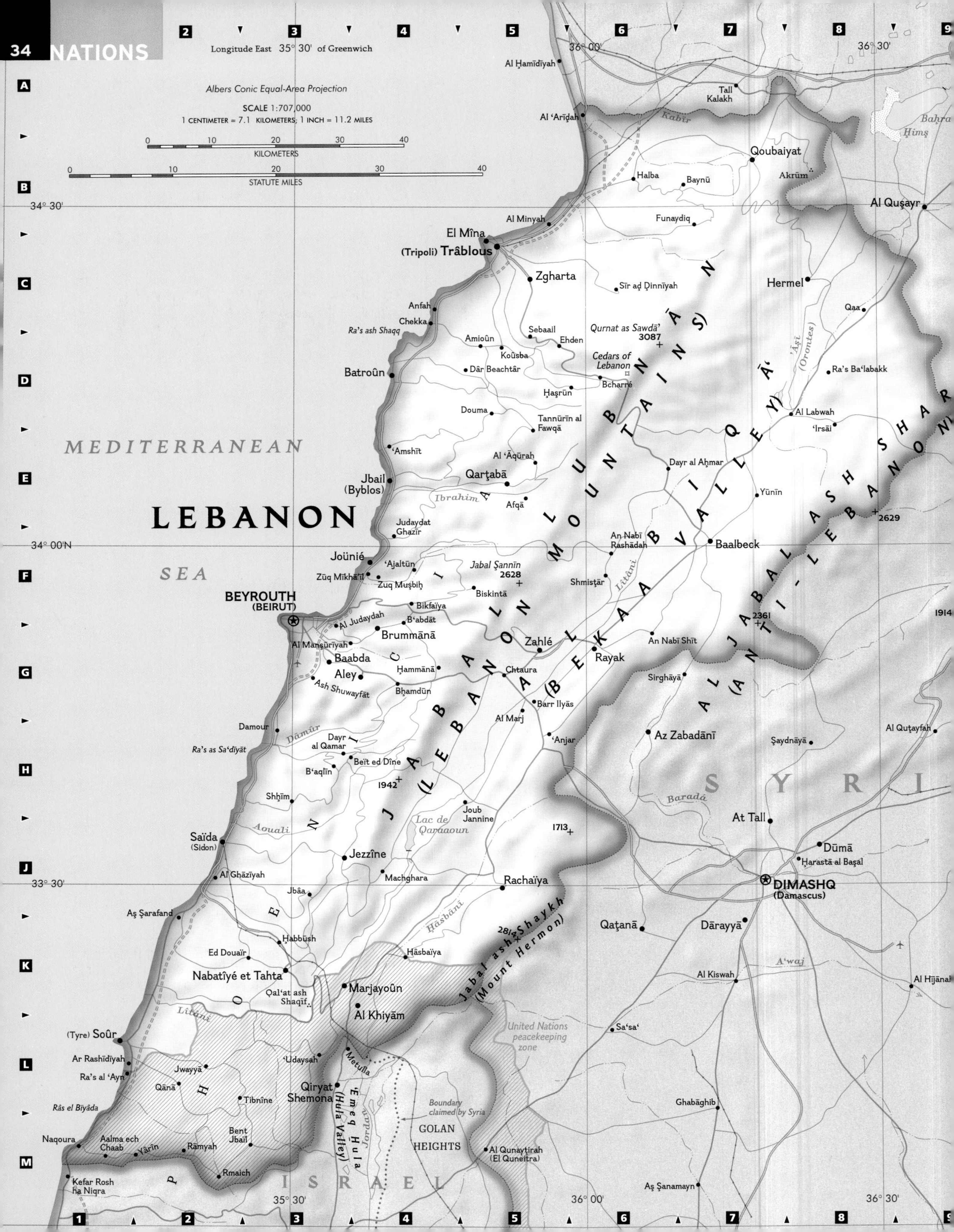
Longitude East 35° 30' of Greenwich
Albers Conic Equal-Area Projection
SCALE 1:707,000
1 CENTIMETER = 7.1 KILOMETERS; 1 INCH = 11.2 MILES
0 10 20 30 40
KILOMETERS
0 10 20 30 40
STATUTE MILES
34° 30'
34° 00'N
33° 30'
36° 00'
36° 30'
35° 30'
MEDITERRANEAN
SEA
LEBANON
S Y R I
ISRAEL
GOLAN HEIGHTS
BEYROUTH
(BEIRUT)
DIMASHQ
(Damascus)
Al Ḩamīdīyah
Tall Kalakh
Al ʻArīḑah
Kabīr
Baḩra Ḩimş
Qoubaiyat
Halba
Baynū
Akrūm
Al Quşayr
Al Minyah
Funaydiq
El Mîna
(Tripoli) Trâblous
Zgharta
Sīr aḑ Ḑinnīyah
Hermel
Qaa
Anfah
Chekka
Ra's ash Shaqq
Sebaail
Ehden
Qurnat as Sawdā'
3087
Amioûn
Koûsba
Cedars of Lebanon
Bcharré
Dâr Beachtâr
Batroûn
'Āşī (Orontes)
Ra's Baʻlabakk
Ḩaşrūn
Douma
Tannūrīn al Fawqā
Al Labwah
ʻIrsāi
ʻAmshīt
Al ʻĀqūrah
Dayr al Aḩmar
Jbail
(Byblos)
Qarţabā
Ibrahim
Afqā
Yūnīn
Judaydat Ghazīr
2629
An Nabī Rashādah
Baalbeck
Jounié
ʻAjaltūn
Jabal Şannīn
2628
Zūq Mīkhā'īl
Zuq Muşbiḩ
Shmistār
Līṭānī
Biskintā
Bikfaïya
Al Judaydah
Bʻabdāt
2361
1914
Brummānā
An Nabī Shīt
Al Manşūrīyah
Zahlé
Rayak
Baabda
Aley
Ḩammānā
Chtaura
Sirghāyā
Ash Shuwayfāt
Bḩamdūn
Barr Ilyās
Al Marj
Damour
Dāmūr
ʻAnjar
Az Zabadānī
Şaydnāyā
Al Quţayfah
Dayr al Qamar
Ra's as Saʻdīyāt
Beït ed Dîne
Bʻaqlīn
1942
Shḩīm
Joub Jannine
Baradá
At Tall
Lac de Qaraaoun
Aouali
1713
Saïda
(Sidon)
Dūmā
Jezzîne
Ḩarastā al Başal
Al Ghāzīyah
Machghara
Rachaïya
Jbâa
Aş Şarafand
Ḩāsbānī
2814
Qaţanā
Dārayyā
Ḩabbūsh
Ed Douaïr
Hâsbaïya
Jabal ash Shaykh (Mount Hermon)
Aʻwaj
Nabatîyé et Tahta
Al Kiswah
Al Hijānah
Marjayoûn
Qalʻat ash Shaqīf
Al Khiyām
Līṭānī
United Nations peacekeeping zone
(Tyre) Soûr
Sa'sa'
Ar Rashīdīyah
ʻUdaysah
Metulla
Ra's al ʻAyn
Jwayyā
Qānā
Qiryat Shemona
ʻEmeq Hula (Hula Valley)
Tibnîne
Rās el Bīyāda
Boundary claimed by Syria
Ghabāghib
Jordan
Bent Jbaïl
Naqoura
Aalma ech Chaab
Yārīn
Rāmyah
Al Qunayţirah
(El Quneitra)
Rmaich
Kefar Rosh ha Niqra
Aş Şanamayn
JABAL LUBNĀN (LEBANON MOUNTAINS)
AL BIQĀʻ (BEKAA VALLEY)
AL JABAL ASH SHARQĪ (ANTI-LEBANON)
JABAL LUBNĀN (LEBANON MOUNTAINS)
A B C D E F G H J K L M
1 2 3 4 5 6 7 8 9

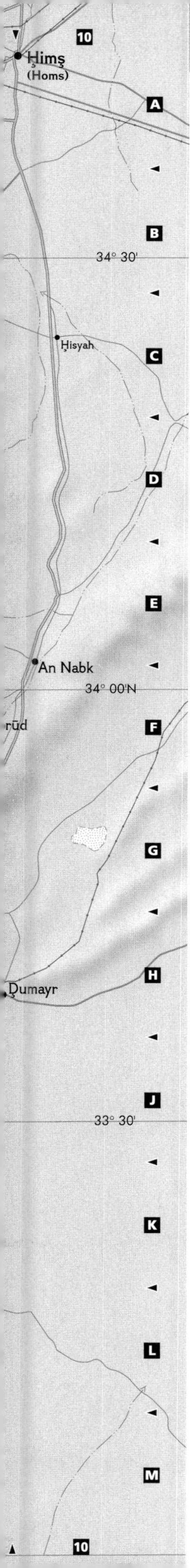

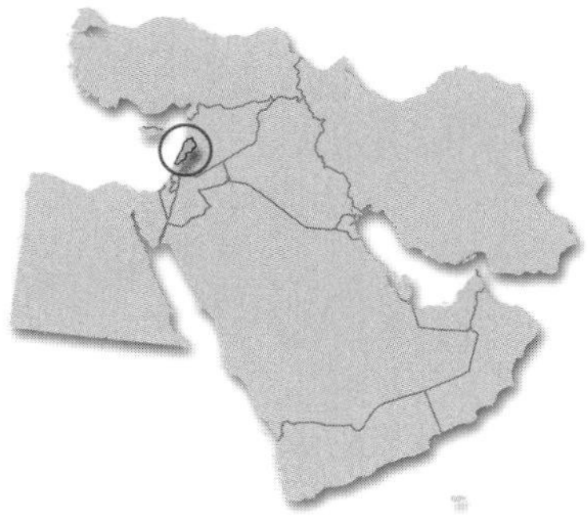

Lebanon

LEBANESE REPUBLIC

AREA	10,400 sq km (4,015 sq mi)
POPULATION	4,300,000
CAPITAL	Beyrouth (Beirut) 2,115,000
RELIGION	(percent of population): Muslim 70% (Shiite, Sunni, Druze), Christian 30% (Maronite, Orthodox)
LANGUAGE	Arabic (official), French, English, Armenian
LITERACY	86.4%
LIFE EXPECTANCY	73 years
TROOPS	Active: 71,800
GDP PER CAPITA	$5,200
CRUDE OIL RESERVES	None or negligible
ECONOMY	IND: banking; food processing; jewelry; cement; textiles; mineral and chemical products; wood and furniture products; oil refining; metal fabricating. AGR: citrus, grapes, tomatoes, apples, vegetables, potatoes, olives, tobacco; sheep, goats. EXP: foodstuffs and tobacco, textiles, chemicals, precious stones, metal, electrical equipment and products, jewelry, and paper.
AREA COMPARISON	Lebanon encompasses 0.13% of the 48 contiguous United States.

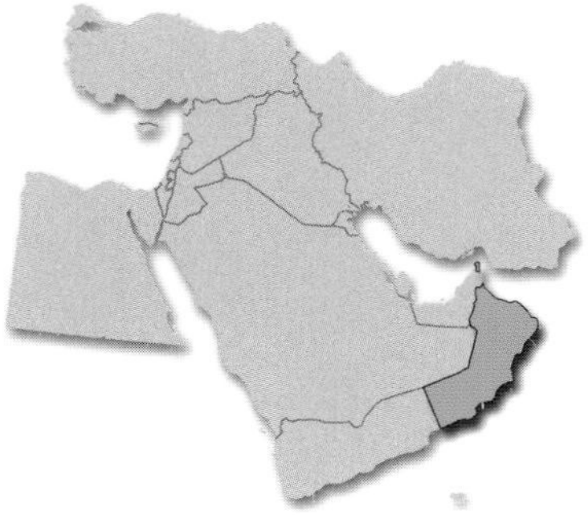

Oman

SULTANATE OF OMAN

AREA 212,460 sq km (82,031 sq mi)

POPULATION 2,600,000

CAPITAL Maşqat (Muscat) 540,000

RELIGION (percent of population): Muslim 88% (mostly Ibadhi, Sunni 25%), Hindu 8%, Christian 4%

LANGUAGE Arabic (official), English, Baluchi, Urdu, Indian dialects

LITERACY approaching 80%

LIFE EXPECTANCY 73 years

TROOPS Active: 43,400

GDP PER CAPITA $8,200

CRUDE OIL RESERVES 5,500,000,000 barrels

ECONOMY IND: crude oil production and refining, natural gas production, construction, cement, copper. AGR: dates, limes, bananas, alfalfa, vegetables; camels, cattle; fish. EXP: petroleum, reexports, fish, metals, textiles.

AREA COMPARISON Oman encompasses 2.6% of the 48 contiguous United States.

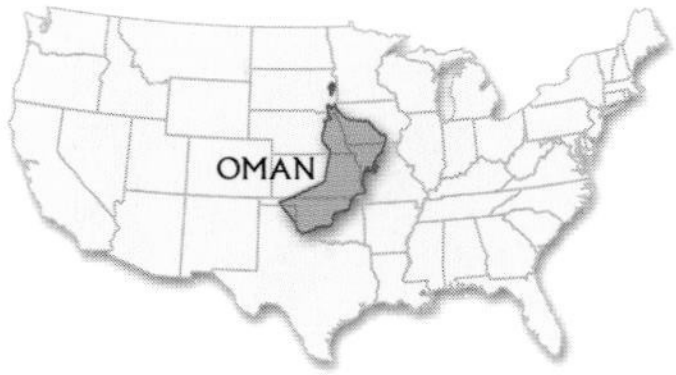

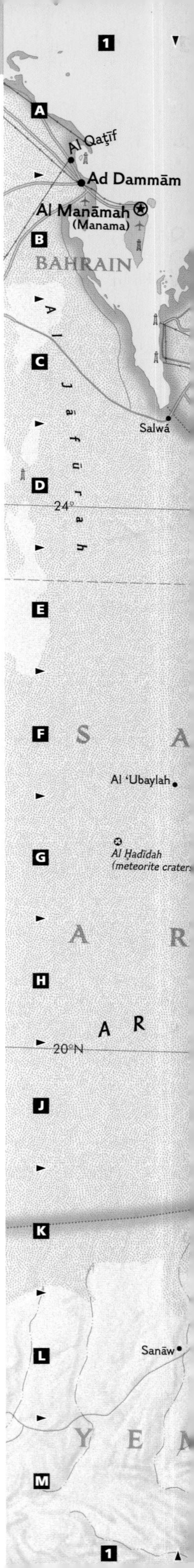

PERSIAN GULF
GULF OF OMAN
ARABIAN SEA
IRAN
QATAR
UNITED ARAB EMIRATES
SAUDI ARABIA
OMAN
AR RUB' AL KHĀLĪ (EMPTY QUARTER)
ENCLAVES
An enclave is a territory surrounded by another country. Madha is an Omani enclave surrounded by the United Arab Emirates, but Madha in turn encircles the tiny U.A.E. enclave of Nahwa.
MADHA Oman
NAHWA U.A.E.
Strait of Hormuz
TROPIC OF CANCER
Bandar-e 'Abbās
Masqaṭ (Muscat)
Abū Ẓaby (Abu Dhabi)
Ad Dawḥah (Doha)
Dubayy (Dubai)
Ash Shāriqah (Sharjah)
Ajmān
Umm al Qaywayn
Ra's al Khaymah
Al Fujayrah
Mīnā' Jabal 'Alī
Al 'Ayn
Al Buraymī
Ṣuḥār
Maṭraḥ
Ruwī
Nizwá
Bahlah
Ṣūr
Ra's al Ḥadd
Ramlat Āl Wahībah
Jazīrat Maṣīrah (Masira)
Khalīj Maṣīrah
Ghubbat Ṣawqirah
Ẓufār
Ṣalālah
Ṭāqah
Mirbāṭ
Ra's Mirbāṭ
Jabal Samḥān 1463
Jazā'ir Khurīyā Murīyā (Kuria Muria Islands)
Ra's ash Sharbatāt
Ra's al Madrakah
Madrakah
Duqm
Haymā'
Al Ghābah
Mughshin
Thamarīt
Rakhyūt
Al Ghayḍah
Ḥabarūt
'Urūq Ibn Ḥamūdah
Umm as Samīm
Wādī Aswad
Wādī Shiḥan
Al Jabal al Akhḍar
Jabal ash Shām 2980
Jabal Ḥafīt 1166
Jabal Ghawīl 1461
Jabal al Ḥarīm 2087
Ra's Musandam
Liwā
Boundary Undefined
De Facto Boundary
Lambert Conformal Conic Projection
SCALE 1:4,630,000
1 CENTIMETER = 46.3 KILOMETERS; 1 INCH = 73.1 MILES
KILOMETERS
STATUTE MILES
Longitude East 56° of Greenwich

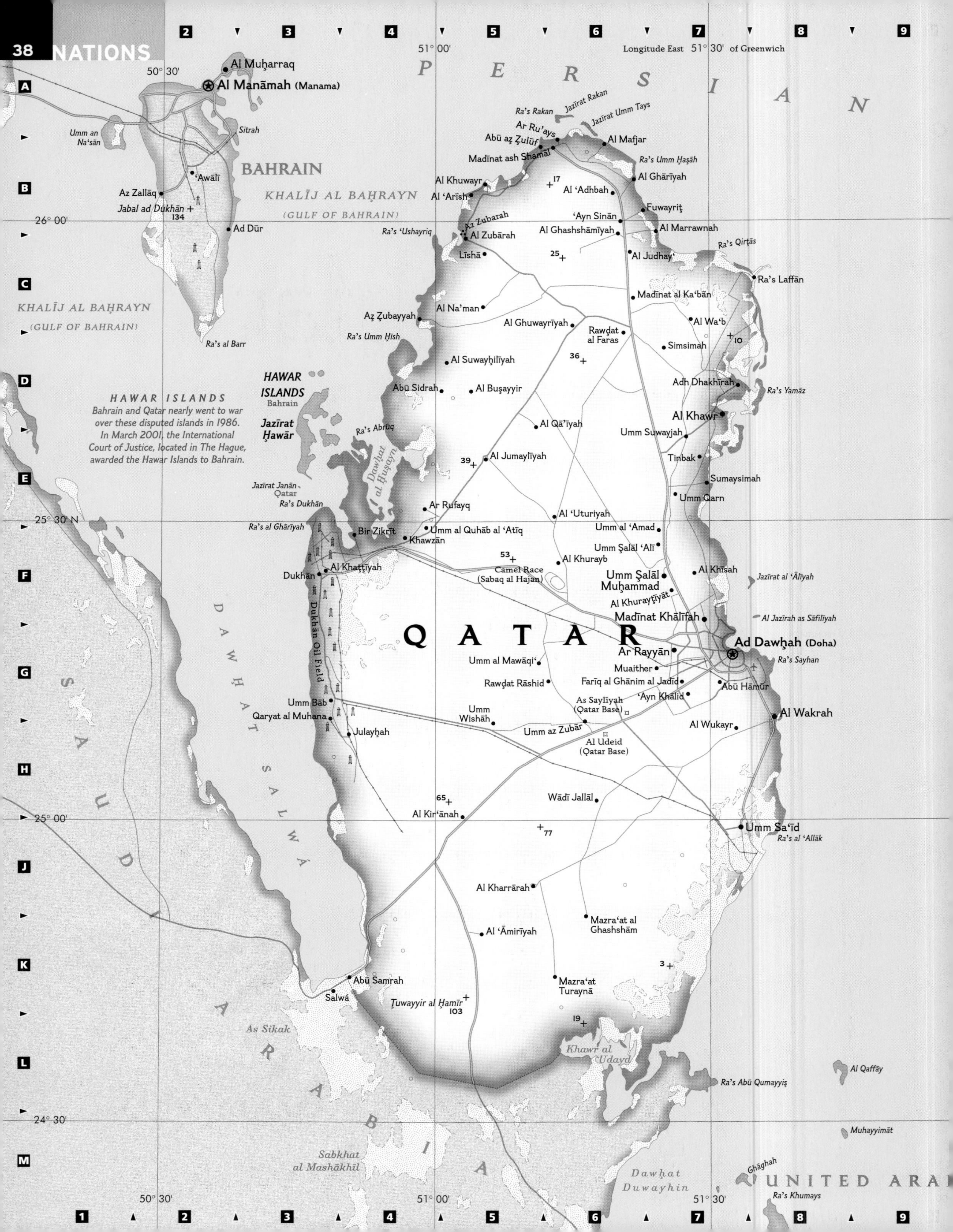
Longitude East 51° 30' of Greenwich
51° 00'
50° 30'
26° 00'
25° 30' N
25° 00'
24° 30'
P E R S I A N
Al Muḩarraq
Al Manāmah (Manama)
Umm an Na'sān
Sitrah
BAHRAIN
'Awālī
Az Zallāq
Jabal ad Dukhān
134
Ad Dūr
KHALĪJ AL BAḨRAYN
(GULF OF BAHRAIN)
Ra's al Barr
HAWAR ISLANDS
Bahrain and Qatar nearly went to war over these disputed islands in 1986. In March 2001, the International Court of Justice, located in The Hague, awarded the Hawar Islands to Bahrain.
HAWAR ISLANDS
Bahrain
Jazīrat Ḩawār
Jazīrat Janān
Qatar
Ra's Dukhān
Ra's al Ghārīyah
Ra's Abrūq
Dawḩat al Ḩuşayn
Ra's Rakan
Jazīrat Rakan
Jazīrat Umm Tays
Ar Ru'ays
Abū az Ẓulūf
Madīnat ash Shamāl
Al Mafjar
Ra's Umm Ḩaşāh
Al Ghārīyah
Al Khuwayr
Al 'Arīsh
Al 'Adhbah
Fuwayriţ
'Ayn Sinān
Al Ghashshāmīyah
Al Marrawnah
Ra's 'Ushayriq
Az Zubārah
Al Zubārah
Līshā
Al Judhay'
Ra's Qirţās
Ra's Laffān
Madīnat al Ka'bān
Al Na'man
Az Zubayyah
Ra's Umm Ḩīsh
Al Ghuwayrīyah
Rawḑat al Faras
Al Wa'b
Simsimah
Al Suwayḩilīyah
Abū Sidrah
Al Buşayyir
Adh Dhakhīrah
Ra's Yamāz
Al Khawr
Al Qā'īyah
Umm Suwayjah
Al Jumaylīyah
Tinbak
Sumaysimah
Umm Qarn
Ar Rufayq
Al 'Uturiyah
Bir Zikrīt
Umm al Quhāb al 'Atīq
Khawzān
Umm al 'Amad
Umm Şalāl 'Alī
Camel Race (Sabaq al Hajan)
Al Khurayb
Al Khaţţīyah
Dukhān
Al Khīsah
Jazīrat al 'Āliyah
Umm Şalāl Muḩammad
Al Khuraytīyāt
Madīnat Khalīfah
Al Jazīrah as Sāfilīyah
Dukhān Oil Field
QATAR
Ad Dawḩah (Doha)
Ar Rayyān
Ra's Sayhan
Umm al Mawāqi'
Muaither
Rawḑat Rāshid
Farīq al Ghānim al Jadīd
Abū Hāmūr
As Saylīyah (Qatar Base)
'Ayn Khālid
Umm Bāb
Qaryat al Muhana
Umm Wishāh
Al Wakrah
Umm az Zubār
Al Wukayr
Julayḩah
Al Udeid (Qatar Base)
DAWḨAT SALWÁ
Wādī Jallāl
Al Kir'ānah
Umm Sa'īd
Ra's al 'Allāk
Al Kharrārah
Mazra'at al Ghashshām
Al 'Āmirīyah
Mazra'at Turaynā
Abū Samrah
Salwá
Ţuwayyir al Ḩamīr
103
As Sikak
Khawr al 'Udayd
Al Qaffāy
Ra's Abū Qumayyiş
Muhayyimāt
SAUDI ARABIA
Sabkhat al Mashākhīl
Dawḩat Duwayhin
Ghāghah
UNITED ARA
Ra's Khumays

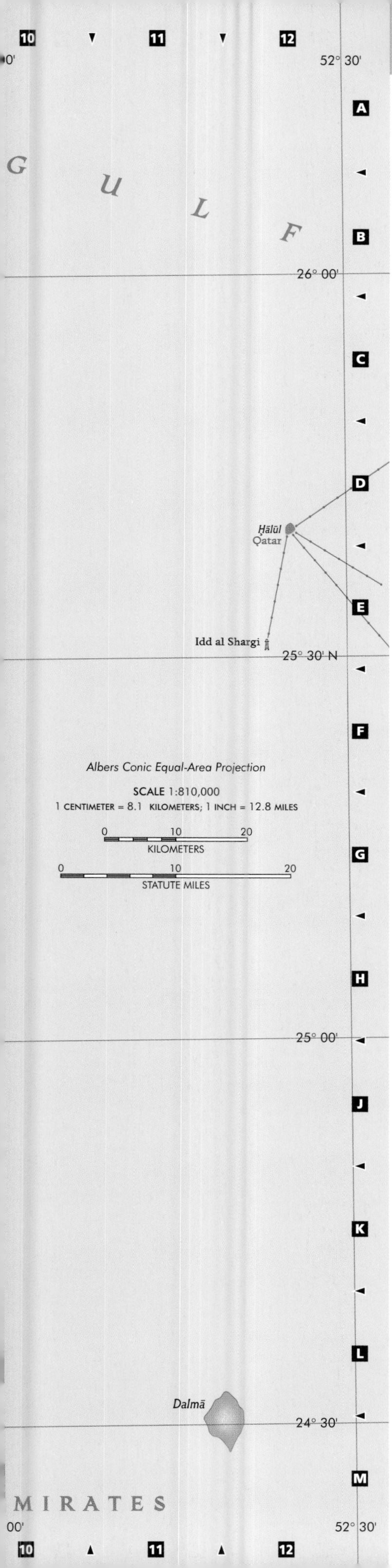
52° 30'
G U L F
26° 00'
Ḩālūl
Qatar
Idd al Shargi
25° 30' N
Albers Conic Equal-Area Projection
SCALE 1:810,000
1 CENTIMETER = 8.1 KILOMETERS; 1 INCH = 12.8 MILES
0 10 20
KILOMETERS
0 10 20
STATUTE MILES
25° 00'
Dalmā
24° 30'
MIRATES
52° 30'

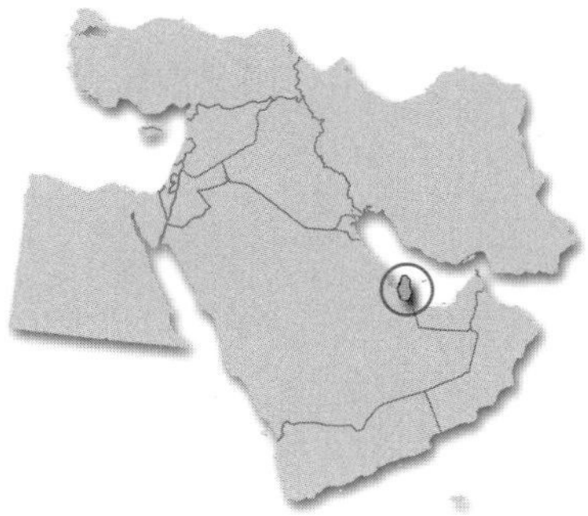

Qatar

STATE OF QATAR

AREA	11,437 sq km (4,416 sq mi)
POPULATION	600,000
CAPITAL	Ad Dawḩah (Doha) 285,000
RELIGION	(percent of population): Muslim 83% (mostly Sunni), Christian 10%, Hindu 3%, other 4%
LANGUAGE	Arabic (official), English commonly used as a second language
LITERACY	79%
LIFE EXPECTANCY	72 years
TROOPS	Active: 12,300
GDP PER CAPITA	$21,200
CRUDE OIL RESERVES	15,200,000,000 barrels
ECONOMY	IND: crude oil production and refining, fertilizers, petrochemicals, steel reinforcing bars, cement. AGR: fruits, vegetables; poultry, dairy products, beef; fish. EXP: petroleum products 80%, fertilizers, steel.
AREA COMPARISON	Qatar encompasses 0.14% of the 48 contiguous United States.

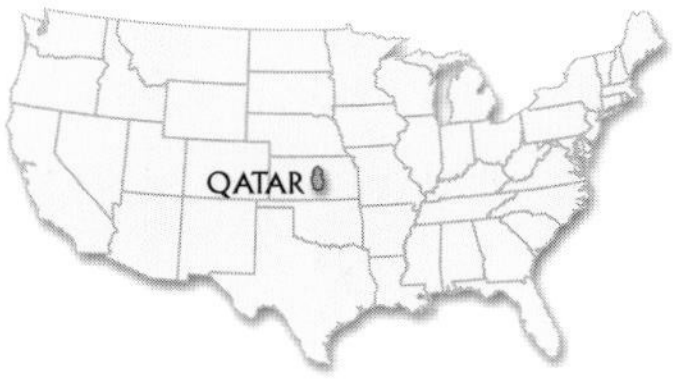
QATAR

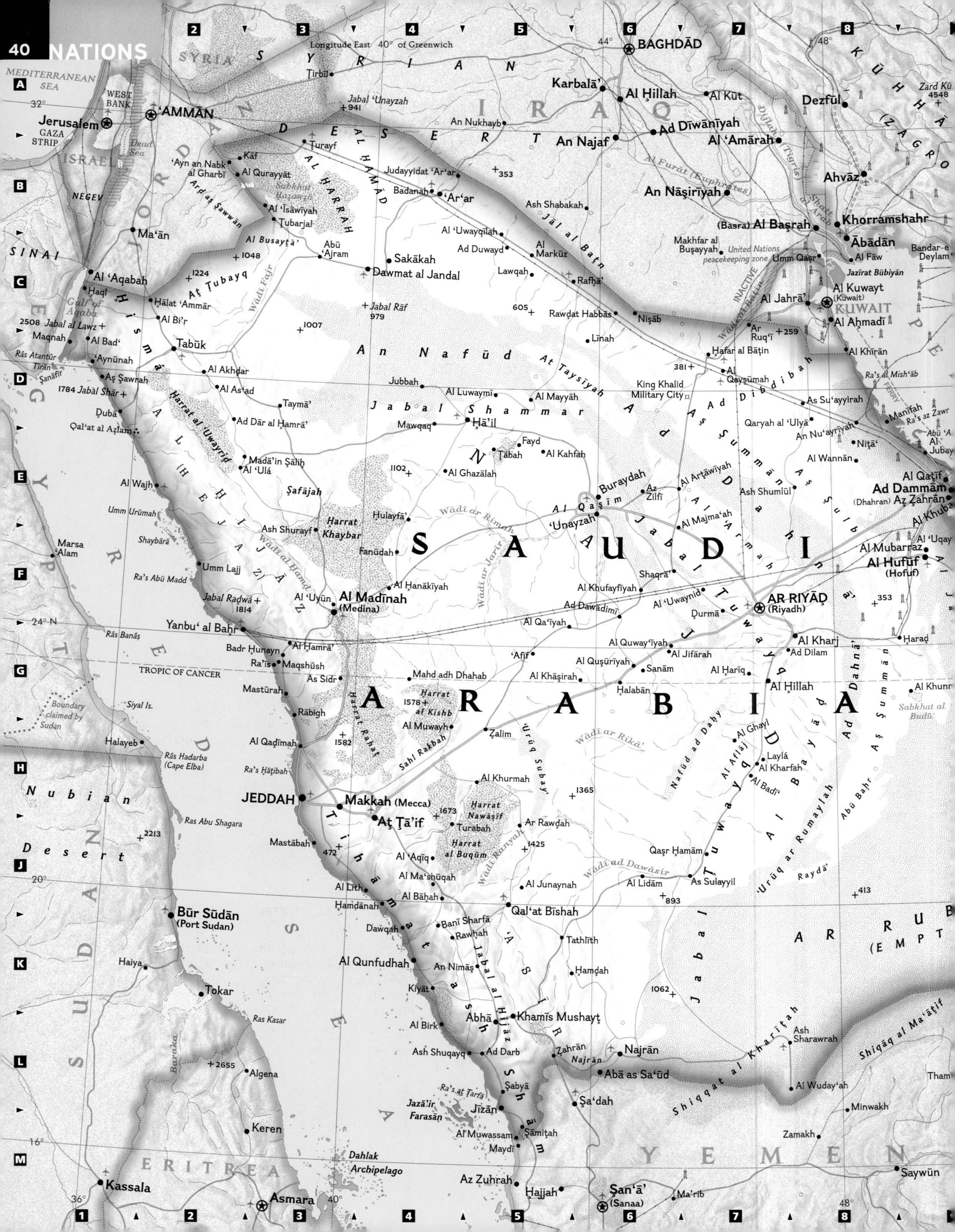

Longitude East 40° of Greenwich
MEDITERRANEAN SEA
SYRIA
SYRIAN DESERT
IRAQ
JORDAN
ISRAEL
WEST BANK
GAZA STRIP
Jerusalem
'AMMĀN
BAGHDĀD
Karbalā'
Al Ḥillah
Al Kūt
Ad Dīwānīyah
An Najaf
Al 'Amārah
An Nāṣirīyah
(Basra) Al Baṣrah
Khorramshahr
Ābādān
Ahvāz
Dezfūl
KUWAIT
Al Kuwayt (Kuwait)
Al Jahrā'
Al Aḥmadī
SINAI
NEGEV
Al 'Aqabah
Gulf of Aqaba
Tabūk
An Nafūd
Jabal Shammar
Ḥā'il
Sakākah
Dawmat al Jandal
Buraydah
'Unayzah
SAUDI ARABIA
AR RIYĀḌ (Riyadh)
Al Hufūf (Hofuf)
Ad Dammām
Al Madīnah (Medina)
Yanbu' al Baḥr
TROPIC OF CANCER
JEDDAH
Makkah (Mecca)
Aṭ Ṭā'if
Qal'at Bīshah
Abhā
Khamīs Mushayṭ
Najrān
Jīzān
Jazā'ir Farasān
Būr Sūdān (Port Sudan)
Nubian Desert
SUDAN
ERITREA
Asmara
Kassala
Keren
Dahlak Archipelago
YEMEN
Ṣan'ā' (Sanaa)
Ṣa'dah
Ḥajjah
Ma'rib
Saywūn
AR RUB' (EMPT
Ad Dahnā'
Aṣ Ṣummān
Jabal Ṭuwayq
Ḥarrat Khaybar
Ḥarrat Rahat
Tihāmat 'Asīr
Al Ḥijāz
Wādī ad Dawāsir
Wādī ar Rimah
Wādī al Baṭin
Al Furāt (Euphrates)
Dijlah (Tigris)
United Nations peacekeeping zone

Saudi Arabia

KINGDOM OF SAUDI ARABIA

AREA 1,960,582 sq km (756,985 sq mi)

POPULATION 24,000,000

CAPITAL Ar Riyāḑ (Riyadh) 4,761,000

RELIGION (percent of population): Muslim 94% (mostly Sunni), Christian 4%, other 2% (Hindu, Buddhist)

LANGUAGE Arabic (official)

LITERACY 78%

LIFE EXPECTANCY 72 years

TROOPS Active: 201,200; Reserves: 20,000

GDP PER CAPITA $10,600

CRUDE OIL RESERVES 261,800,000,000 barrels

ECONOMY IND: crude oil production, petroleum refining, basic petrochemicals, cement, construction, fertilizer, plastics. AGR: wheat, barley, tomatoes, melons, dates, citrus; mutton, chickens, eggs, milk. EXP: petroleum and petroleum products 90%.

AREA COMPARISON Saudi Arabia encompasses 24.4% of the 48 contiguous United States.

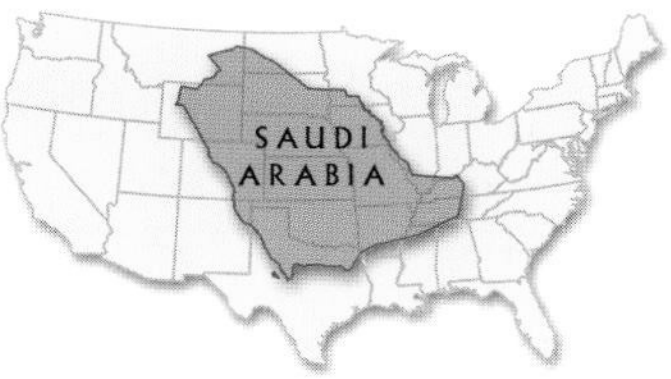

Longitude East 40° of Greenwich
38°
36° N
34°
36°
38°
40°
T U R K E Y
S Y R I A
L E B A N O N
J O R D A N
S Y R I A N D E S E R T
MEDITERRANEAN SEA
Türkoğlu
Yavuzeli
Halfeti
Bozova
Atatürk Barajı
Viranşehir
Kızıltepe
Bahçe
Sakçagöze
Ceyhan
Osmaniye
Fevzipaşa
İslâhiye
Gaziantep
Şanlıurfa
(Edessa)
Çamlıdere
Akdoğan
Oğuzeli
Nizip
Birecik
Suruç
Dörtyol
Musabeyli
Kargamış
(Carchemish)
Jarābulus
'Ayn al 'Arab
Arsalān Ṭāsh
Mürşitpınar
Şehit
Nusretbey
Ceylanpınar
Ra's al 'Ayn
Yumurtalık
Yakacık
(Payas)
Hassa
Maydān Ikbis
Doğanpınar
Shuyūkh Fawqānī
Büyüktaş
Massah
Kānlī
Kilis
Elbeyli
Zawghar
Tall al Aḥmar
(Til Barsip)
Yağmuralan
Akçakale
Tall
Ḥalaf
İskenderun
(Alexandretta)
Aktepe
(Güvenç)
Nur Dağları
A'zāz
Jawbān Bayk
Mandik
Tall al Abyaḍ al 'Atiq
Salūq
Tall Tamir
Top Boğazı
(Syrian Gates)
Kırıkhan
'Afrīn
Jabal Sim'ān
Akhtarīn
Manbij
Wādī al Ḥimar
Tall Rif'at
Dayr Sim'ān
Hamam
Jubb Ḥasan Aghā
Abū Daghmah
Qushlat Yūsuf Bāshā
Sharaqraq
922
Jabal 'Abd al 'Az
Akıncı Burnu
Kızıl Dağ
1795
Reyhanlı
Māyir
555
Muslimīyah
Al Bāb
Tall al Ḥudān
Al Furāt (Euphrates)
Balīkh
870
(Antioch) Hatay
Ḥārim
ḤALAB (Aleppo)
Dayr Ḥāfir
Samandağı
(Seleucia)
Salqīn
Altınözü
847
Al Atārib
Ūrmā aṣ Ṣughrá
Jabbūl
As Safīrah
Khirbat 'Uqlah
Ma'arrat Miṣrīn
Maskanah
(Meskéné)
Buḥayrat al Asad
Ar Raqqah
(Nicephorium)
Karbeyaz
Kassab
Yayladağı
Qanāyah
Idlib
Taftanāz
'Aqrabah
Sabkhat al Jabbūl
Dibsī Faraj
Ra's al Basīṭ
419
Arīḥā
Saraqib
Al Ḥājib
638
Tall Mardīkh (Ebla)
Madīnat ath Thawrah
Al Manṣūrah
Wata al Khān
Ṣarāyā
Jisr ash Shughūr
Abū aḍ Ḍuhūr
Khanāṣir
As Sabkhah
Ma'dīn Jadīd
Al Ḥaffah
Qal'at Ṣahyūn
Jabal al 'Alawīyīn
1562
Ra's Shamrah
(Ugarit)
Ma'arrat an Nu'mān
Wādī Shatnat as Salmās
Zenobia
Ar Ruṣāfah
At Tibnī
Khirbat al Andarīn
Al Lādhiqīyah
(Latakia)
Qal'at al Maḍīq
Apamea
Khān Shaykhūn
Jablah
Ṣuqaylabīyah
'Arab al Mulk
Ṣūrān
Kharsān
Khirbat Isrīyah
867
Jabal Bishrī
Dayr az Zawr
Al Qudayr
Bāniyās
1359
Dayr Shumayyil at Taḥtānī
Muḥradah
Al 'Āṣī (Orontes)
As Sa'an
Wādī Sanīmah
Al Kawm
Ḥamāh
(Hamath)
Al Qadmūs
Maṣyāf
691
'Uqayribāt
Qudaym
Qaṣr al Ḥayr ash Sharqī
Al Mayādīn
Ash Shaykh Badr
Bīrīn
Kafr Buhum
Salamīyah
Ṭarṭūs
(Tortosa)
Duraykīsh
Ar Rastan
(Arethusa)
Tall al Qaṭā
1387
'Amrīt
(Marathus)
Ṣāfītā
Kafrūn Bashūr
Talbīsah
Al Mashrafah
Jubb al Jarrāḥ
As Sukhnah
Wādī Dubayah
Al 'Ashāra
Krak des Chevaliers
Al Khuraybah
Shīn
1325
Wādī Ṭarfāwī
Wādī 'Awarid
Al Ḥamīdīyah
Ḥimṣ (Homs)
Ḥarrākah
Tall Kalakh
Abū Dālī
Liftāyā
Shinshār
Furqlus
Wādī al Miyāh
Qoubaiyat
Tiyās
Tadmur
(Palmyra)
Dār al 'Abīd as Sūd
El Mîna
Trâblous
(Tripoli)
Al Quṣayr
Qunayyah
Riblah
Shayrāt
Zgharta
Hermel
Ḥisyah
Ghunthur
Qaṣr al Ḥayr al Gharbī
Sabkhat al Mūḥ
Batroûn
Ra's Ba'labakk
Ṣadad
Lubnān Mts.
Al Qaryatayn
Wādī al 'Annān
Jbail (Byblos)
Qārah
1406
Jabal ar Ruwāq
Wādī al Wa'r
463
Baalbeck
Dayr 'Aṭīyah
An Nabk
BEYROUTH
(Beirut)
Jabal ash Sharq
(Anti-Lebanon)
Jabal Lubnān
(Lebanon Mts.)
Al Biqā'
(Bekaa Valley)
Yabrūd
1020
795
2361
Wādī 'Ukāsh
An Nāṣirīyah
Ma'lūlā
Jayrūd
1390
Sab' Ābār
Sirghāyā
Wādī as Ṣawāb
'Anjar
Az Zabadānī
Ṣaydnāyā
Al Quṭayfah
Baḥr Ṣayqal
'Akāshāt
At Tall
Ḍumayr
Khān Abū Shāmāt
690
Rachaïya
Dūmā
Dārayyā
DIMASHQ
(Damascus)
Buḥayrat al 'Utaybah
Jabal at Tanf
772
At Tanf
Qaṭanā
2814
Jabal ash Shaykh
(Mt. Hermon)
Al Hījānah
979
Buḥayrat al Hījānah
Al Khiyām
Ein Qunya
Sa'sa'
UN peacekeeping zone
GOLAN HEIGHTS
The "heights" is an arid volcanic plateau. Part of Syria when it achieved independence in 1946, it was captured by Israel in 1967. Some 18,000 Israelis live here today with about 17,000 Arabs. Syria still claims the region, and UN peacekeepers patrol the Syrian frontier.
'Emeq Hula
(Hula Valley)
Al Qunayṭirah
(El Quneitra)
Burāq
Al Mismīyah
Boundary claimed by Syria
Aṣ Ṣanamayn
GOLAN HEIGHTS
ISRAEL
Ar Rafīd
Al Lajā
Ar Ruṭbah
Nawā
Shaqqā
Sea of Galilee
(Sea of Kinnereth)
Shaykh Miskīn
Izra'
Shahbā' (Philippopolis)
Wādī Shuayb
Ṭafas
Khirbat al Ghazālah
Qanawāt
Al Mushannaf
Ṭirbīl
Yarmūk
Dar'ā
As Suwaydā'
Jabal ad Durūz
1803
Irbid
(Arbela)
Ar Ramthā
Al Qurayyah
Al Ḥiṣn
Buṣrá ash Shām
Ṣalkhad
Mallāḥ
Ar Ruwayshid
Sama
Al Ghāriyah
Imtān
'Ajlūn
Al Mafraq
Al 'Ānāt
Jarash
(Gerasa)
Ṣabḥā
Jabal ar Rimāḥ 1262

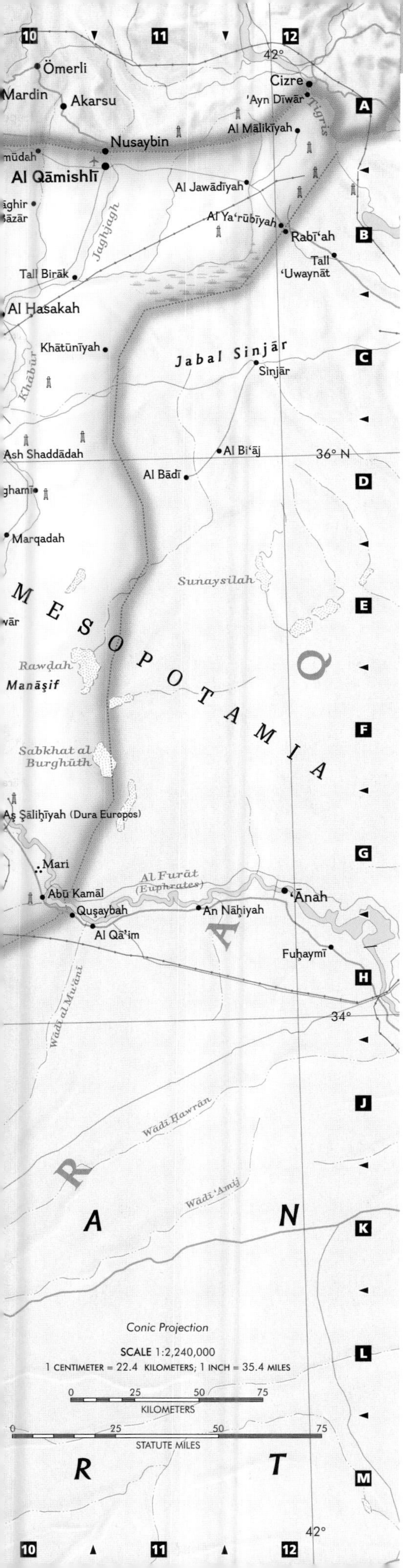

10
11
12
42°
Ömerli
Mardin
Akarsu
Cizre
'Ayn Dīwār
Tigris
A
Al Mālikīyah
Nusaybin
Al Qāmishlī
Al Jawādīyah
Jaghjagh
Al Ya'rūbīyah
Rabī'ah
B
Tall 'Uwaynāt
Tall Birāk
Al Ḩasakah
Khātūnīyah
Jabal Sinjār
Sinjār
Khābūr
C
Ash Shaddādah
Al Bi'āj
36° N
Al Bādī
D
Marqadah
Sunaysilah
E
MESOPOTAMIA
Rawḑah
Manāşif
F
Sabkhat al Burghūth
Aş Şāliḩīyah (Dura Europos)
G
Mari
Al Furāt (Euphrates)
Abū Kamāl
'Ānah
Quşaybah
An Nāḩiyah
Al Qā'im
Fuḩaymī
H
Wādī al Mu'ānī
34°
Wādī Ḩawrān
J
Wādī 'Amij
K
IRAQ
L
M
Conic Projection
SCALE 1:2,240,000
1 CENTIMETER = 22.4 KILOMETERS; 1 INCH = 35.4 MILES
0 25 50 75
KILOMETERS
0 25 50 75
STATUTE MILES

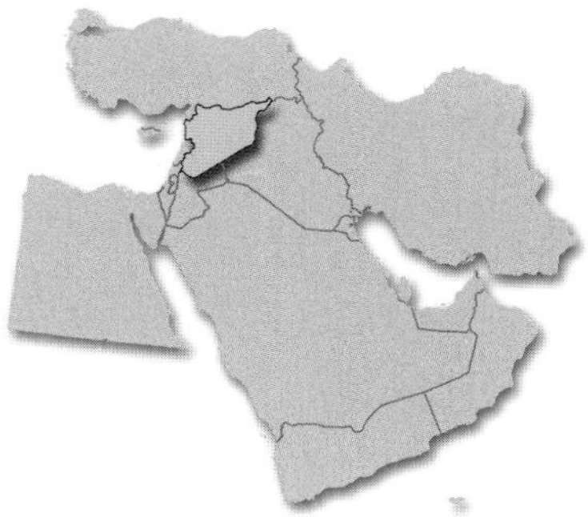

Syria

SYRIAN ARAB REPUBLIC

AREA	185,180 sq km (71,498 sq mi)
POPULATION	17,200,000
CAPITAL	Dimashq (Damascus) 2,195,000
RELIGION	(percent of population): Muslim 89% (mostly Sunni, Alawite 12%, Druze 3%), Christian 10%, other 1%
LANGUAGE	Arabic (official); Kurdish, Armenian, Aramaic, Circassian widely understood; French, English somewhat understood
LITERACY	70.8%
LIFE EXPECTANCY	70 years
TROOPS	Active: 321,000; Reserves: 354,000
GDP PER CAPITA	$3,200
CRUDE OIL RESERVES	2,500,000,000 barrels
ECONOMY	IND: petroleum, textiles, food processing, beverages, tobacco, phosphate rock mining. AGR: wheat, barley, cotton, lentils, chickpeas, olives, sugar beets; beef, mutton, eggs, poultry, milk. EXP: crude oil 68%, textiles 7%, fruits and vegetables 6%, raw cotton 4% (1998 est.).
AREA COMPARISON	Syria encompasses 2.3% of the 48 contiguous United States.

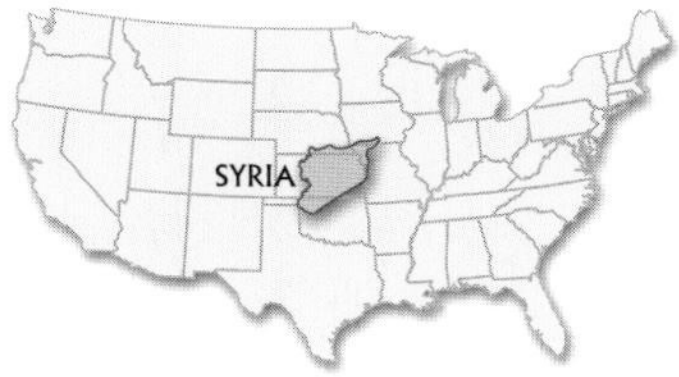
SYRIA

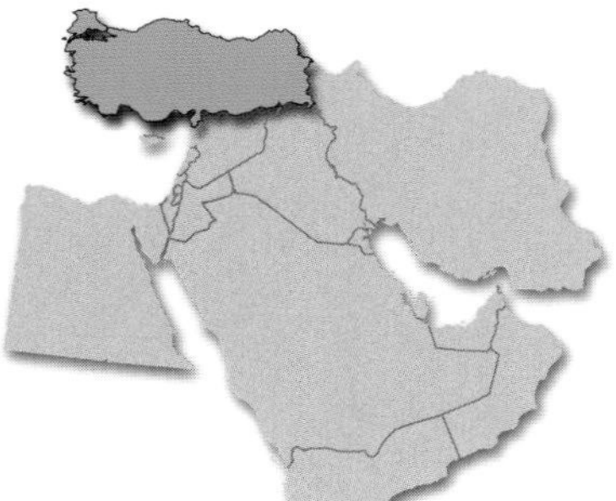

Turkey

REPUBLIC OF TURKEY

AREA 780,580 sq km (301,383 sq mi)

POPULATION 67,300,000

CAPITAL Ankara (Angora) 3,208,000

RELIGION (percent of population): Muslim 97%, (mostly Sunni, Alevi 15 to 30%), Christian 1%, other 2%

LANGUAGE Turkish (official), Kurdish, Arabic, Armenian, Greek

LITERACY 85%

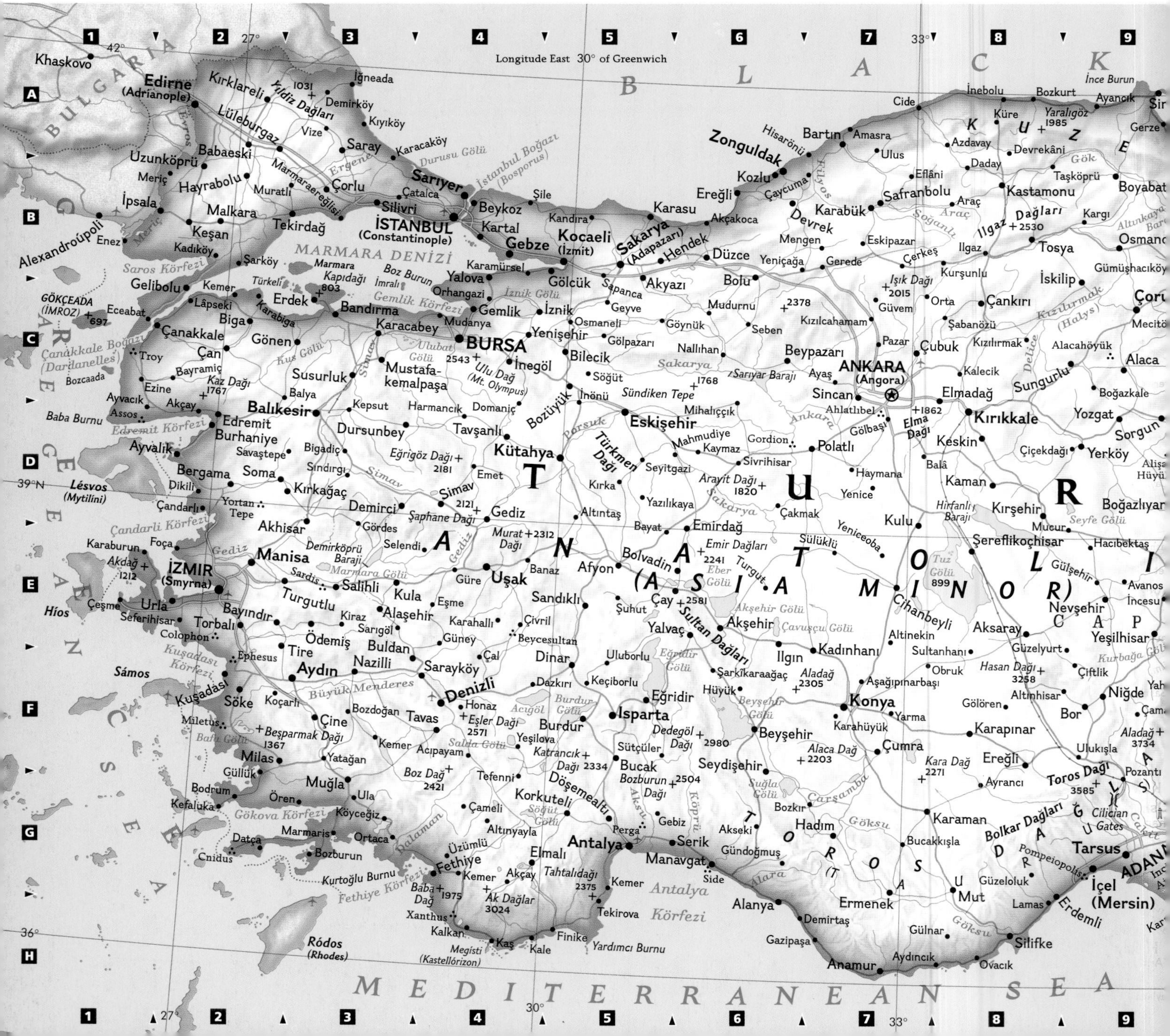

LIFE EXPECTANCY 69 years

TROOPS Active: 515,000; Reserves: 378,700

GDP PER CAPITA $6,700

CRUDE OIL RESERVES 300,000,000 barrels

ECONOMY IND: textiles, food processing, autos, mining (coal, chromite, copper, boron), steel, petroleum, construction, lumber, paper. AGR: tobacco, cotton, grain, olives, sugar beets, pulse, citrus; livestock. EXP: apparel 24.8%, foodstuffs 12.8%, textiles 12.7%, metal manufactures 8.8%, transport equipment 8.5% (2000).

AREA COMPARISON Turkey encompasses 9.7% of the 48 contiguous United States.

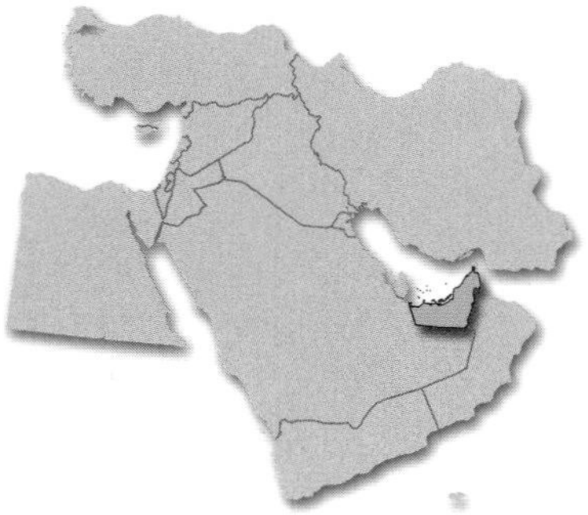

United Arab Emirates

UNITED ARAB EMIRATES

AREA 82,880 sq km (32,000 sq mi)

POPULATION 3,500,000

CAPITAL Abū Z̧aby (Abu Dhabi) 471,000

RELIGION (percent of population): Muslim 70% (mostly Sunni), Hindu 18%, Christian 7%, other 5%

LANGUAGE Arabic (official), Persian, English, Hindi, Urdu

LITERACY 79.2%

LIFE EXPECTANCY 74 years

TROOPS Active: 65,000

GDP PER CAPITA $21,100

CRUDE OIL RESERVES 97,800,000,000 barrels

ECONOMY IND: petroleum, fishing, petrochemicals, construction materials, some boatbuilding, handicrafts, pearling. AGR: dates, vegetables, watermelons; poultry, eggs, dairy products; fish. EXP: crude oil 45%, natural gas, reexports, dried fish, dates.

AREA COMPARISON U.A.E. encompasses 1.03% of the 48 contiguous United States.

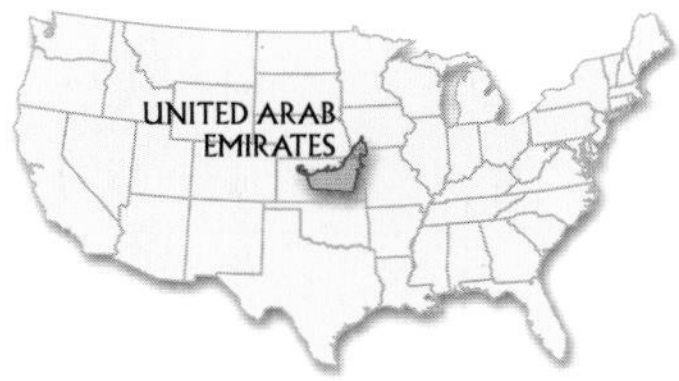

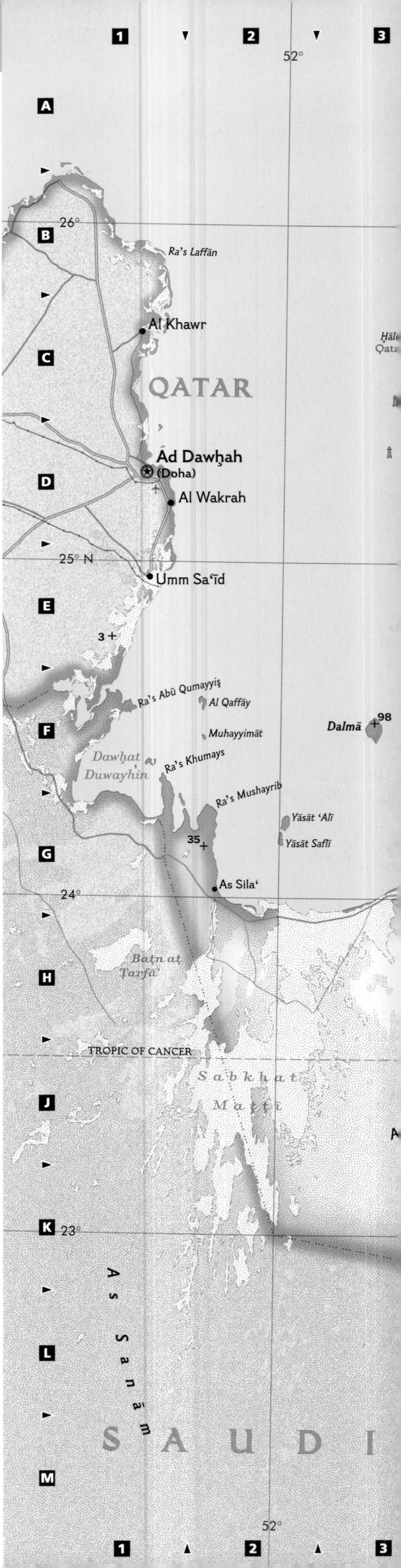

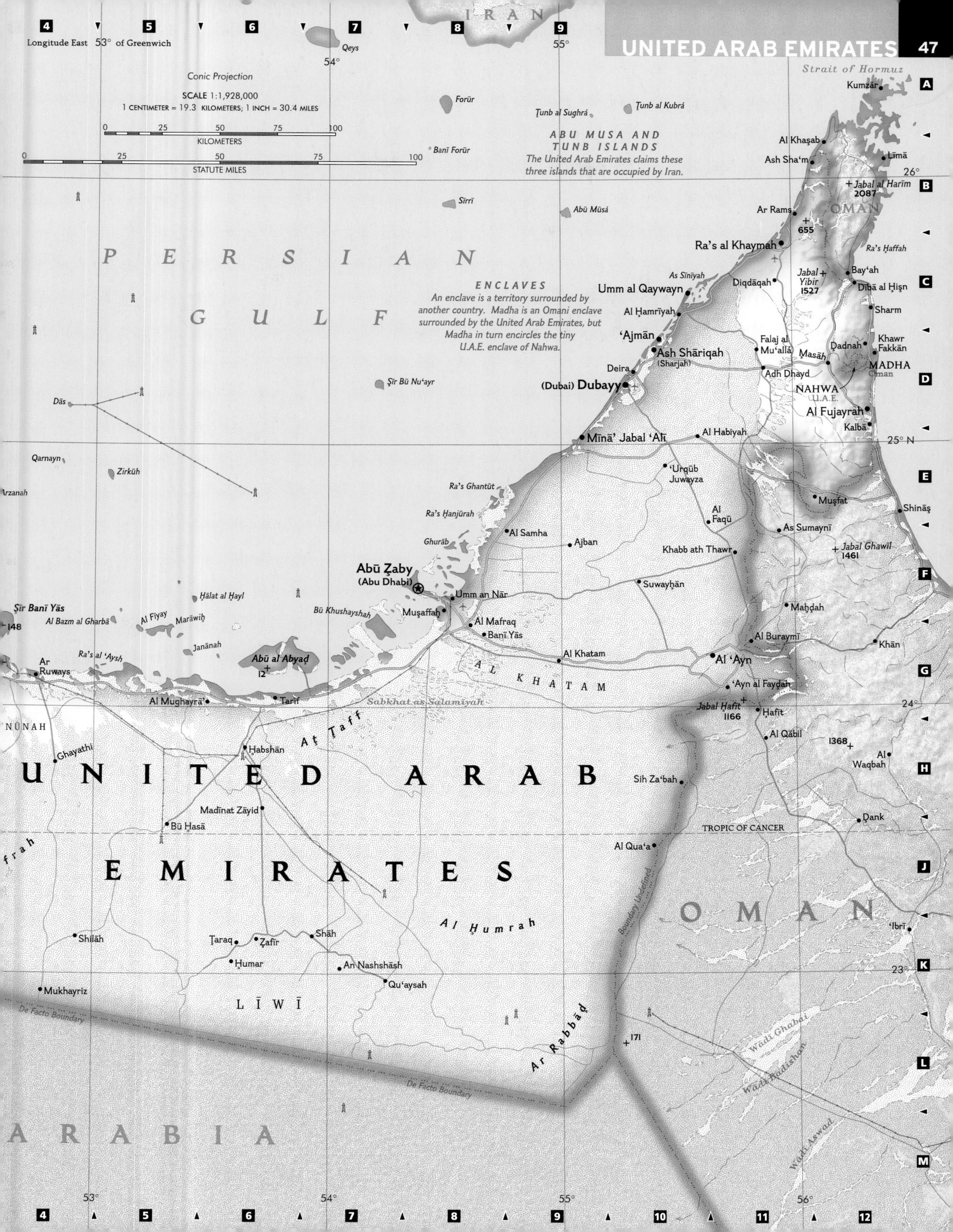
Longitude East 53° of Greenwich
Conic Projection
SCALE 1:1,928,000
1 CENTIMETER = 19.3 KILOMETERS; 1 INCH = 30.4 MILES
0 25 50 75 100
KILOMETERS
0 25 50 75 100
STATUTE MILES
IRAN
Qeys
Forūr
Banī Forūr
Ṭunb al Sughrá
Ṭunb al Kubrá
ABU MUSA AND TUNB ISLANDS
The United Arab Emirates claims these three islands that are occupied by Iran.
Sīrrī
Abū Mūsá
Strait of Hormuz
Kumzār
Al Khaṣab
Līmā
Ash Sha'm
26°
Jabal al Ḩarīm 2087
OMAN
Ar Rams
655
Ra's al Khaymah
Ra's Ḩaffah
PERSIAN GULF
ENCLAVES
An enclave is a territory surrounded by another country. Madha is an Omani enclave surrounded by the United Arab Emirates, but Madha in turn encircles the tiny U.A.E. enclave of Nahwa.
As Sīnīyah
Umm al Qaywayn
Diqdāqah
Jabal Yibir 1527
Bay'ah
Dibā al Ḩiṣn
Al Ḩamrīyah
Sharm
'Ajmān
Ash Shāriqah (Sharjah)
Falaj al Mu'allā
Masāh
Ḑadnah
Khawr Fakkān
MADHA Oman
Deira
Adh Dhayd
(Dubai) Dubayy
NAHWA U.A.E.
Al Fujayrah
Kalbā
Ṣīr Bū Nu'ayr
Dās
Mīnā' Jabal 'Alī
Al Habiyah
25° N
Qarnayn
Zirkūh
Arzanah
'Urqūb Juwayza
Ra's Ghantūt
Muşfat
Shināṣ
Ra's Ḩanjūrah
Al Faqū
As Sumaynī
Al Samha
Ghurāb
Ajban
Jabal Ghawīl 1461
Khabb ath Thawr
Abū Ẓaby (Abu Dhabi)
Suwayḩān
Ḩālat al Ḩayl
Umm an Nār
Ṣīr Banī Yās
148
Al Fiyay
Marāwiḩ
Bū Khushayshah
Muşaffaḩ
Maḩḑah
Al Bazm al Gharbī
Al Mafraq
Banī Yās
Al Buraymī
Jananah
Khān
Ra's al 'Aysh
Abū al Abyaḑ 12
Al Khatam
Ar Ruways
Al 'Ayn
AL KHATAM
'Ayn al Fayḑah
Al Mughayrā'
Ṭarīf
Sabkhat as Salamīyah
Jabal Ḩafīt 1166
Ḩafīt
24°
NŪNAH
At Taff
Al Qābil
Ghayathi
1368
Al Waqbah
Ḩabshān
UNITED ARAB EMIRATES
Sih Za'bah
Madīnat Zāyid
Bū Hasā
Ḑank
TROPIC OF CANCER
Al Qua'a
OMAN
Boundary Undefined
Al Ḩumrah
'Ibrī
Shilāh
Ṭaraq
Ẓafīr
Shāh
23°
Ḩumar
An Nashshāsh
Qu'aysah
Mukhayriz
LĪWĀ
De Facto Boundary
Ar Rabbād
171
Wadi Ghabai
Wadi Ḩadishah
De Facto Boundary
ARABIA
Wadi Aswad
53°
54°
55°
56°
4 5 6 7 8 9 10 11 12
A B C D E F G H J K L M

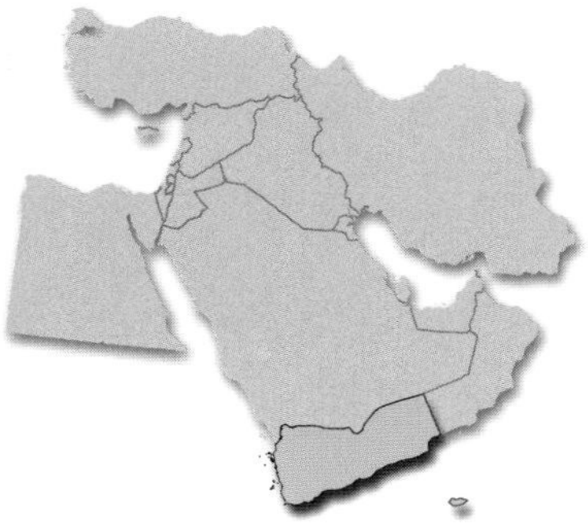

Yemen

REPUBLIC OF YEMEN

AREA 527,970 sq km (203,850 sq mi)
POPULATION 18,600,000
CAPITAL Şan‘ā’ (Sanaa) 1,410,000
RELIGION (percent of population): Muslim 99% (mostly Sunni, Shiite 40%), other 1%
LANGUAGE Arabic (official)
LITERACY 38%

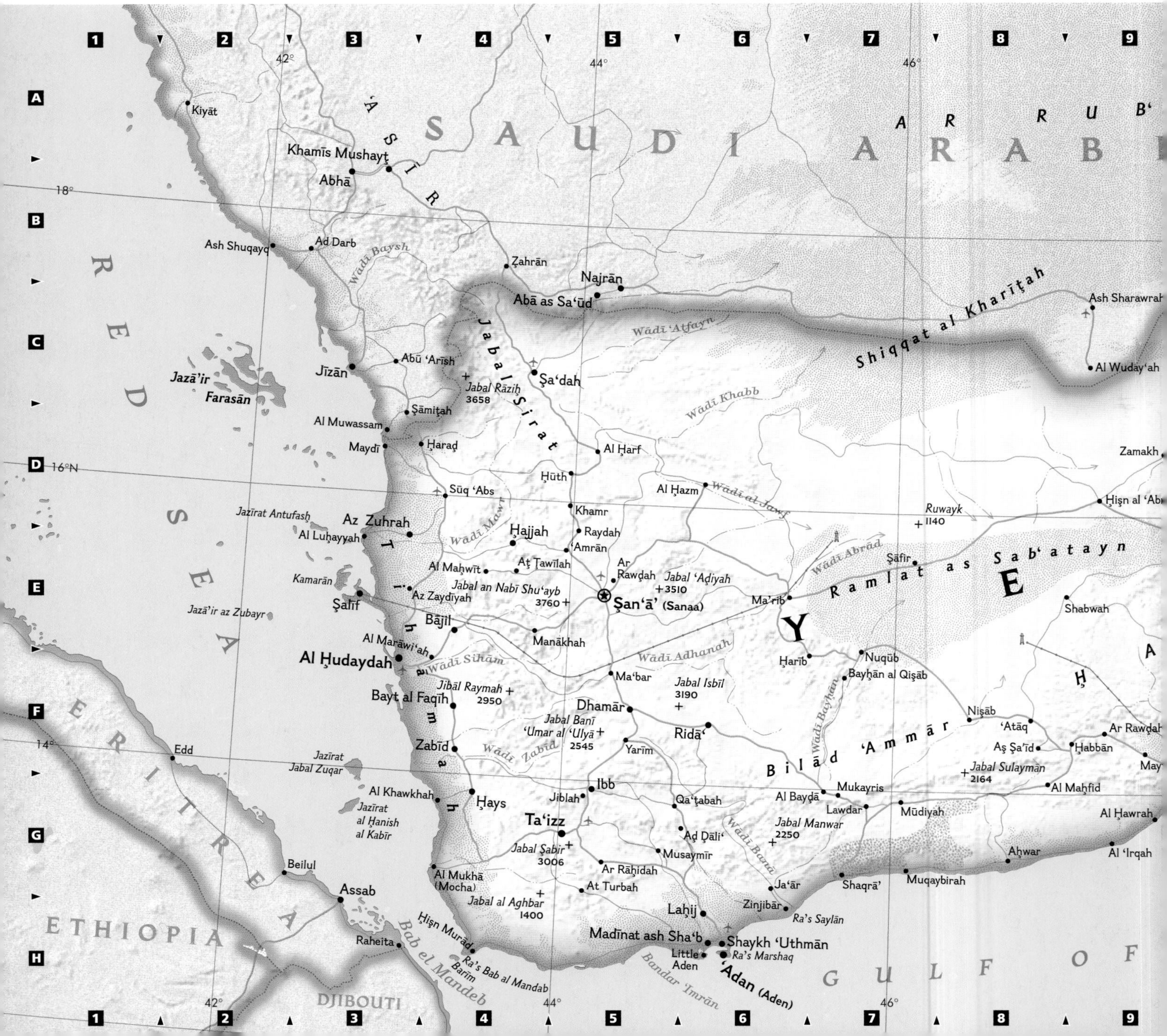
1
2
3
4
5
6
7
8
9
A
B
C
D
E
F
G
H
42°
44°
46°
18°
16°N
14°
SAUDI ARABIA
AR RUB‘
‘ASĪR
Kiyāt
Khamīs Mushayţ
Abhā
Ash Shuqayq
Ad Darb
Wādī Baysh
Z̧ahrān
Najrān
Abā as Sa‘ūd
Shiqqat al Kharīţah
Ash Sharawrah
Al Wuday‘ah
Wādī ‘Atfayn
Wādī Khabb
RED SEA
Jazā’ir Farasān
Jīzān
Abū ‘Arīsh
Jabal Rāziḩ
3658
Şa‘dah
Jabal Şirat
Şāmiţah
Al Muwassam
Maydī
Ḩaraḑ
Al Ḩarf
Zamakh
Ḩūth
Al Ḩazm
Wādī al Jawf
Sūq ‘Abs
Khamr
Ḩişn al ‘Abr
Ruwayk
1140
Jazīrat Antufash
Az Zuhrah
Al Luḩayyah
Wādī Mawr
Ḩajjah
Raydah
‘Amrān
Şāfir
Ramlat as Sab‘atayn
Wādī Abrād
Al Maḩwīt
Aţ Ţawīlah
Ar Rawḑah
Jabal ‘Aḑīyah
3510
Kamarān
Jabal an Nabī Shu‘ayb
3760
Az Zaydīyah
Şan‘ā’ (Sanaa)
Ma’rib
YEMEN
Shabwah
Jazā’ir az Zubayr
Şalīf
Tihāmah
Bājil
Manākhah
Al Marāwi‘ah
Al Ḩudaydah
Wādī Sihām
Wādī Adhanah
Ḩarīb
Nuqūb
Bayḩān al Qişāb
Ma‘bar
Jabal Isbīl
3190
Jibāl Raymah
2950
Bayt al Faqīh
Dhamār
Ridā‘
Wādī Bayḩān
Nişāb
‘Ataq
Ar Rawḑah
Jabal Banī ‘Umar al ‘Ulyā
2545
Yarīm
Bilād ‘Ammār
Aş Şa‘īd
Ḩabbān
Zabīd
Wādī Zabīd
ERITREA
Edd
Jazīrat Jabal Zuqar
Jabal Sulaymān
2164
Al Maḩfid
Al Khawkhah
Ibb
Jiblah
Mukayris
Al Bayḑā
Jazīrat al Ḩanish al Kabīr
Ḩays
Qa‘ţabah
Lawdar
Mūdiyah
Al Ḩawrah
Ta‘izz
Jabal Manwar
2250
Aḑ Ḑāli‘
Wādī Banā
Jabal Şabir
3006
Musaymīr
Aḩwar
Al ‘Irqah
Beilul
Al Mukhā (Mocha)
Ar Rāḩidah
Ja‘ār
Shaqrā’
Muqaybirah
Assab
At Turbah
Jabal al Aghbar
1400
Zinjibār
Laḩij
Ra’s Saylān
ETHIOPIA
Ḩişn Murād
Madīnat ash Sha‘b
Shaykh ‘Uthmān
Raheita
Bab el Mandeb
Ra’s Bab al Mandab
Barīm
Little Aden
Ra’s Marshaq
‘Adan (Aden)
Bandar Imrān
GULF OF
DJIBOUTI

LIFE EXPECTANCY 59 years

TROOPS Active: 54,000; Reserves: 40,000

GDP PER CAPITA $820

CRUDE OIL RESERVES 4,000,000,000 barrels

ECONOMY IND: crude oil production and petroleum refining; small-scale production of cotton textiles and leather goods; food processing; handicrafts; small aluminum products factory; cement. AGR: grain, fruits, vegetables, pulses, qat (mildly narcotic shrub), coffee, cotton; dairy products, livestock (sheep, goats, cattle, camels), poultry; fish. EXP: crude oil, coffee, dried and salted fish.

AREA COMPARISON Yemen encompasses 6.6% of the 48 contiguous United States.

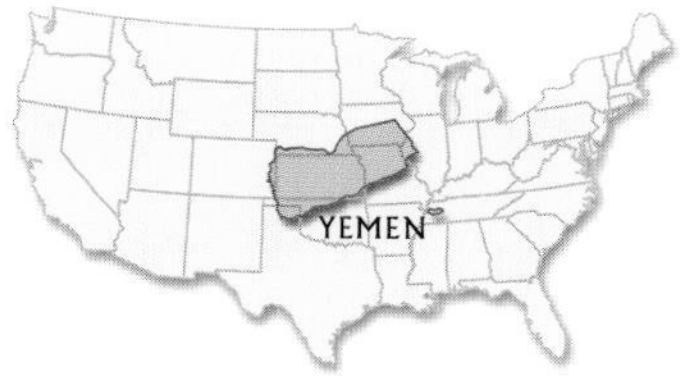

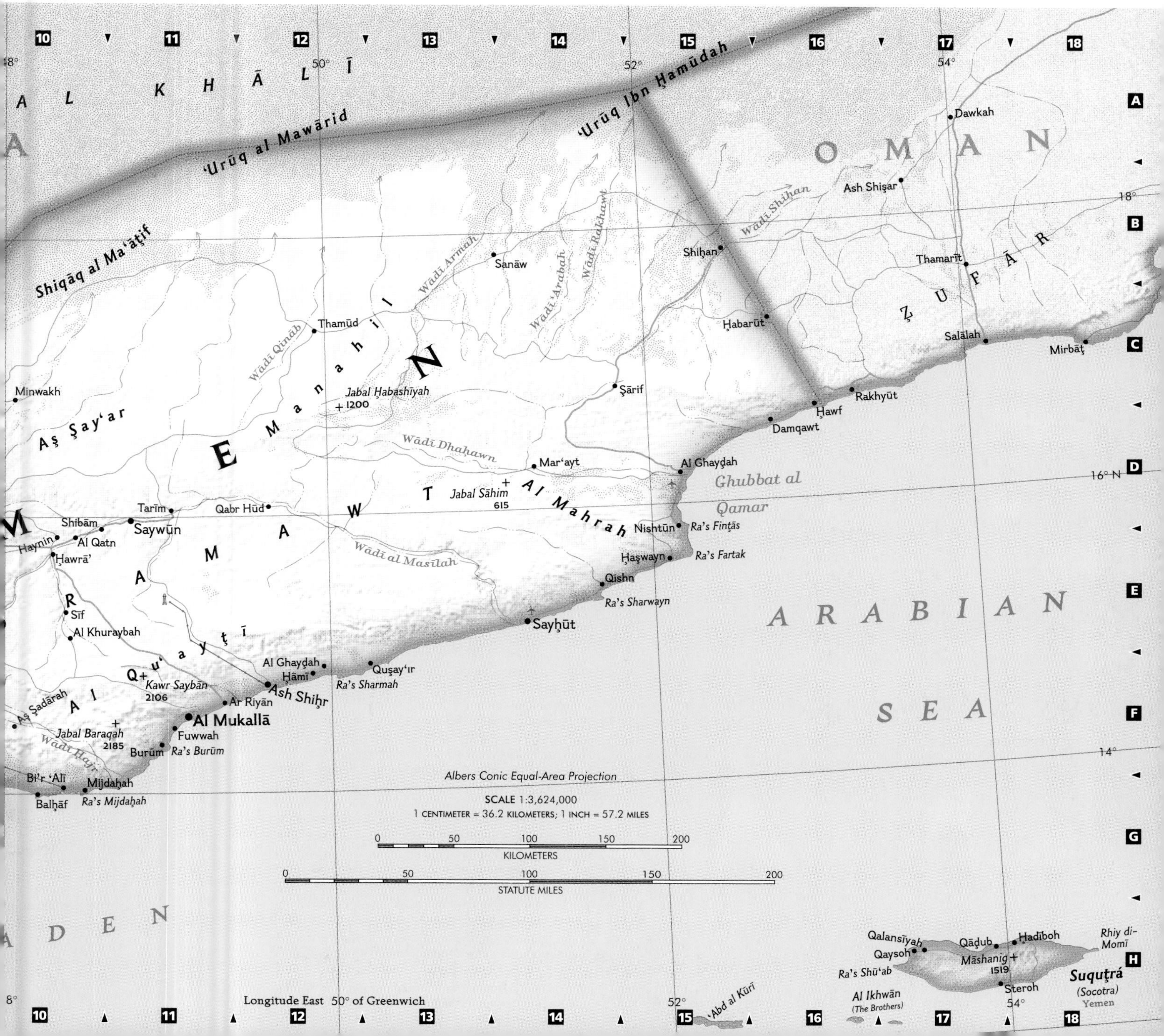

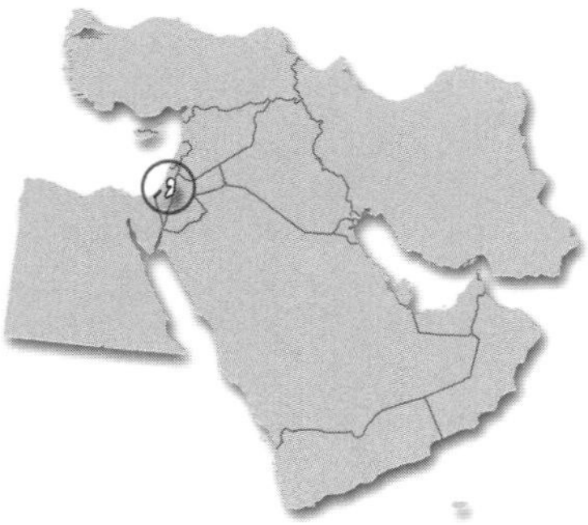

Occupied Territories

OCCUPIED TERRITORIES: WEST BANK AND GAZA STRIP

AREA West Bank: 5,860 sq km (2,263 sq mi); Gaza Strip: 360 sq km (139 sq mi)

POPULATION West Bank: 2,576,000; Gaza Strip: 1,107,000

RELIGION West Bank: Muslim 89%, (mostly Sunni), Jewish 9%, Christian 2%; Gaza Strip: Muslim 99% (mostly Sunni), other 1%

LANGUAGE Arabic, Hebrew (spoken by Israeli settlers and many Palestinians, English (widely understood)

LITERACY Data not available

LIFE EXPECTANCY 72 years

TROOPS No active military

GDP PER CAPITA $1,000 West Bank; $625 Gaza Strip

CRUDE OIL RESERVES None or negligible

ECONOMY IND: generally small family businesses that produce cement, textiles, soap, olive-wood carvings, and mother-of-pearl souvenirs; the Israelis have established some small-scale, modern industries. AGR: olives, citrus, vegetables; beef, dairy products. EXP: olives,fruit, vegetables, limestone, citrus, flowers.

AREA COMPARISON Occupied Territories encompass 0.08% of the 48 contiguous United States.

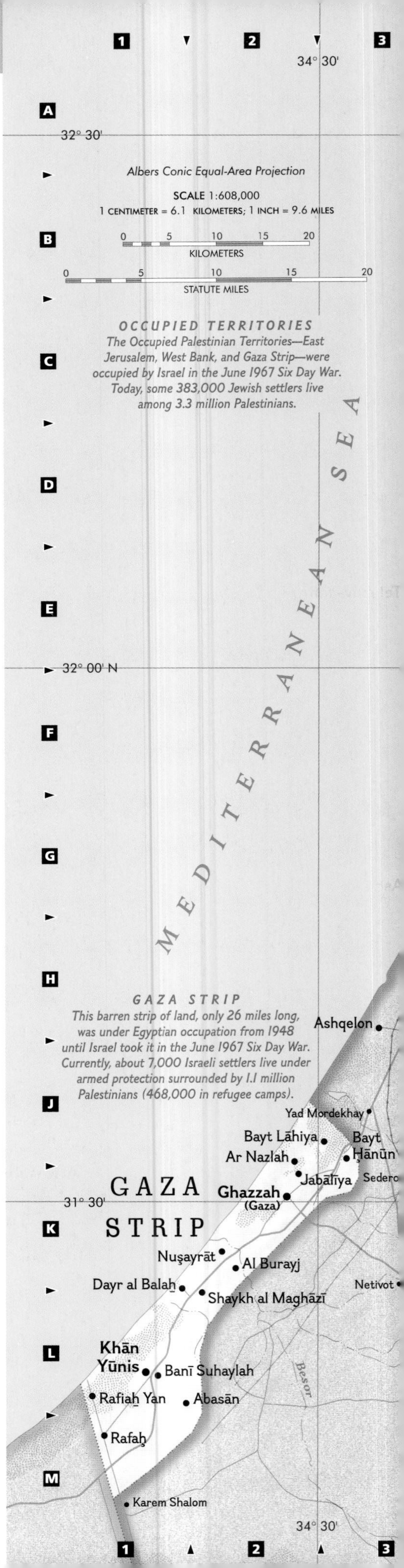

Longitude East 35° of Greenwich
35° 30'
Megiddo
Irbid
(Arbela)
32° 30'
Bet She'an
(Beth Shan)
Yāmūn
Ya'bad
(Jenin) Janīn
Dayr Abū Da'īf
Ḩadera
PLAIN OF SHARON
Hadera
'Arrābah
Dothan
Qabāţīyah
Zabābida
'Attīl
Meholа
WEST BANK
Jordan annexed this part of Palestine on the Jordan River's west bank after the 1948-49 war with Israel—but lost it to Israel in the 1967 Six Day War. It is known as Judaea and Samaria to Israelis. Israeli-Palestinian agreements from 1993 to 1999 provided for Israeli withdrawal and Palestinian self-rule; but by 2002, rising violence brought Israeli troops back.
Meithalūn
Netanya
Jaba'
Ţūlkarm
'Anabtā
Ţūbās
Burqā
Jarash
(Gerasa)
Sabasţīyah
(Samaria)
Tammūn
National Water Carrier
'Aşīrah ash Shamālīyah
Bayt Ibā
Tirza
Jordan
(Nablus) Nābulus
Khirbat Balāţah
(Shechem)
Jabal aţ Ţūr +
(Mt. Gerizim)
881
Qalqīlyah
Qarne Shomeron
'Azzūn
Kefar Sava
Bayt Fūrīk
SAMARIA
Argaman
Jammā'īn
'Aqrabah
WEST
Biddyā
Elqana
Ari'el
Qabalān
Dāmiya
Alexandrium
Petah Tiqwa
Tel Aviv-Yafo
Dayr Ballūţ
Salfīt
Shiloh
As Salţ
Şuwaylih
Holon
Gilgal
'Aţţārah
Silwād
32° 00' N
1016 +
Niran
Qiryat Sefer
BANK
'AMMĀN
(Philadelphia)
Baytīn
No'omi
JORDAN
Rām Allāh
(Ramallah)
Al Bīrah
Tal as Sulţān
ALLENBY BRIDGE
Nā'ūr
Bayt Liqyā
Ar Rām
Al Jīb
(Jericho) Arīhā
Hajalah Ford
Ashdod
Ma'ale Adummim
Jerusalem
Al 'Ayzarīyah
(Bethany)
ISRAEL
Khirbat Qumrān
Mādabā
Bayt Jālā
Bayt Laḩm (Bethlehem)
Betar 'Illit
Bayt Sāḩūr
JERUSALEM
A city holy to Jews, Christians, and Muslims, its access and control is at the center of the Arab-Israeli conflict. Israel proclaimed Jerusalem its capital in 1949 and annexed East Jerusalem after the 1967 war. Palestinians insist that it be their capital, too.
Kefar 'Ezyon
Efrata
JUDAEA
Qiryat Gat
Dead Sea
Ḩalḩūl
Si'īr
Mizpe Shalem
Tarqūmiyah
Idnah
Qiryat Arba'
Al Khalīl
(Hebron)
Banī Na'īm
Dūrā
-416
(-1365 ft)
'Arugot
31° 30'
Hever
'En Gedi
Yaţţah
Karmel
Carmel
Hevron
Az Zāhirīyah
As Samū'
Mezadot Yehuda
Be'er Sheva'
(Beersheba)
'Arad
Be'er Sheva'
35° 00'
35° 30'
36° 00'
4 5 6 7 8 9 10 11 12
A B C D E F G H J K L M

Baghdad

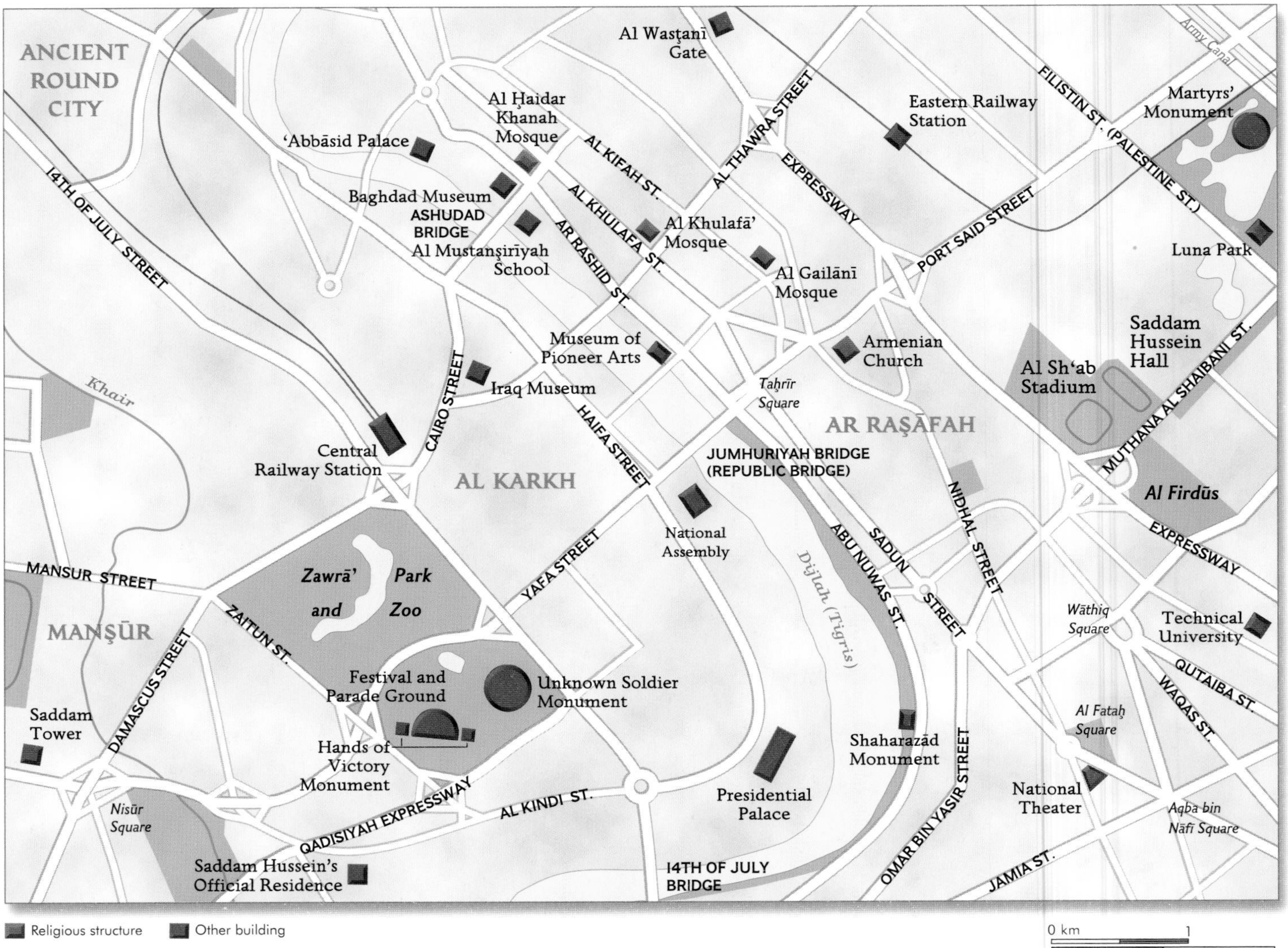
ANCIENT ROUND CITY
Al Wasṭanī Gate
Al Ḥaidar Khanah Mosque
'Abbāsid Palace
Baghdad Museum
ASHUDAD BRIDGE
Al Mustanṣirīyah School
AL KIFAH ST.
AL KHULAFA ST.
AR RASHID ST.
AL THAWRA STREET
EXPRESSWAY
Eastern Railway Station
FILISTIN ST. (PALESTINE ST.)
Army Canal
Martyrs' Monument
Luna Park
14TH OF JULY STREET
Al Khulafā' Mosque
Al Gailānī Mosque
PORT SAID STREET
Museum of Pioneer Arts
Iraq Museum
CAIRO STREET
Armenian Church
Taḥrīr Square
Al Sh'ab Stadium
Saddam Hussein Hall
MUTHANA AL SHAIBANI ST.
Khair
Central Railway Station
AL KARKH
HAIFA STREET
JUMHURIYAH BRIDGE (REPUBLIC BRIDGE)
AR RAṢĀFAH
Al Firdūs
National Assembly
NIDHAL STREET
SADUN STREET
ABU NUWAS ST.
EXPRESSWAY
MANSUR STREET
Zawrā' Park and Zoo
YAFA STREET
Dijlah (Tigris)
Wāthiq Square
Technical University
MANṢŪR
ZAITUN ST.
DAMASCUS STREET
QUTAIBA ST.
WAQAS ST.
Festival and Parade Ground
Unknown Soldier Monument
Saddam Tower
Hands of Victory Monument
Shaharazād Monument
Al Fataḥ Square
OMAR BIN YASIR STREET
National Theater
Presidential Palace
AL KINDI ST.
QADISIYAH EXPRESSWAY
Nisūr Square
Aqba bin Nāfi Square
Saddam Hussein's Official Residence
14TH OF JULY BRIDGE
JAMIA ST.
Religious structure
Other building
0 km 1
0 mi 1

POPULATION	4,958,000
CITY ELEVATION	112 feet 34 meters
LATITUDE	33° 21′ N
LONGITUDE	44° 25′ E
TEMPERATURE Average Daily High/Low °F (°C)	Jan. 61°/39°F (16°/4°C) July 109°/75°F (43°/24°C)
RAINFALL Average Monthly inches (mm)	January 1.1 (27) July 0 (0)
TIME ZONE Greenwich mean time	+3 hours GMT

Young, as Middle Eastern cities go, Baghdad was founded in 762 by Mansur, caliph of the Abbasid dynasty. It soon rose to become one of the most important cities of Islam and a center of Arabic scholarship and arts—notably under caliph Harun ar-Rashid—celebrated in tales of the *Arabian Nights*. Rapidly modernized during the early 1980s, Iraq's capital was heavily bombed during the 1991 Gulf War. Damaged bridges and buildings have been repaired or rebuilt. Saddam Hussein's regime has put up plenty of grandiose monuments, but life is bleak for ordinary citizens.

Baghdad
IRAQ
0 km 200
0 mi 200

Beirut

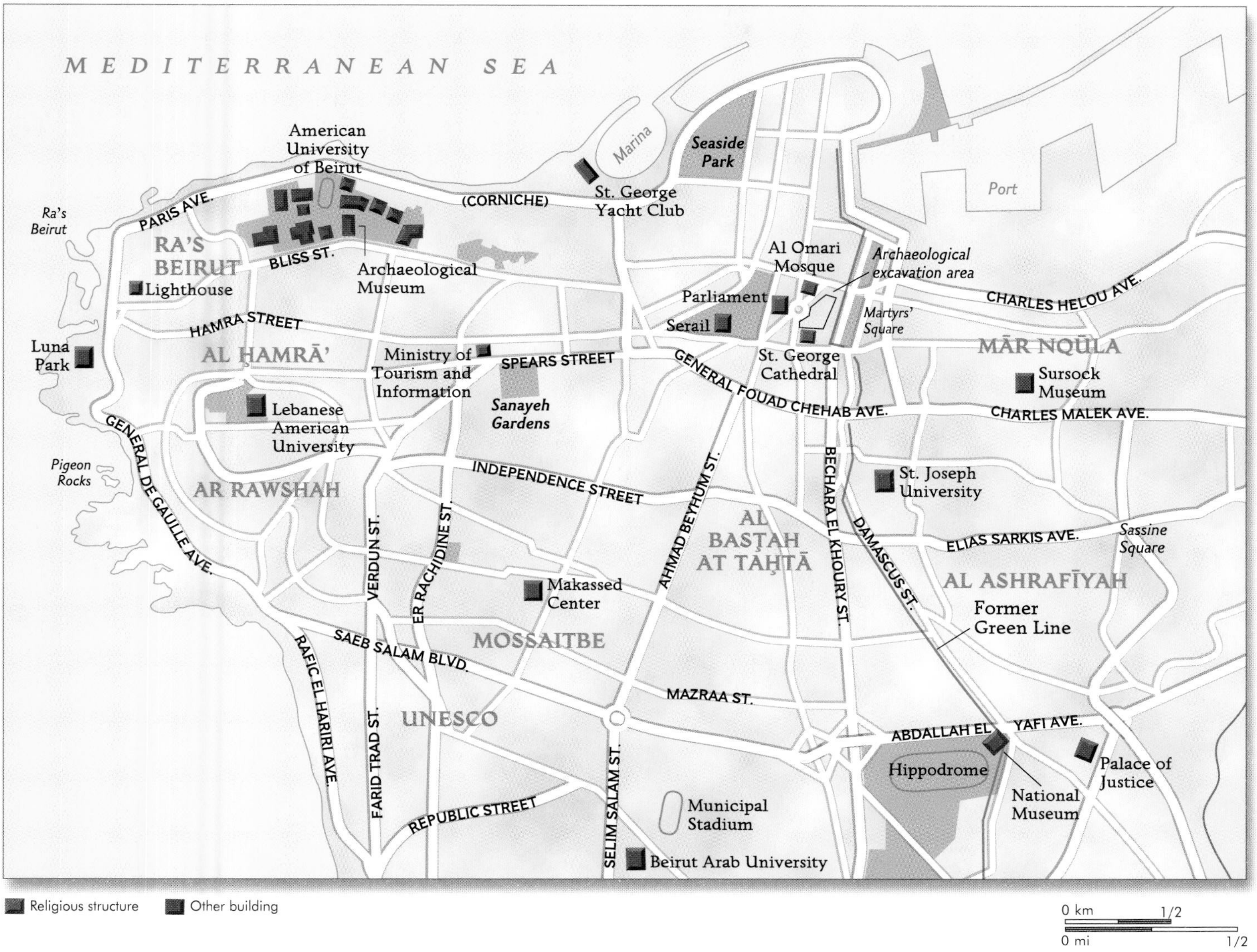
MEDITERRANEAN SEA
Marina
Seaside Park
Port
American University of Beirut
St. George Yacht Club
(CORNICHE)
PARIS AVE.
Ra's Beirut
RA'S BEIRUT
BLISS ST.
Archaeological Museum
Lighthouse
Al Omari Mosque
Archaeological excavation area
Parliament
Serail
Martyrs' Square
CHARLES HELOU AVE.
HAMRA STREET
Luna Park
AL HAMRĀ'
Ministry of Tourism and Information
SPEARS STREET
St. George Cathedral
MĀR NQŪLA
Sursock Museum
GENERAL FOUAD CHEHAB AVE.
CHARLES MALEK AVE.
Lebanese American University
Sanayeh Gardens
GENERAL DE GAULLE AVE.
Pigeon Rocks
AR RAWSHAH
INDEPENDENCE STREET
AHMAD BEYHUM ST.
BECHARA EL KHOURY ST.
St. Joseph University
VERDUN ST.
ER RACHIDINE ST.
AL BASTAH AT TAHTA
DAMASCUS ST.
ELIAS SARKIS AVE.
Sassine Square
AL ASHRAFĪYAH
Makassed Center
Former Green Line
SAEB SALAM BLVD.
RAFIC EL HARIRI AVE.
MOSSAITBE
MAZRAA ST.
UNESCO
FARID TRAD ST.
SELIM SALAM ST.
ABDALLAH EL YAFI AVE.
Hippodrome
Palace of Justice
National Museum
Municipal Stadium
REPUBLIC STREET
Beirut Arab University
Religious structure
Other building
0 km 1/2
0 mi 1/2

POPULATION	2,115,000
CITY ELEVATION	79 feet 24 meters
LATITUDE **LONGITUDE**	33° 53′ N 35° 30′ E
TEMPERATURE Average Daily High/Low °F (°C)	 Jan. 63°/52°F (17°/11°C) July 88°/73°F (31°/23°C)
RAINFALL Average Monthly inches (mm)	 January 7.4 (187) July 0 (0)
TIME ZONE Greenwich mean time	 +2 hours GMT

Massively ravaged during the 1975-1990 civil war, which split the city along the infamous Green Line dividing its Muslim west from its Christian east, Lebanon's capital has been massively rebuilt. Billions of dollars in ongoing renovation have transformed the ruined "Paris of the Middle East" into a fair reflection of what it was before the war: a capital of fashion, banking, trade, international conferences, nightlife, and tourism served by three dozen airlines.

LEBANON
Beirut
0 km 50
0 mi 50

Cairo

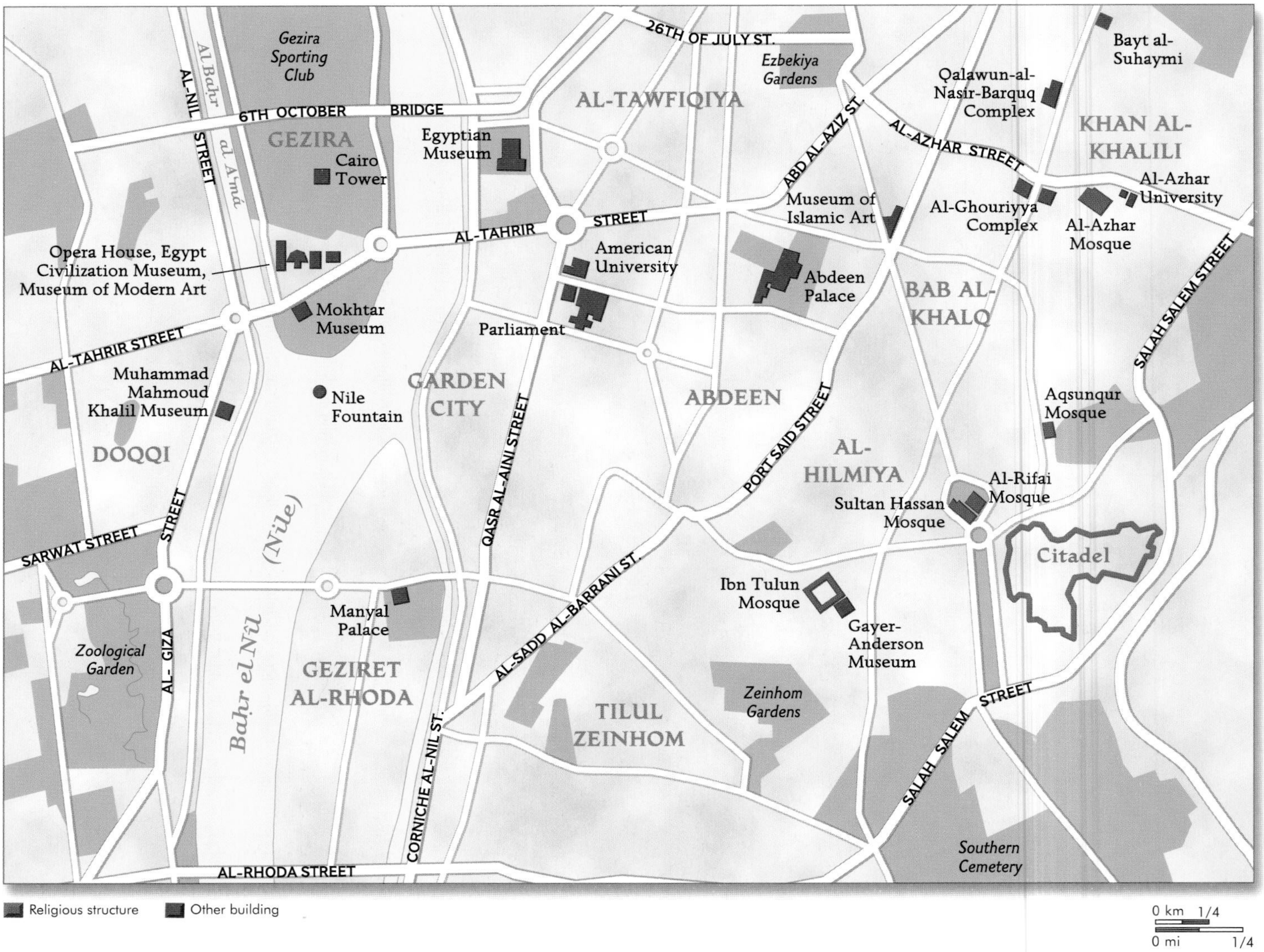
26TH OF JULY ST.
Gezira Sporting Club
Ezbekiya Gardens
Bayt al-Suhaymi
Qalawun-al-Nasir-Barquq Complex
AL-TAWFIQIYA
KHAN AL-KHALILI
AL-NIL STREET
Al Bahr al A'ma
6TH OCTOBER BRIDGE
GEZIRA
Egyptian Museum
Cairo Tower
ABD AL-AZIZ ST.
AL-AZHAR STREET
Museum of Islamic Art
Al-Ghouriyya Complex
Al-Azhar University
Al-Azhar Mosque
AL-TAHRIR STREET
American University
Opera House, Egypt Civilization Museum, Museum of Modern Art
Abdeen Palace
BAB AL-KHALQ
SALAH SALEM STREET
Mokhtar Museum
Parliament
AL-TAHRIR STREET
Muhammad Mahmoud Khalil Museum
Nile Fountain
GARDEN CITY
ABDEEN
Aqsunqur Mosque
DOQQI
QASR AL-AINI STREET
PORT SAID STREET
AL-HILMIYA
(Nile)
Al-Rifai Mosque
Sultan Hassan Mosque
SARWAT STREET
STREET
Citadel
Ibn Tulun Mosque
Manyal Palace
AL-SADD AL-BARRANI ST.
Gayer-Anderson Museum
Zoological Garden
AL-GIZA
Bahr el Nil
GEZIRET AL-RHODA
CORNICHE AL-NIL ST.
TILUL ZEINHOM
Zeinhom Gardens
SALAH SALEM STREET
Southern Cemetery
AL-RHODA STREET
Religious structure
Other building
0 km 1/4
0 mi 1/4

POPULATION	9,586,000
CITY ELEVATION	79 feet 24 meters
LATITUDE	30° 03′ N
LONGITUDE	31° 15′ E
TEMPERATURE Average Daily High/Low °F (°C)	Jan. 66°/48°F (19°/9°C) July 94°/71°F (34°/22°C)
RAINFALL Average Monthly inches (mm)	January .2 (5) July 0 (0)
TIME ZONE Greenwich mean time	+2 hours GMT

Egypt's capital of Cairo, Africa and the Middle East's largest city with more than nine million people, straddles the Nile just south of the river's great delta. Ancient Egyptian, Roman, Arabic, and Turkish monuments proclaim vital links with history; today Cairo's rich contrasts, ancient pyramids, modern skyscrapers, fragrant bazaars, towering palm trees, industry and commerce, suburbs and shantytowns, mosques and minarets, make it the center of Arab culture. Thousand-year-old Al-Azhar University, oldest in the world, still draws students and intellectuals from throughout the Middle East.

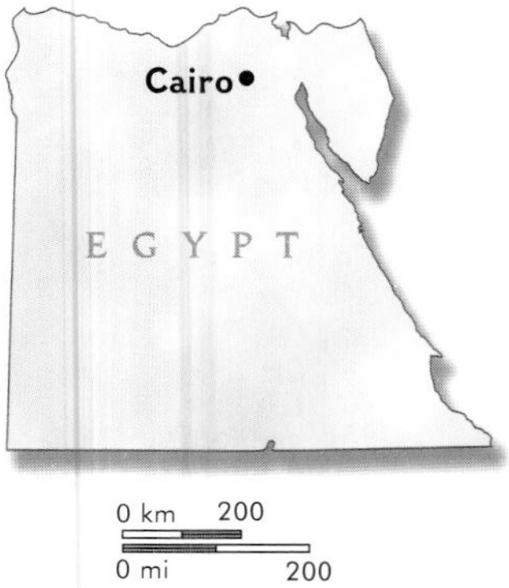
Cairo
EGYPT
0 km 200
0 mi 200

Damascus

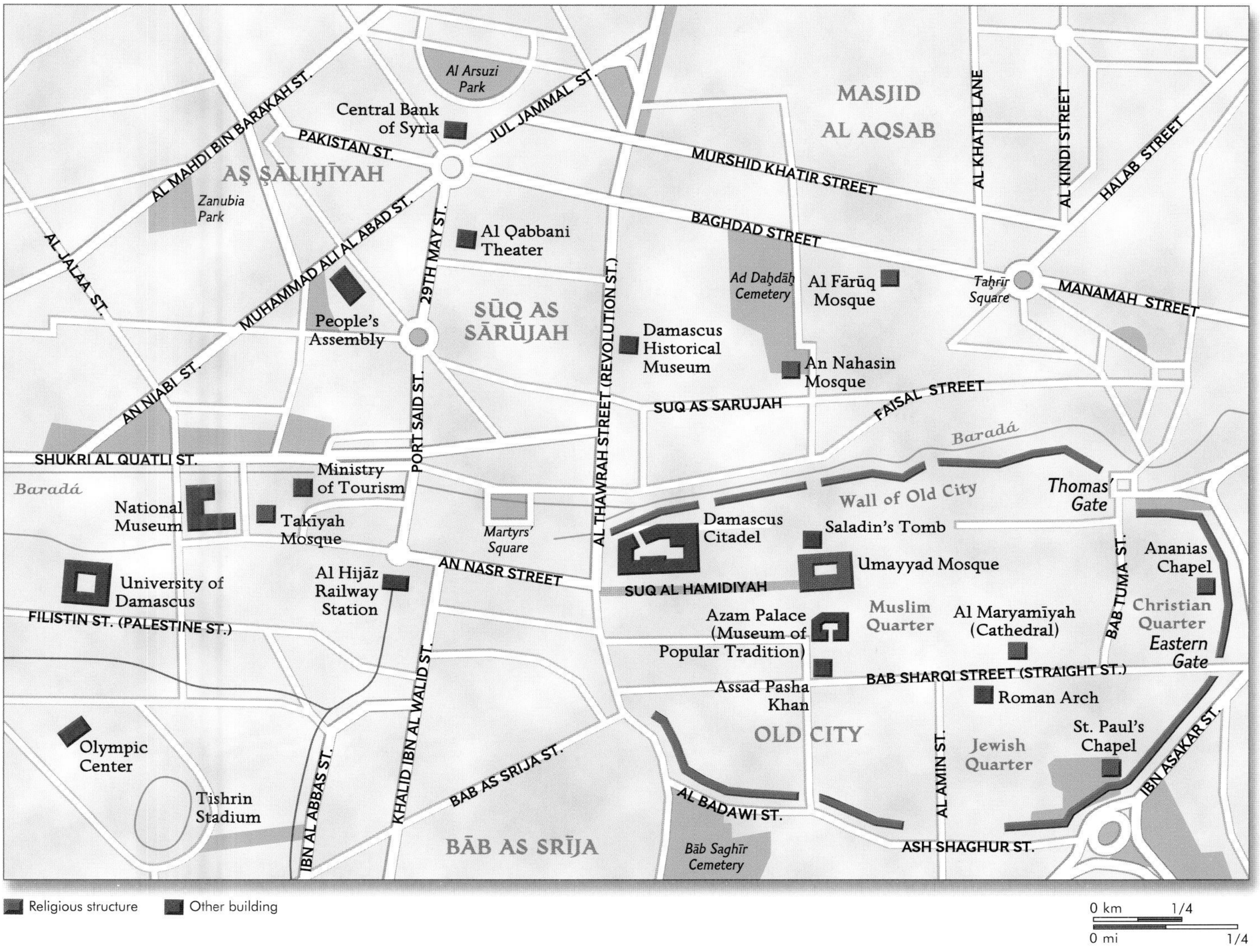
MASJID AL AQSAB
AŞ ŞĀLIḤĪYAH
SŪQ AS SĀRŪJAH
BĀB AS SRĪJA
OLD CITY
Al Arsuzi Park
Central Bank of Syria
Zanubia Park
Al Qabbani Theater
People's Assembly
Ad Daḥdāḥ Cemetery
Al Fārūq Mosque
Taḥrīr Square
Damascus Historical Museum
An Nahasin Mosque
Ministry of Tourism
National Museum
Takīyah Mosque
Martyrs' Square
Damascus Citadel
Saladin's Tomb
Umayyad Mosque
Thomas' Gate
Ananias Chapel
Wall of Old City
University of Damascus
Al Hijāz Railway Station
Azam Palace (Museum of Popular Tradition)
Muslim Quarter
Al Maryamīyah (Cathedral)
Christian Quarter
Eastern Gate
Assad Pasha Khan
Roman Arch
Jewish Quarter
St. Paul's Chapel
Olympic Center
Tishrin Stadium
Bāb Saghīr Cemetery
Baradá
AL MAHDI BIN BARAKAH ST.
PAKISTAN ST.
JUL JAMMAL ST.
MURSHID KHATIR STREET
AL KHATIB LANE
AL KINDI STREET
HALAB STREET
BAGHDAD STREET
MANAMAH STREET
AL JALAA ST.
MUHAMMAD ALI AL ABAD ST.
29TH MAY ST.
AL THAWRAH STREET (REVOLUTION ST.)
AN NIABI ST.
PORT SAID ST.
SUQ AS SARUJAH
FAISAL STREET
SHUKRI AL QUATLI ST.
AN NASR STREET
SUQ AL HAMIDIYAH
FILISTIN ST. (PALESTINE ST.)
BAB TUMA ST.
BAB SHARQI STREET (STRAIGHT ST.)
KHALID IBN AL WALID ST.
IBN AL ABBAS ST.
BAB AS SRIJA ST.
AL BADAWI ST.
AL AMIN ST.
ASH SHAGHUR ST.
IBN ASAKAR ST.
Religious structure
Other building
0 km 1/4
0 mi 1/4

POPULATION	2,195,000
CITY ELEVATION	2,320 feet 707 meters
LATITUDE	33° 30′ N
LONGITUDE	36° 18′ E
TEMPERATURE	
Average Daily High/Low °F (°C)	Jan. 54°/36°F (12°/2°C) July 97°/64°F (36°/18°C)
RAINFALL	
Average Monthly inches (mm)	January 1.5 (39) July 0 (0)
TIME ZONE	
Greenwich mean time	+3 hours GMT

Built on a desert oasis nourished by the Barada River, Syria's capital is among the world's oldest continuously inhabited cities. Conquering armies, kingdoms, dynasties, and empires have swept through for thousands of years, but Damascus has been spared from extensive damage in modern conflicts. The city remains famous for its ancient markets, museums, remnants of Roman walls, and the eighth-century Umayyad Mosque, considered one of the world's finest examples of Islamic architecture.

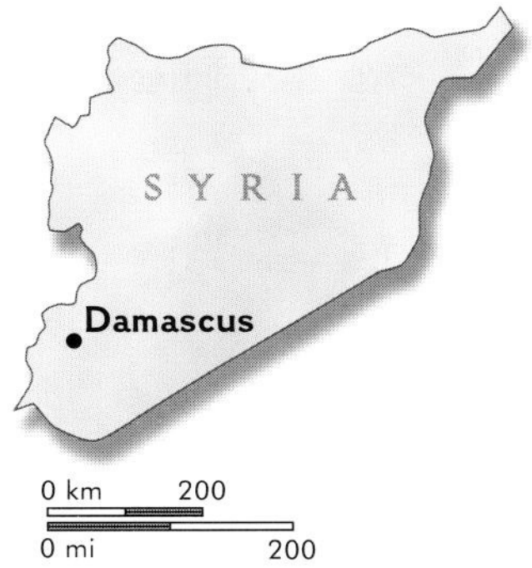
SYRIA
Damascus
0 km 200
0 mi 200

Jerusalem

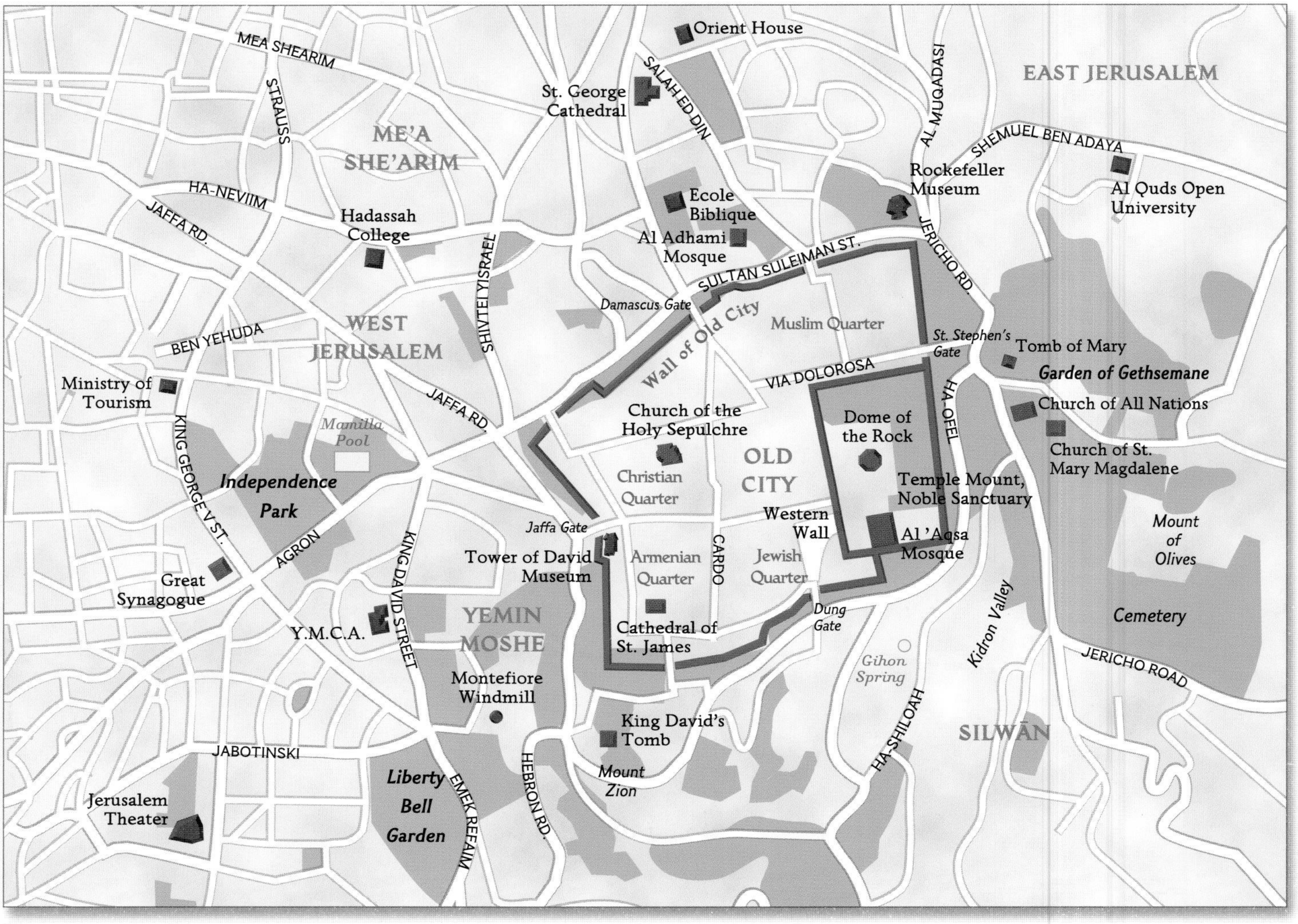
MEA SHEARIM
STRAUSS
ME'A SHE'ARIM
HA-NEVI'IM
JAFFA RD.
Hadassah College
St. George Cathedral
Orient House
SALAH ED DIN
AL MUQADASI
EAST JERUSALEM
SHEMUEL BEN ADAYA
Rockefeller Museum
Al Quds Open University
Ecole Biblique
Al Adhami Mosque
JERICHO RD.
SULTAN SULEIMAN ST.
SHIVTEI YISRAEL
Damascus Gate
Wall of Old City
Muslim Quarter
St. Stephen's Gate
Tomb of Mary
Garden of Gethsemane
BEN YEHUDA
WEST JERUSALEM
Ministry of Tourism
JAFFA RD.
VIA DOLOROSA
Dome of the Rock
HA-OFEL
Church of All Nations
Church of St. Mary Magdalene
Church of the Holy Sepulchre
KING GEORGE V ST.
Mamilla Pool
Independence Park
Christian Quarter
OLD CITY
Temple Mount, Noble Sanctuary
Mount of Olives
AGRON
Jaffa Gate
Western Wall
Al 'Aqsa Mosque
Great Synagogue
KING DAVID STREET
Tower of David Museum
Armenian Quarter
CARDO
Jewish Quarter
Y.M.C.A.
YEMIN MOSHE
Cathedral of St. James
Dung Gate
Kidron Valley
Cemetery
JERICHO ROAD
Gihon Spring
Montefiore Windmill
King David's Tomb
HA-SHILOAH
SILWĀN
JABOTINSKI
Mount Zion
Liberty Bell Garden
EMEK REFAIM
HEBRON RD.
Jerusalem Theater

Religious structure | Other building

0 km 1/4
0 mi 1/4

POPULATION	661,000
CITY ELEVATION	2,658 feet 810 meters
LATITUDE	31° 47′ N
LONGITUDE	35° 14′ E
TEMPERATURE Average Daily High/Low °F (°C)	Jan. 53°/39°F (12°/4°C) July 84°/63°F (29°/17°C)
RAINFALL Average Monthly inches (mm)	January 5.5 (140) July 0 (0)
TIME ZONE Greenwich mean time	+2 hours GMT

Medieval cartographers located Jerusalem at the center of the world, and in the eyes of many the Old City remains so. For Jews, the Western Wall of the Second Temple is the holiest of sites. Above it is the Dome of the Rock, third holiest site in Islam, commemorating the place where Muhammad ascended to heaven. A few blocks away the Church of the Holy Sepulchre marks the traditional site where Jesus was crucified, entombed, and resurrected. Israel claims the city as its eternal capital; Palestinians assert that East Jerusalem should be theirs.

Jerusalem
ISRAEL
0 km 100
0 mi 100

Tehran

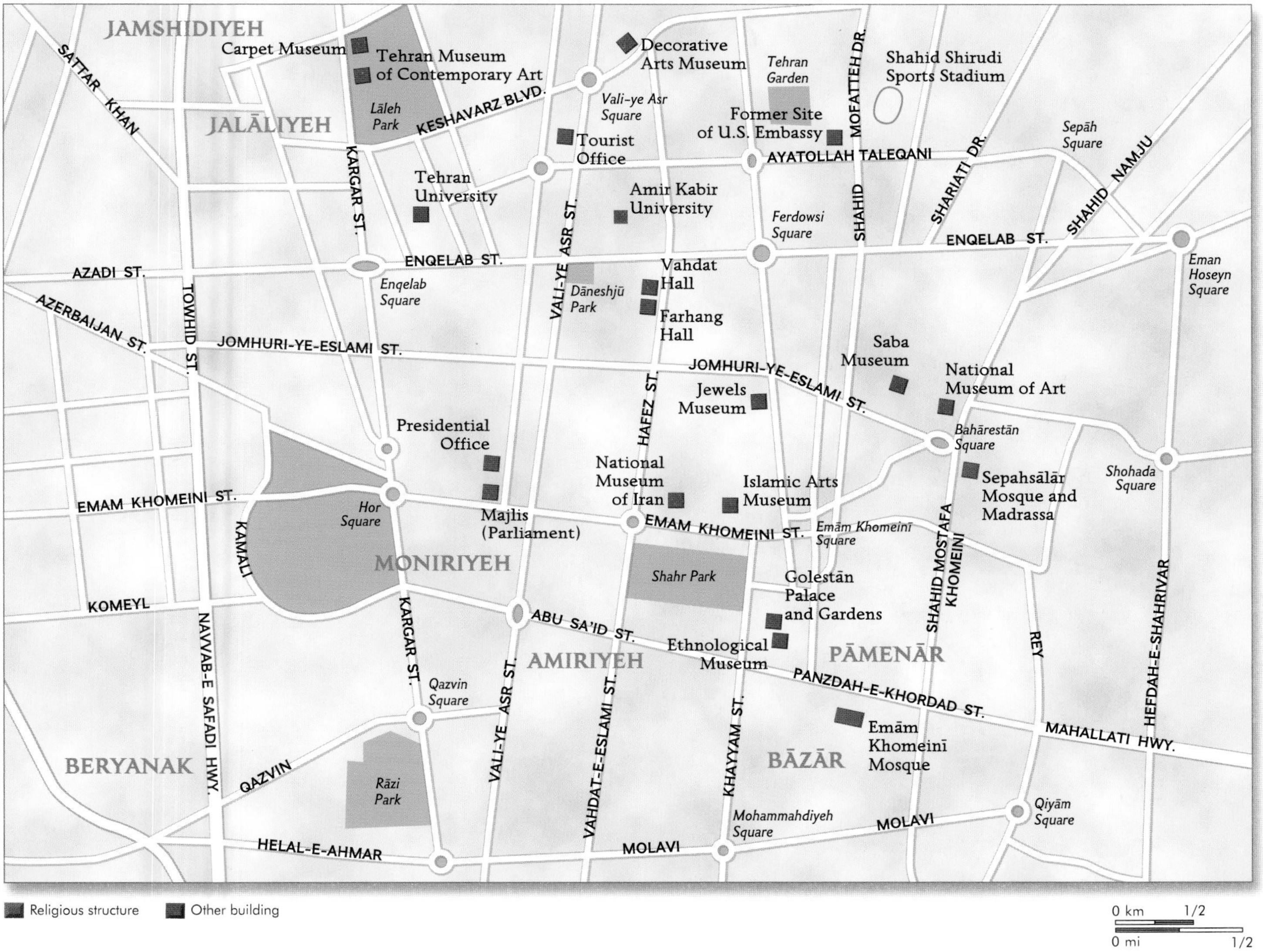

POPULATION	7,038,000
CITY ELEVATION	3,800 feet 1,158 meters
LATITUDE	35° 40′ N
LONGITUDE	51° 26′ E
TEMPERATURE Average Daily High/Low °F (°C)	Jan. 45°/30°F (7°/-1°C) July 98°/75°F (37°/24°C)
RAINFALL Average Monthly inches (mm)	January 1.6 (42) July .1 (2)
TIME ZONE Greenwich mean time	+3.5 hours GMT

Iran's Elburz Mountains overlook the high, expansive capital of Tehran (3,800 feet). The city's Muslim population, a multi-ethnic mix of majority Persians, Azeris, Kurds, Arabs, and tribal groups, grew rapidly in the 1980s; rising birthrates, rural to urban migration, and refugees from Afghanistan and war with Iraq swelled the city. Religious minorities—Armenian and Assyrian Christians, Zoroastrians, and Jews—have lived here for centuries. Iran's Pahlavi dynasty, founded in 1925, ended in 1979 with the establishment of an Islamic Republic under Ayatollah Khomeini.

Tehran
IRAN
0 km 500
0 mi 500

REGIONAL THEMES

LEFT TO RIGHT: Demonstration by Tanzim militiamen in the West Bank city of Ramallah on the occasion of the funeral of a Palestinian; Oil production facilities at the port of Dubayy, United Arab Emirates; Palestinian men playing cards in the West Bank city of Hebron; Sand dunes in Saudi Arabia; In Jerusalem a Jewish family lights candles to celebrate Hanukkah, the Festival of Lights; Flowing water pumped from a well in a village in Syria.

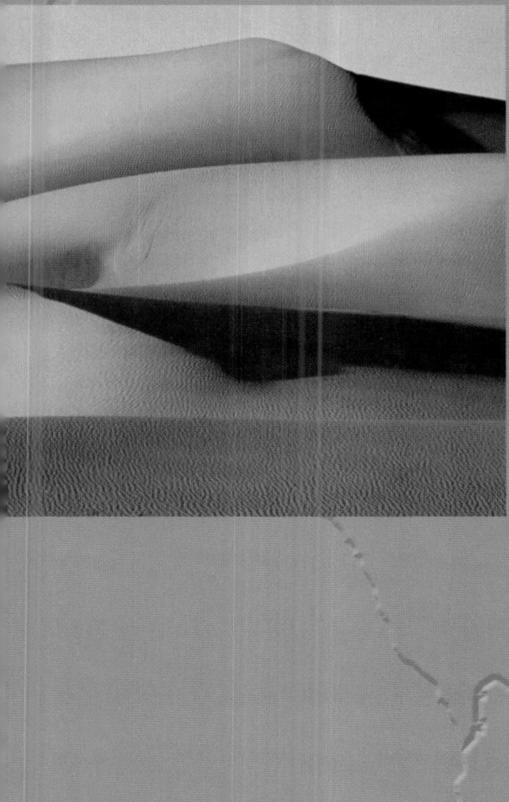

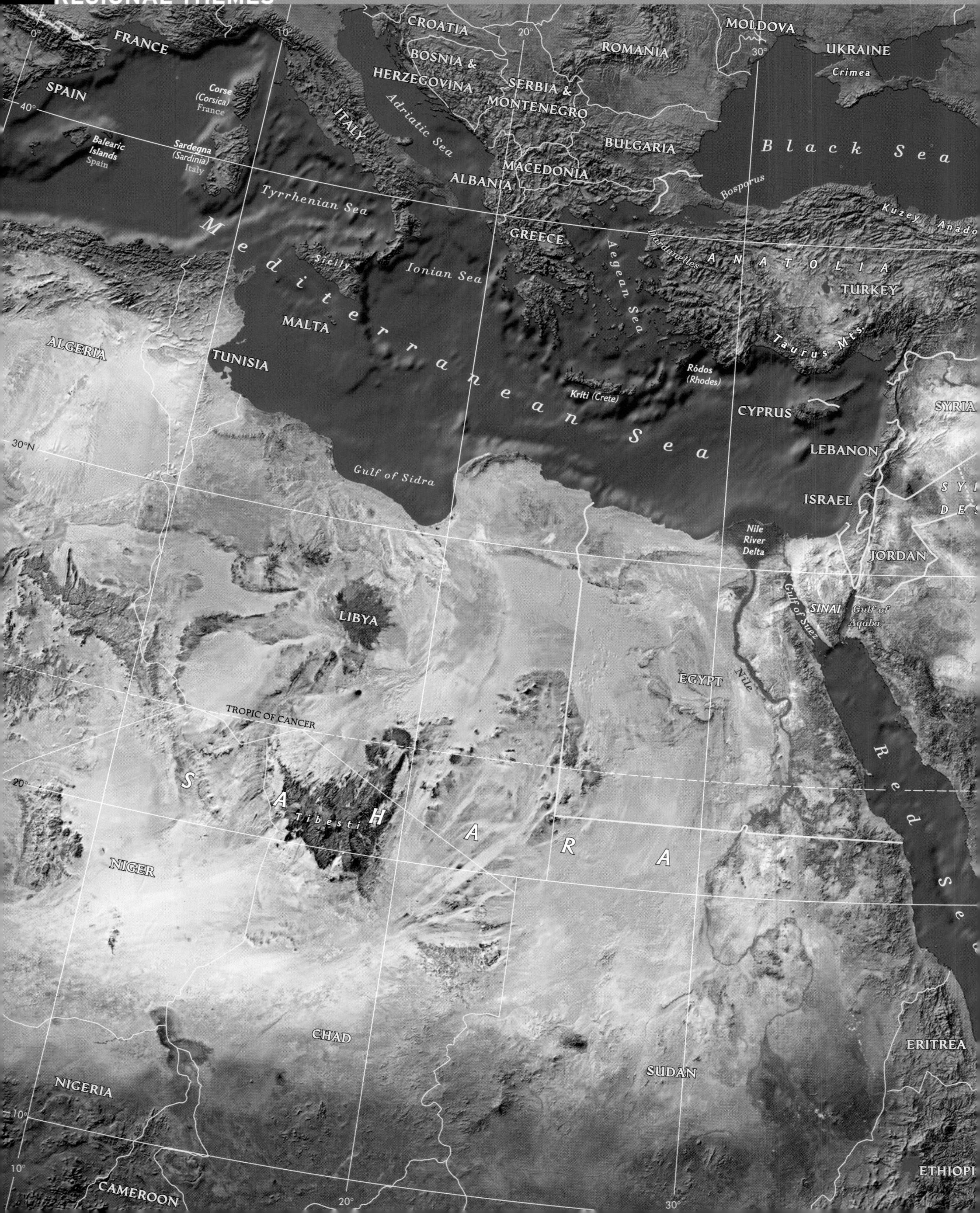
FRANCE
SPAIN
Corse
(Corsica)
France
Balearic
Islands
Spain
Sardegna
(Sardinia)
Italy
CROATIA
BOSNIA &
HERZEGOVINA
SERBIA &
MONTENEGRO
ROMANIA
MOLDOVA
UKRAINE
Crimea
ITALY
Adriatic Sea
BULGARIA
Black Sea
MACEDONIA
ALBANIA
Bosporus
Tyrrhenian Sea
Mediterranean Sea
GREECE
Dardanelles
ANATOLIA
Kuzey Anado
Sicily
Ionian Sea
Aegean Sea
TURKEY
MALTA
Taurus Mts.
ALGERIA
TUNISIA
Ródos
(Rhodes)
Kriti (Crete)
CYPRUS
SYRIA
LEBANON
Gulf of Sidra
ISRAEL
Nile
River
Delta
JORDAN
LIBYA
SINAI
Gulf of Suez
Gulf of Aqaba
EGYPT
Nile
TROPIC OF CANCER
SAHARA
Tibesti
Red Sea
NIGER
CHAD
SUDAN
ERITREA
NIGERIA
CAMEROON
ETHIOPI
40°
30°N
20°
10°
0°
10
20°
30°

RUSSIA
KAZAKHSTAN
KYRGYZSTAN
UZBEKISTAN
CHINA
GEORGIA
ARMENIA
AZERBAIJAN
TURKMENISTAN
TAJIKISTAN
Caspian Sea
Elburz Mountains
Hindu Kush
Karakoram Ra.
HIMALAYA
AFGHANISTAN
Tigris
Euphrates
Zagros Mountains
IRAN
IRAQ
PAKISTAN
Indus
INDIA
KUWAIT
Persian Gulf
Str. of Hormuz
Oman
Rann of Kutch
Nafūd
Ad Dahnā'
BAHRAIN
QATAR
SAUDI ARABIA
Gulf of Oman
TROPIC OF CANCER
UNITED ARAB EMIRATES
Ra's al Ḩadd
ARABIAN PENINSULA
AR RUB' AL KHĀLĪ
Jazīrat Maşīrah
OMAN
ARABIAN SEA
YEMEN
Ḩaḑramawt
Albers Conic Equal-Area Projection
SCALE 1:16,246,000
1 CENTIMETER = 162 KILOMETERS; 1 INCH = 256 MILES
0 100 200 300 400 500 600
KILOMETERS
0 100 200 300 400 500 600
STATUTE MILES
Bab al Mandab
Gulf of Aden
Suquṭrá (Socotra) Yemen
DJIBOUTI
SOMALIA
50°
60°
70°
40°
30°N
20°
10°
Longitude East 60° of Greenwich

Climate

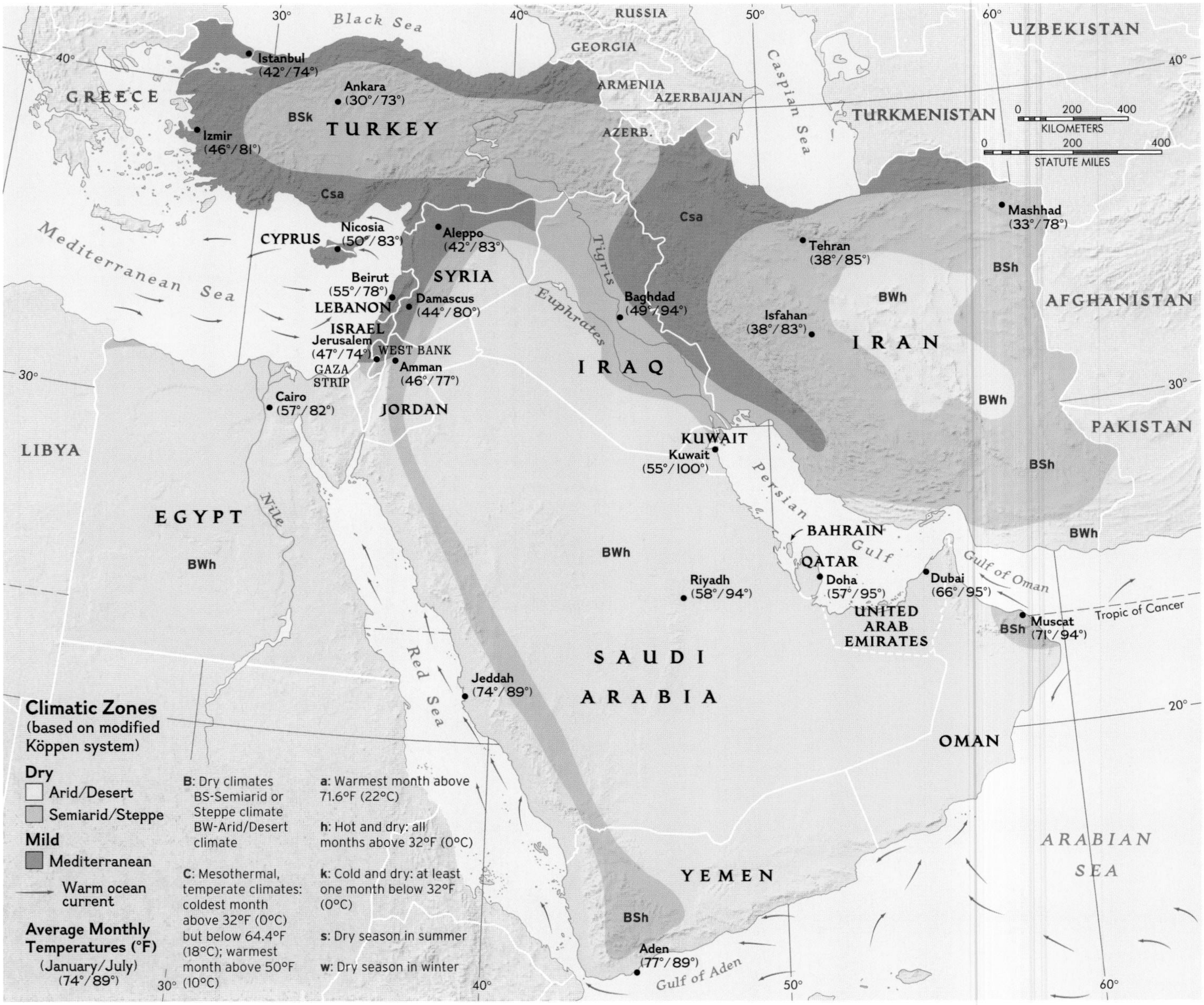

CLIMATE TYPES OF THE MIDDLE EAST

ARID / DESERT

Centered between 20 and 30 degrees north and south latitude, this climate type is typically the result of a persistent high-pressure area. Rainfall amounts in arid/desert areas are negligible, and there is some seasonal variation in temperature. Vegetation is typically sparse. Fifty percent of the Middle East can be classified as arid or desert.

SEMIARID / STEPPE

Regions with a semiarid or steppe climate have a much greater range in monthly temperatures and receive significantly more rain than arid/desert areas. These climates are often found in inland regions, in the rain shadow of mountain ranges. Annual rainfall amounts support mainly grasses and small shrubs. Twenty percent of the Middle East has this climate type.

MEDITERRANEAN

This term describes the climate of much of the Mediterranean region. In the Middle East, it is also found in areas east of the Tigris River and along the Caspian and Black Seas. Summer months are typically warm to hot with dry conditions, while winter months are cool (but not cold) and provide modest precipitation. Thirty percent of the Middle East falls into this category.

MEAN JANUARY TEMPERATURE

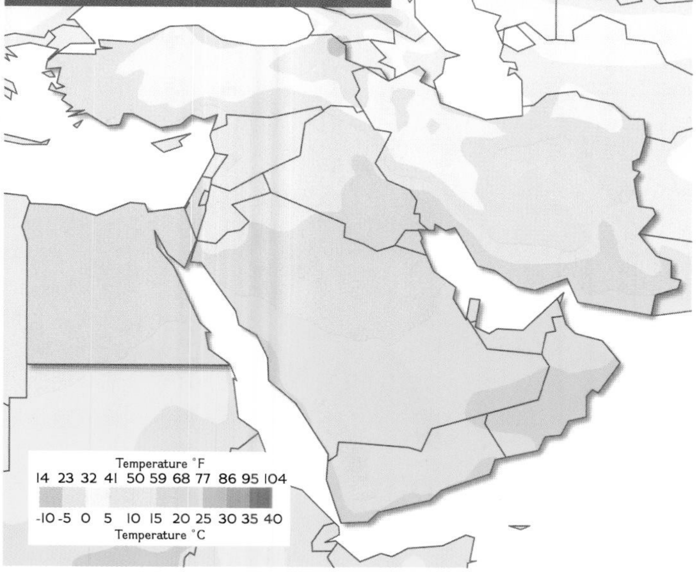
Temperature °F
14 23 32 41 50 59 68 77 86 95 104
-10 -5 0 5 10 15 20 25 30 35 40
Temperature °C

MEAN JANUARY PRECIPITATION

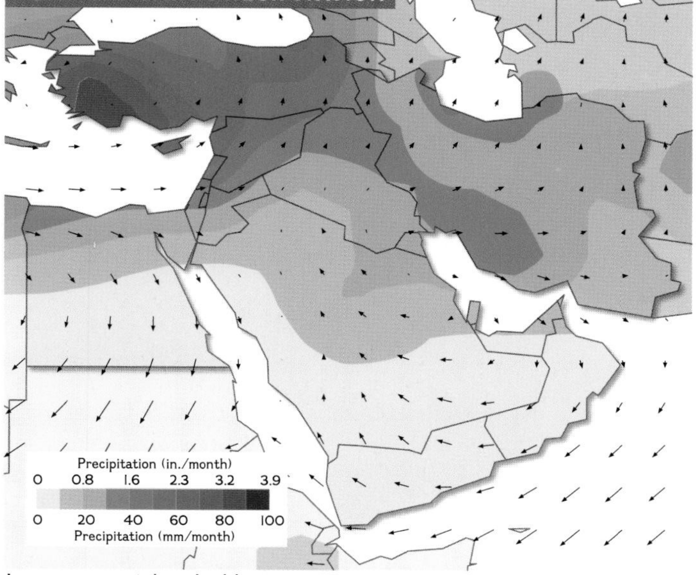
Precipitation (in./month)
0 0.8 1.6 2.3 3.2 3.9
0 20 40 60 80 100
Precipitation (mm/month)

Arrows represent wind speed and direction

MEAN JULY TEMPERATURE

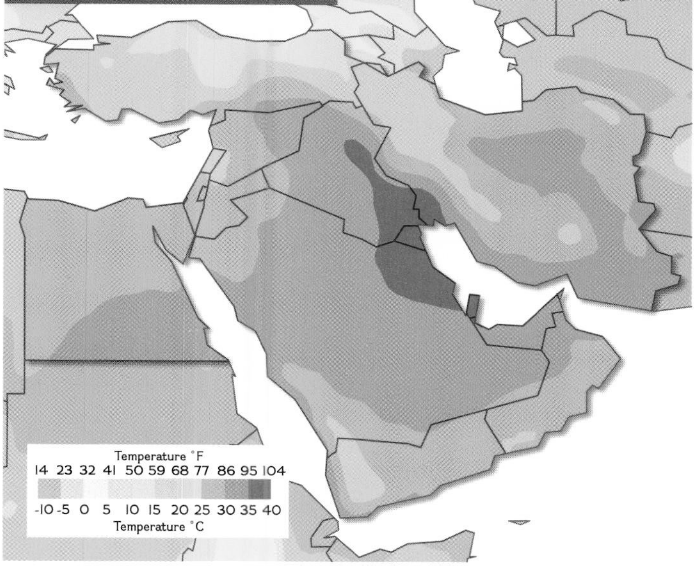
Temperature °F
14 23 32 41 50 59 68 77 86 95 104
-10 -5 0 5 10 15 20 25 30 35 40
Temperature °C

MEAN JULY PRECIPITATION

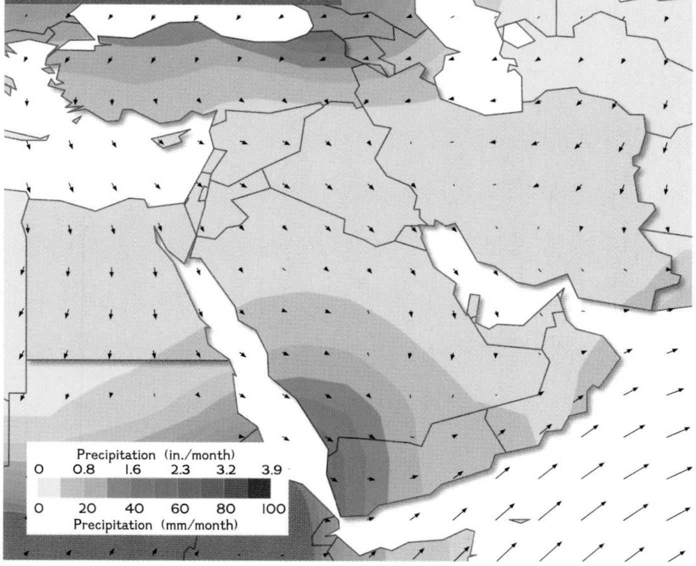
Precipitation (in./month)
0 0.8 1.6 2.3 3.2 3.9
0 20 40 60 80 100
Precipitation (mm/month)

MEAN DAILY TEMPERATURES AND ANNUAL RAINFALL FOR SELECTED CITIES

Highs / lows (°F)	Jan	Feb	Mar	Apr	May	Jun	Jul	Aug	Sep	Oct	Nov	Dec	Rainfall
Aleppo, Syria	50 / 35	55 / 37	62 / 42	72 / 49	84 / 56	92 / 64	97 / 70	97 / 69	92 / 64	80 / 55	65 / 44	54 / 38	13.2 in.
Amman, Jordan	54 / 38	57 / 39	63 / 43	73 / 49	81 / 55	87 / 62	89 / 65	90 / 65	87 / 61	80 / 56	68 / 47	57 / 40	10.7 in.
Baghdad, Iraq	61 / 39	64 / 43	72 / 48	84 / 57	97 / 66	106 / 73	109 / 75	109 / 75	104 / 70	91 / 61	77 / 52	64 / 43	6.1 in.
Beirut, Lebanon	63 / 52	63 / 52	66 / 54	72 / 57	79 / 64	82 / 70	88 / 73	90 / 73	86 / 73	81 / 70	73 / 61	64 / 55	34.4 in.
Cairo, Egypt	66 / 48	69 / 50	74 / 53	83 / 58	90 / 64	94 / 69	94 / 71	93 / 71	91 / 69	85 / 64	76 / 57	68 / 51	1.0 in.
Dubai, UAE	75 / 57	76 / 58	82 / 63	90 / 68	98 / 74	102 / 79	105 / 84	105 / 85	102 / 79	95 / 73	87 / 65	79 / 60	3.7 in.
Istanbul, Turkey	48 / 37	49 / 38	53 / 40	62 / 46	71 / 54	79 / 61	83 / 65	83 / 65	77 / 60	68 / 53	60 / 47	52 / 42	27.4 in.
Jerusalem, Israel	53 / 39	56 / 40	61 / 43	70 / 49	77 / 54	82 / 59	84 / 63	84 / 63	82 / 61	77 / 57	66 / 49	57 / 42	23.2 in
Riyadh, Saudi Arabia	68 / 47	73 / 51	82 / 58	90 / 66	102 / 76	107 / 79	109 / 81	109 / 81	104 / 75	94 / 67	81 / 58	71 / 49	4.0 in.
Tehran, Iran	45 / 30	50 / 33	60 / 41	71 / 52	82 / 61	93 / 70	98 / 75	96 / 73	89 / 67	75 / 55	62 / 44	50 / 34	9.0 in.

Fahrenheit to Celsius conversion: subtract 32, then multiply by 5/9 (.55)

Population

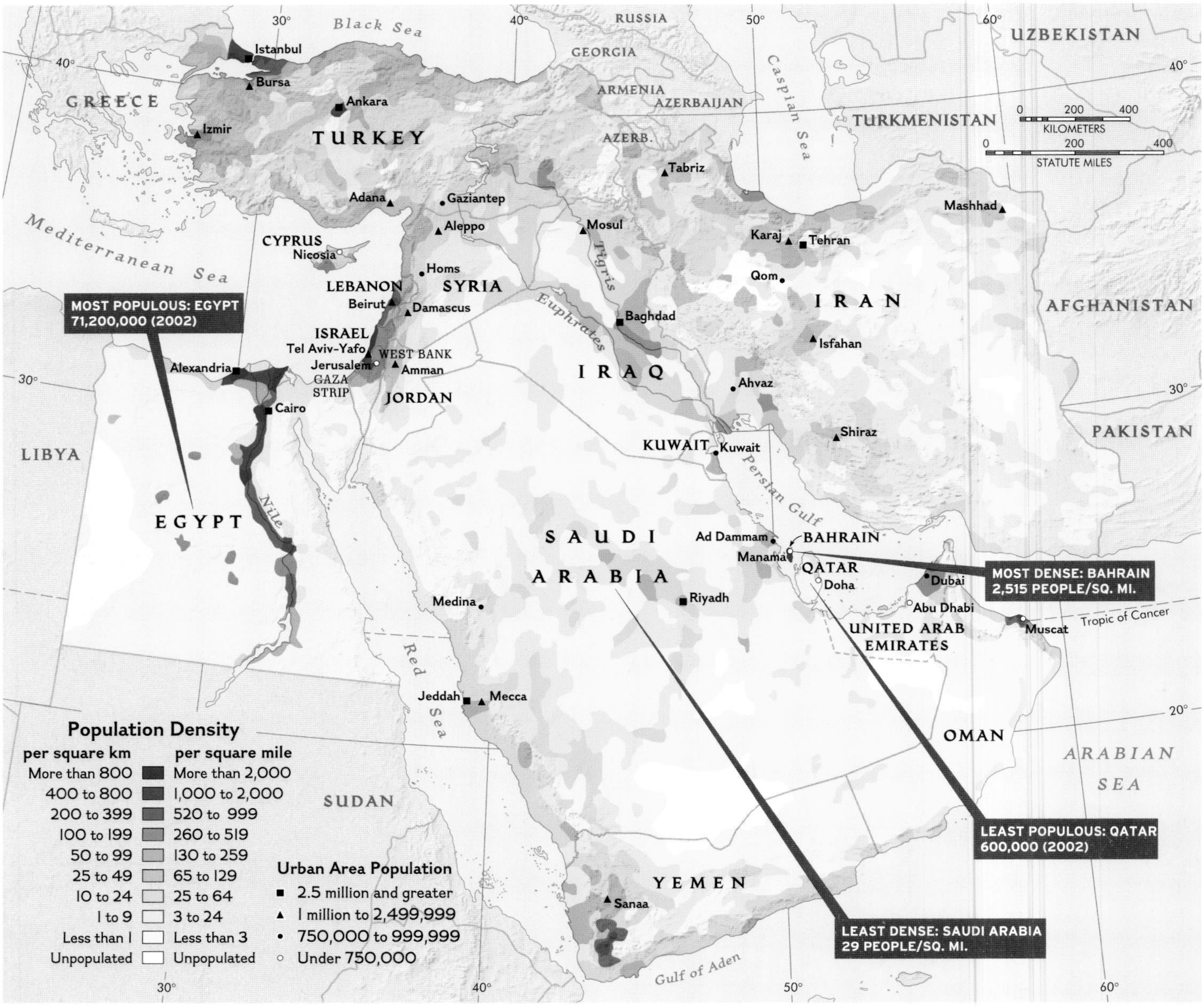

POPULATION GROWTH IN THE MIDDLE EAST, 1950-2000

Between 1950 and 2000, the Middle East grew by 380%—more than any other world region.

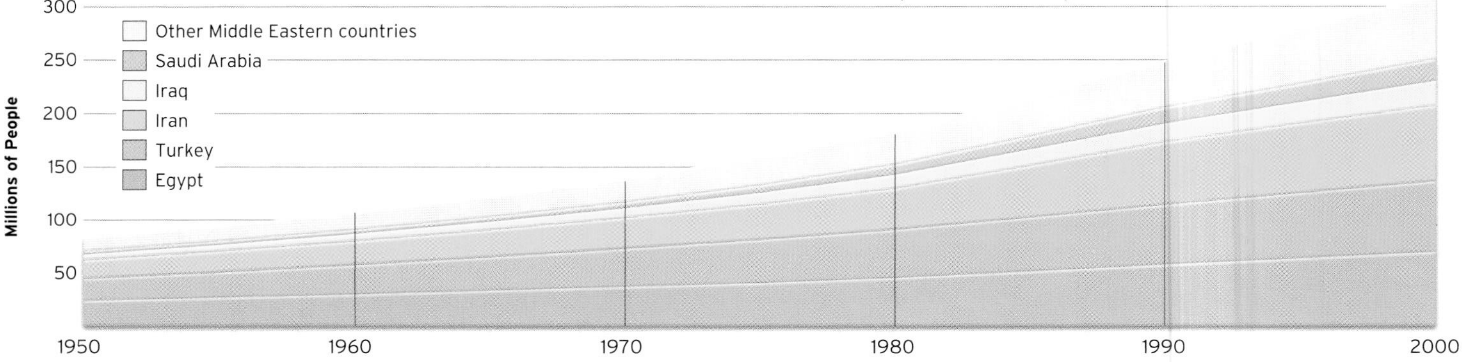

FERTILITY

Average number of children born to women in a given population

Yemen	7.2	Egypt	3.5
Occupied Terr.	5.9	UAE	3.5
Saudi Arabia	5.7	Israel	2.9
Iraq	5.4	Bahrain	2.8
Oman	4.7	Iran	2.5
Kuwait	4.3	Turkey	2.5
Syria	4.1	Lebanon	2.4
Qatar	3.9	Cyprus	1.7
Jordan	3.6	World average	2.8

LIFE EXPECTANCY

Life expectancy at birth, in years

Israel	78	Saudi Arabia	72
Cyprus	77	Jordan	70
Kuwait	76	Syria	70
Bahrain	74	Iran	69
UAE	74	Turkey	69
Lebanon	73	Egypt	66
Oman	73	Yemen	59
Occupied Terr.	72	Iraq	58
Qatar	72	World average	67

URBAN POPULATION

Percentage of population living in urban areas

Kuwait	100	Iraq	68
Israel	91	Cyprus	66
Qatar	91	Iran	66
Lebanon	88	Turkey	66
Bahrain	87	Occupied Terr.	57
Saudi Arabia	83	Syria	50
Jordan	79	Egypt	43
UAE	78	Yemen	26
Oman	72	World average	47

MIGRANT POPULATION

Migrants (persons residing in a country other than where born) as % of total population

UAE	73.8	Lebanon	18.1
Qatar	72.4	Cyprus	6.3
Kuwait	57.9	Syria	5.6
Occupied Terr.	52.2	Iran	3.3
Bahrain	39.8	Turkey	2.3
Jordan	39.6	Yemen	1.4
Israel	37.4	Iraq	0.6
Oman	26.9	Egypt	0.2
Saudi Arabia	25.8	World average	2.9

POPULATION BY AGE AND GENDER (world and selected countries)

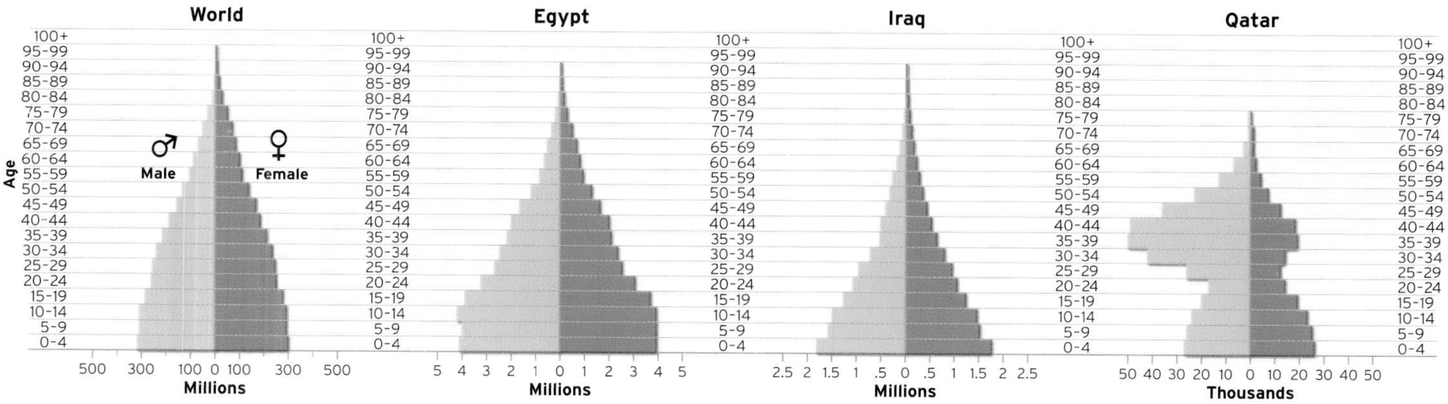

(All figures reflect 2000 data)

POPULATIONS OF MAJOR CITIES

City	1950	2000
Cairo, Egypt	2,410,000	9,462,000
Istanbul, Turkey	1,077,000	8,953,000
Tehran, Iran	1,042,000	6,979,000
Baghdad, Iraq	579,000	4,865,000
Riyadh, Saudi Arabia	111,000	4,549,000
Alexandria, Egypt	1,038,000	3,506,000
Jeddah, Saudi Arabia	119,000	3,192,000
Ankara, Turkey	542,000	3,155,000
Aleppo, Syria	320,000	2,229,000

City	1950	2000
Izmir, Turkey	480,000	2,214,000
Damascus, Syria	367,000	2,144,000
Beirut, Lebanon	327,000	2,070,000
Tel Aviv-Yafo, Israel	418,000	2,001,000
Sanaa, Yemen	46,000	1,327,000
Amman, Jordan	90,000	1,148,000
Mecca, Saudi Arabia	148,000	1,335,000
Tabriz, Iran	235,000	1,274,000
Bursa, Turkey	148,000	1,166,000

Religion

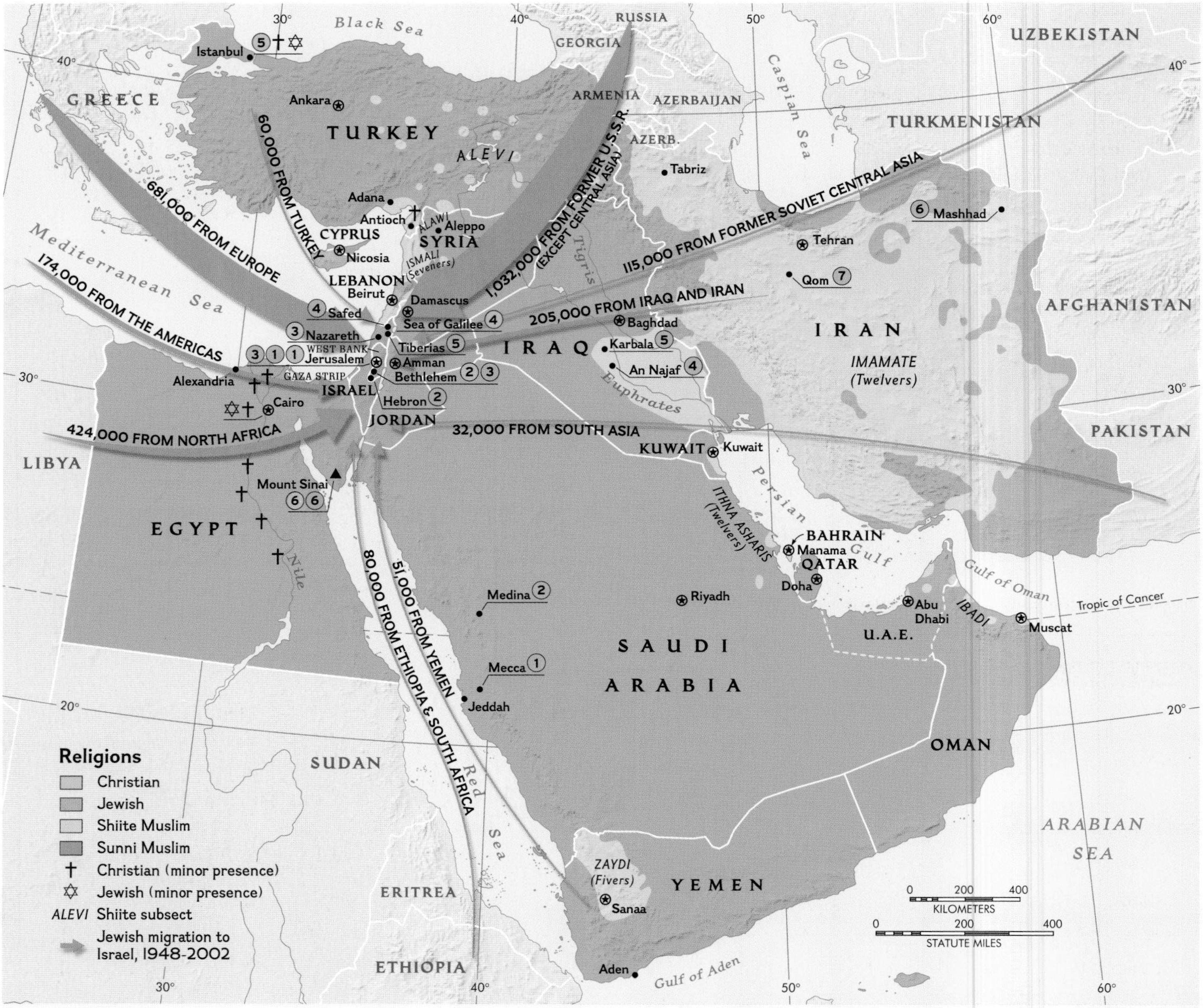

Sacred Places

Christian

1. Jerusalem: Church of the Holy Sepulchre, Jesus's crucifixion
2. Bethlehem: Jesus's birthplace
3. Nazareth: Where Jesus grew up
4. Sea of Galilee: Where Jesus gave the Sermon on the Mount
5. Istanbul (Constantinople): Dedicated as the capital of the newly-Christian Roman Empire (A.D. 300) by Constantine the Great
6. Mount Sinai: Site of God's revelation, where God appeared to Moses and gave him the Ten Commandments

Jewish

1. Jerusalem: Location of the Western Wall and first and second temples; City of David; the ancient and modern capital of Israel
2. Hebron: Burial spot of patriarchs and matriarchs
3. Bethlehem: Site of Rachel's tomb
4. Safed: Where Kabbalah (Jewish mysticism) flourished
5. Tiberias: Where Talmud (source of Jewish law) was first composed
6. Mount Sinai: Site of God's revelation, where God appeared to Moses and gave him the Ten Commandments

Muslim

1. Mecca: Muhammad's birthplace; destination of the pilgrimage, or *hajj*; houses the Kaaba (shrine that Muslims face when praying)
2. Medina: City of Muhammad's flight, or *hegira*
3. Jerusalem: Dome of the Rock, Muhammad's stepping-stone to heaven
4. An Najaf (Shiite): Tomb of Imam Ali
5. Karbala (Shiite): Tomb of Imam Hoseyn
6. Mashhad (Shiite): Location of the shrine to Imam Reza
7. Qom (Shiite): Houses the shrine of Fatima (Imam Reza's sister); location of the Islamic University, a major religious center

TOP 10 NATIONAL JEWISH POPULATIONS

	Jewish population	% of total pop.
1. United States	5,621,000	2.0%
2. Israel	5,346,000	81.0%
3. Russia	951,000	0.7%
4. France	591,000	1.0%
5. Argentina	490,000	1.3%
6. Canada	403,000	1.3%
7. Brazil	357,000	0.2%
8. United Kingdom	302,000	0.5%
9. West Bank & Gaza Strip	239,000	6.5%
10. Ukraine	220,000	0.5%

RELIGIOUS ADHERENTS IN THE MIDDLE EAST

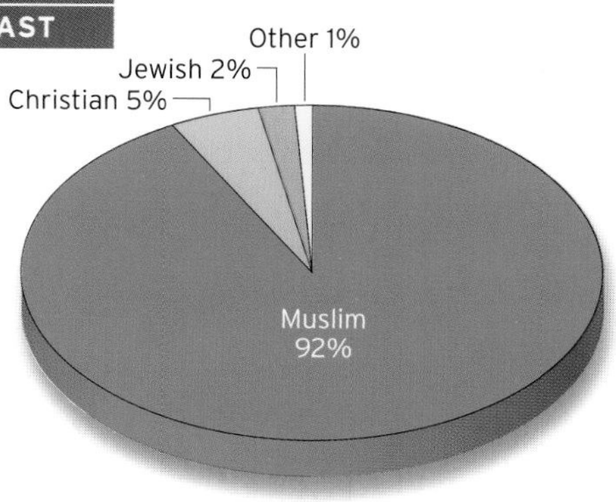
Other 1%
Jewish 2%
Christian 5%
Muslim 92%

TOP 10 NATIONAL MUSLIM POPULATIONS

	Muslim population	% of total pop.
1. Indonesia	181,368,000	83.6%
2. Pakistan	141,650,000	98.7%
3. India	123,960,000	11.8%
4. Bangladesh	110,805,000	82.9%
5. Turkey	65,281,000	97.0%
6. Iran	64,944,000	99.0%
7. Egypt	63,368,000	89.0%
8. Nigeria	63,300,000	48.7%
9. China	38,208,000	3.0%
10. Algeria	30,690,000	97.7%

Note: No Middle Eastern countries fall within the top ten populations for any other religions.

BRANCHES OF ISLAM IN THE MIDDLE EAST

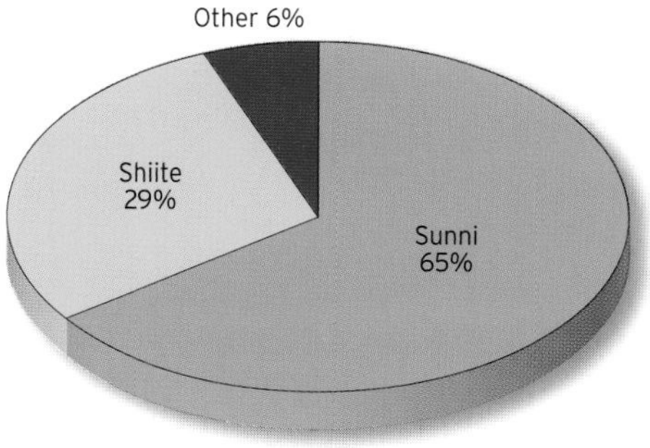
Other 6%
Shiite 29%
Sunni 65%

ADHERENTS BY POLITICAL AREA

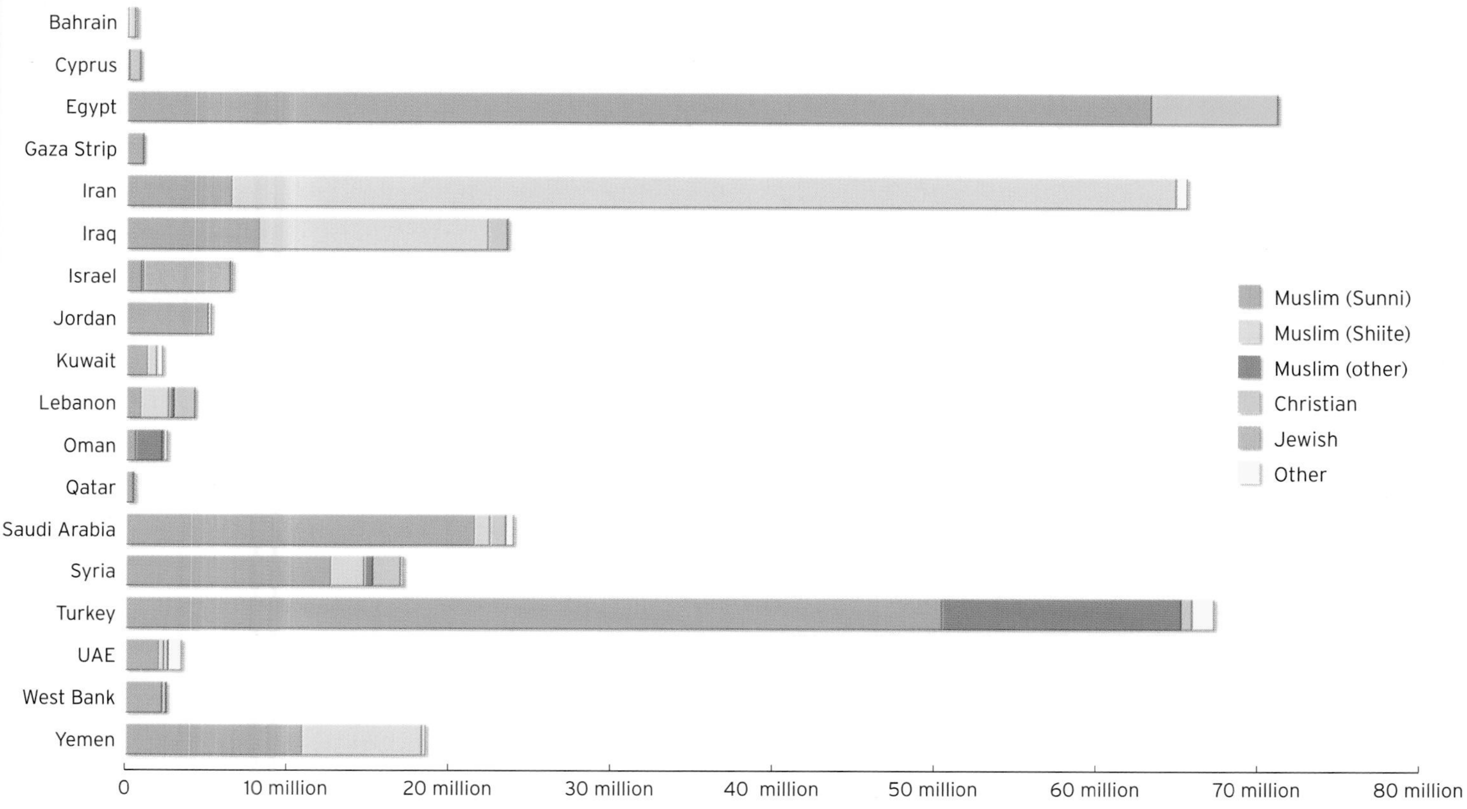

Ethnic and Linguistic Groups

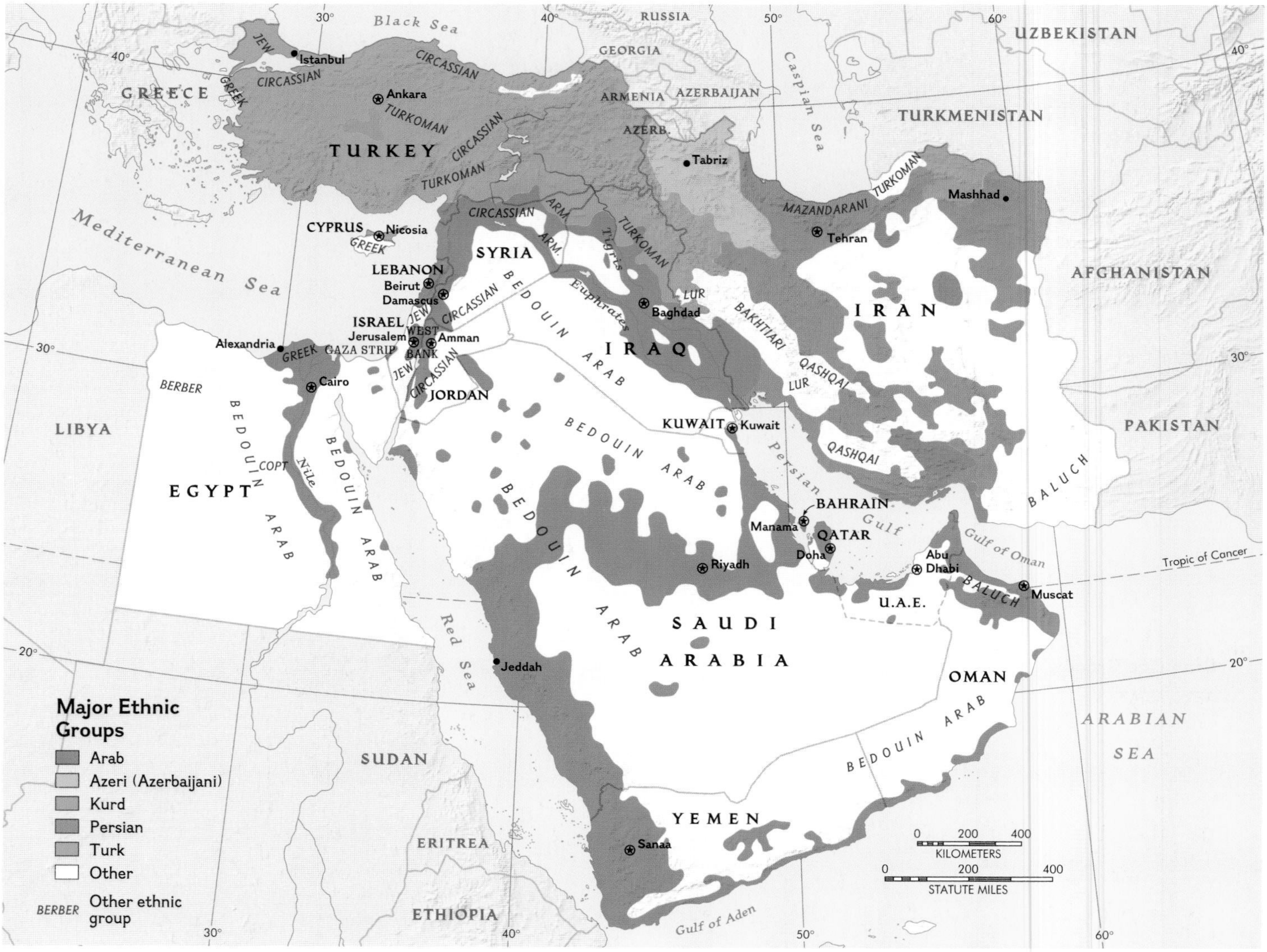

ETHNIC COMPOSITION OF THE MIDDLE EAST

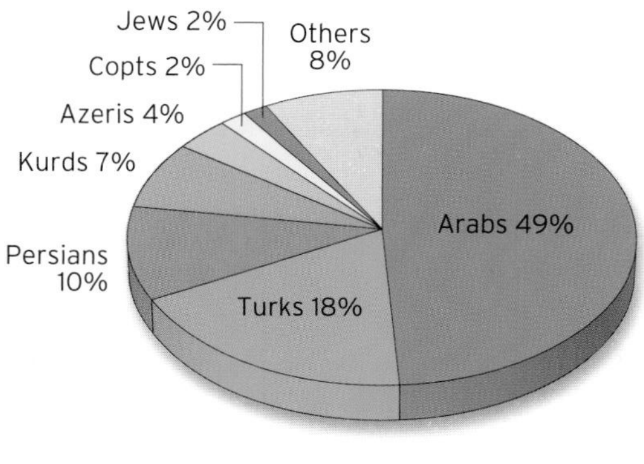

FOREIGN-BORN POPULATION

Figures shown reflect the total number of non-native residents as a percentage of the overall population.

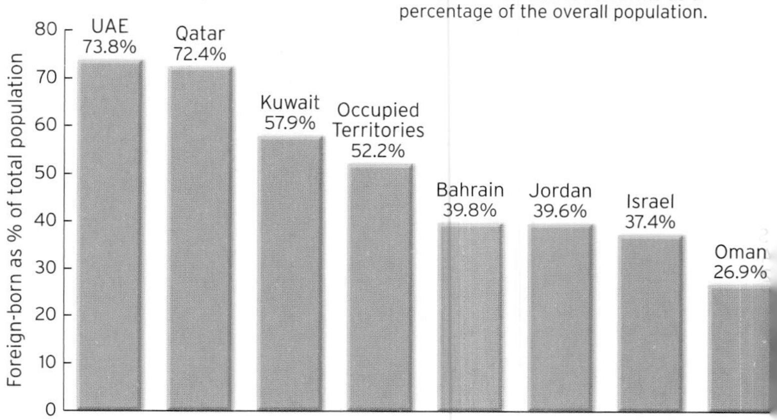

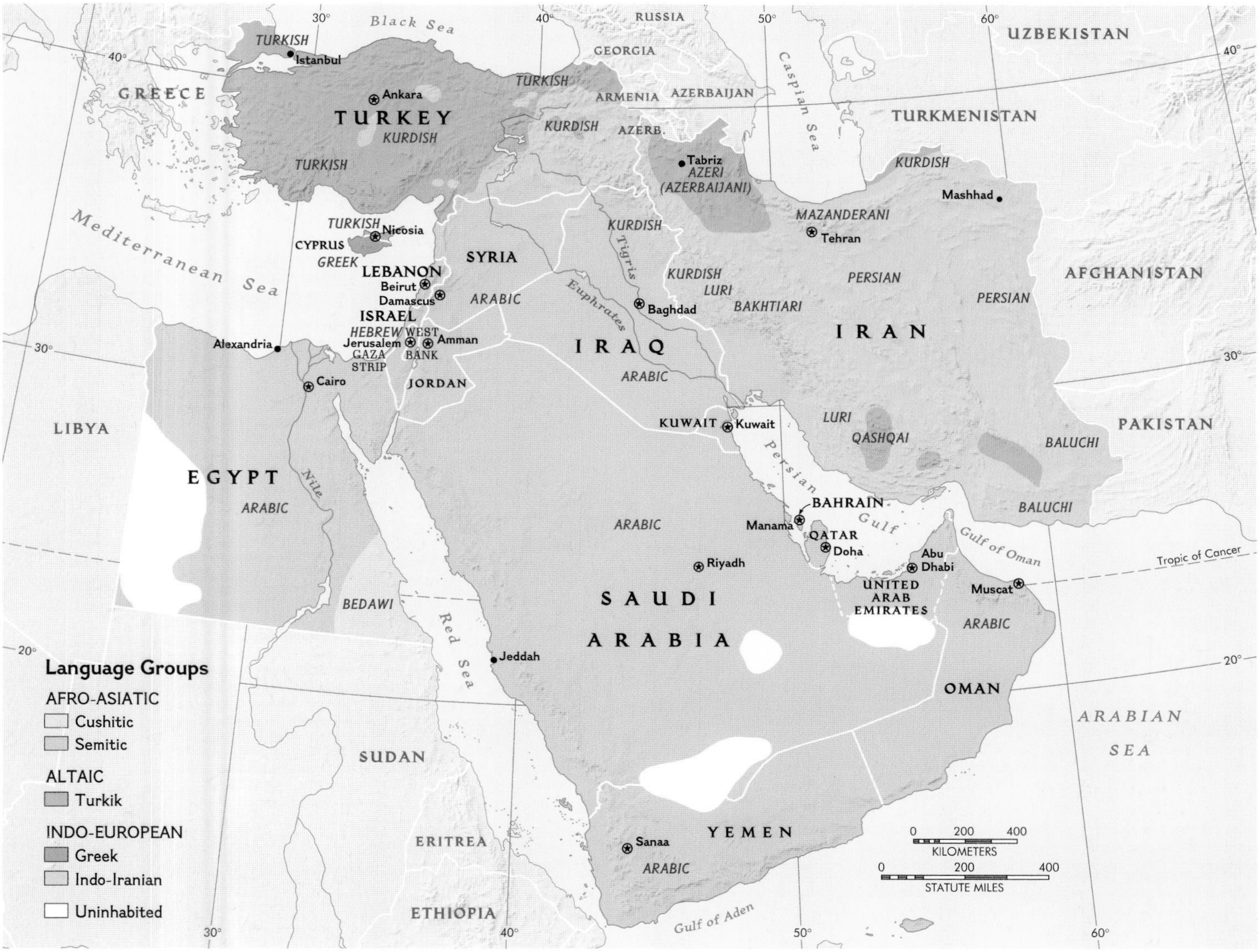

MAIN LANGUAGES OF THE MIDDLE EAST (in order of number of speakers):

1 Arabic
2 Turkish
3 Persian
4 Kurdish
5 Azeri (Azerbaijani)
6 Hebrew

LANGUAGE GROUPS AND SUBGROUPS ON MAP ABOVE:

AFRO-ASIATIC/CUSHITIC
Bedawi

AFRO-ASIATIC/SEMITIC
Arabic, Hebrew

ALTAIC/TURKIC
Azeri (Azerbaijani), Turkish

INDO-EUROPEAN/GREEK
Greek

INDO-EUROPEAN/INDO-IRANIAN
Armenian, Baluchi, Kurdish, Luri, Mazanderani, Persian, Qashqai

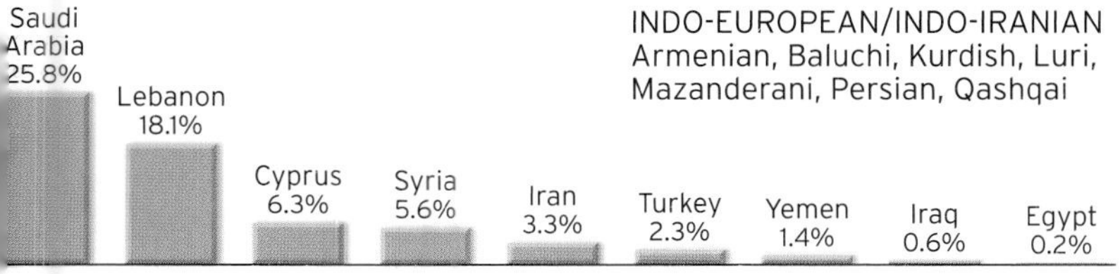

LANGUAGES	Official language	Total number of languages
Bahrain	Arabic	3
Cyprus	Greek, Turkish	4
Egypt	Arabic	11 (1 extinct)
Iran	Persian	71 (2 extinct)
Iraq	Arabic	23
Israel	Hebrew	36 (3 extinct)
Jordan	Arabic	9
Kuwait	Arabic	3
Lebanon	Arabic	5
Oman	Arabic	11
Qatar	Arabic	3
Saudi Arabia	Arabic	5
Syria	Arabic	17 (2 extinct)
Turkey	Turkish	36 (2 extinct)
UAE	Arabic	6
Yemen	Arabic	7

Oil

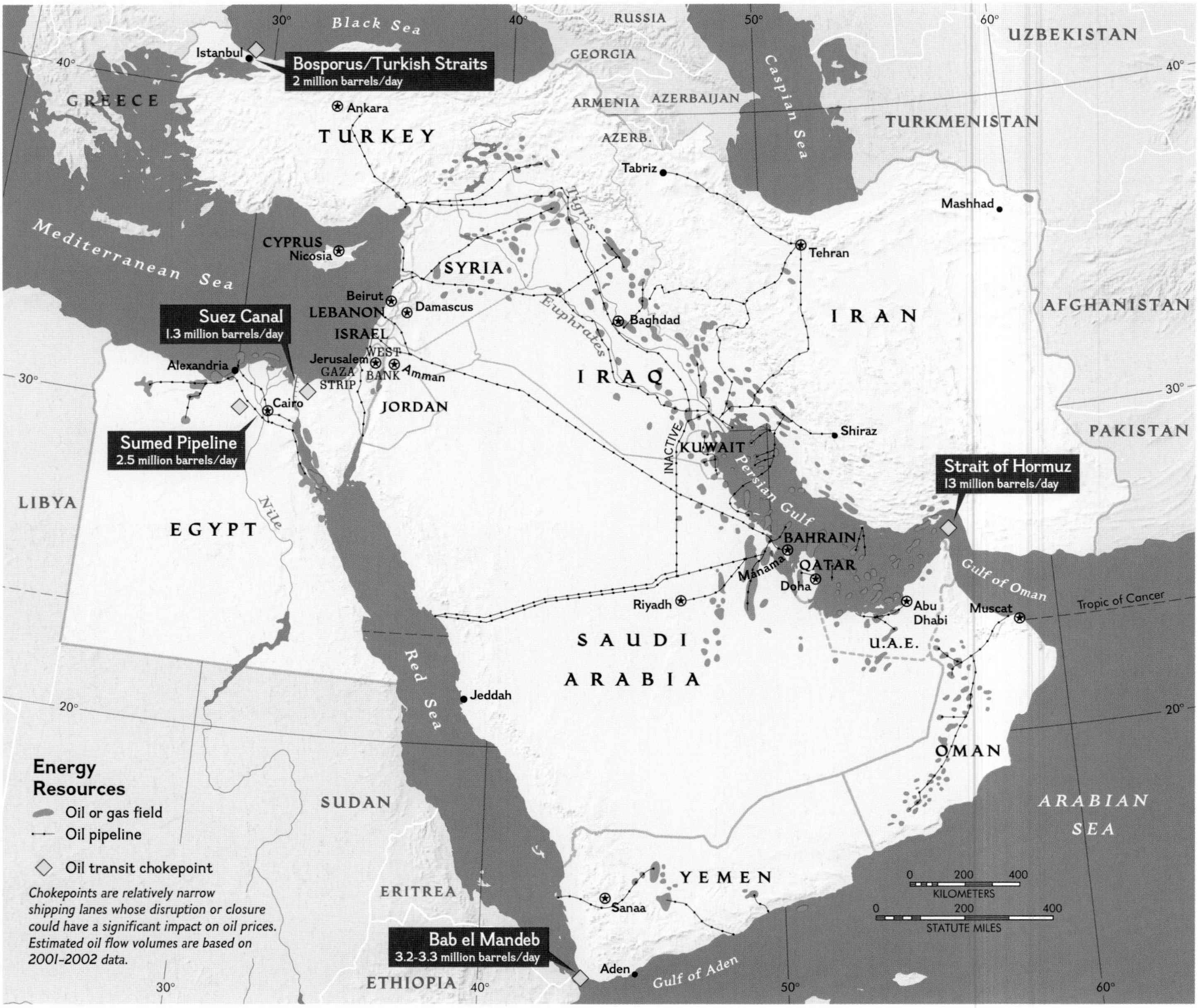
Black Sea
RUSSIA
GEORGIA
UZBEKISTAN
Istanbul
Bosporus/Turkish Straits
2 million barrels/day
GREECE
Ankara
ARMENIA
AZERBAIJAN
AZERB.
Caspian Sea
TURKEY
TURKMENISTAN
Tabriz
Mashhad
Mediterranean Sea
CYPRUS
Nicosia
Tehran
SYRIA
Tigris
Beirut
LEBANON
Damascus
ISRAEL
Euphrates
Baghdad
IRAN
AFGHANISTAN
Suez Canal
1.3 million barrels/day
Alexandria
Jerusalem
WEST BANK
GAZA STRIP
Amman
IRAQ
Cairo
JORDAN
Sumed Pipeline
2.5 million barrels/day
INACTIVE
KUWAIT
Shiraz
PAKISTAN
Persian Gulf
Strait of Hormuz
13 million barrels/day
LIBYA
EGYPT
Nile
BAHRAIN
Manama
QATAR
Doha
Gulf of Oman
Riyadh
Abu Dhabi
Muscat
Tropic of Cancer
U.A.E.
SAUDI ARABIA
Red Sea
Jeddah
OMAN
Energy Resources
Oil or gas field
Oil pipeline
Oil transit chokepoint
Chokepoints are relatively narrow shipping lanes whose disruption or closure could have a significant impact on oil prices. Estimated oil flow volumes are based on 2001-2002 data.
SUDAN
ARABIAN SEA
YEMEN
ERITREA
Sanaa
0 200 400 KILOMETERS
0 200 400 STATUTE MILES
Bab el Mandeb
3.2-3.3 million barrels/day
Aden
Gulf of Aden
ETHIOPIA
30°
40°
50°
60°
20°

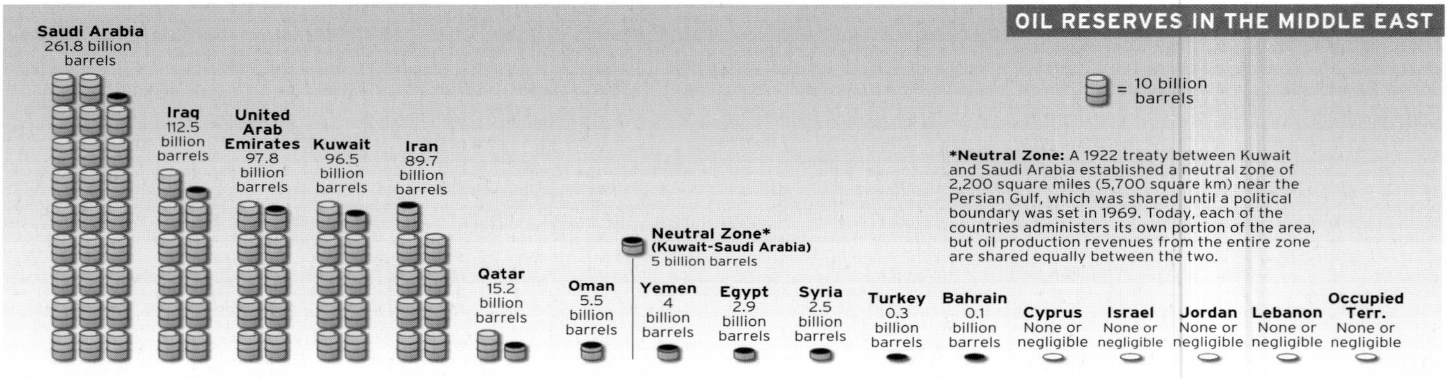
OIL RESERVES IN THE MIDDLE EAST
= 10 billion barrels
Saudi Arabia 261.8 billion barrels
Iraq 112.5 billion barrels
United Arab Emirates 97.8 billion barrels
Kuwait 96.5 billion barrels
Iran 89.7 billion barrels
Qatar 15.2 billion barrels
Oman 5.5 billion barrels
Neutral Zone* (Kuwait-Saudi Arabia) 5 billion barrels
Yemen 4 billion barrels
Egypt 2.9 billion barrels
Syria 2.5 billion barrels
Turkey 0.3 billion barrels
Bahrain 0.1 billion barrels
Cyprus None or negligible
Israel None or negligible
Jordan None or negligible
Lebanon None or negligible
Occupied Terr. None or negligible
*Neutral Zone: A 1922 treaty between Kuwait and Saudi Arabia established a neutral zone of 2,200 square miles (5,700 square km) near the Persian Gulf, which was shared until a political boundary was set in 1969. Today, each of the countries administers its own portion of the area, but oil production revenues from the entire zone are shared equally between the two.

REGIONAL SHARE OF WORLD OIL RESERVES

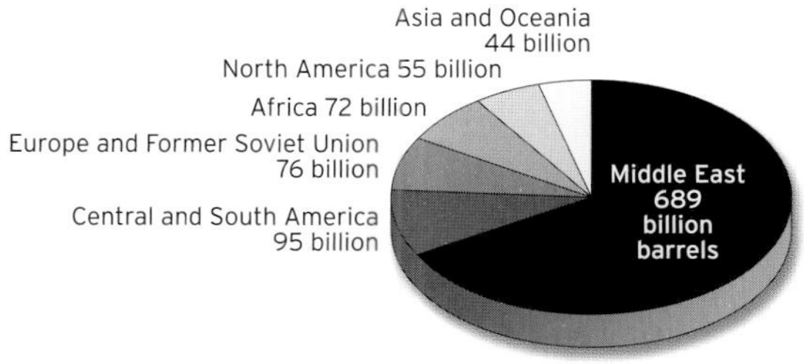
Asia and Oceania
44 billion
North America 55 billion
Africa 72 billion
Europe and Former Soviet Union
76 billion
Central and South America
95 billion
Middle East
689
billion
barrels

REGIONAL SHARE OF WORLD CRUDE OIL PRODUCTION

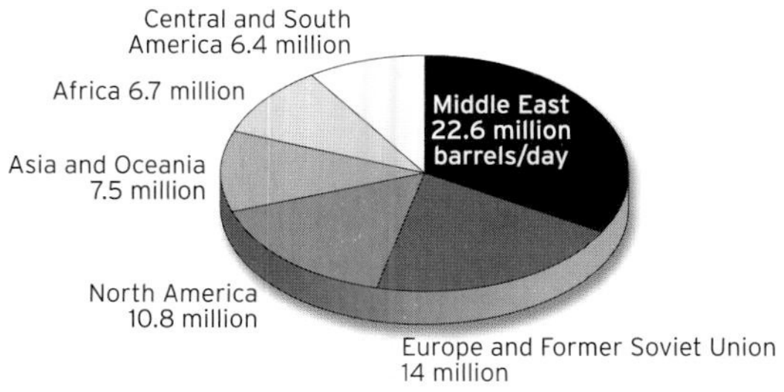
Central and South
America 6.4 million
Africa 6.7 million
Asia and Oceania
7.5 million
North America
10.8 million
Europe and Former Soviet Union
14 million
Middle East
22.6 million
barrels/day

LEADING CRUDE OIL PRODUCERS IN THE MIDDLE EAST, 1970-2000

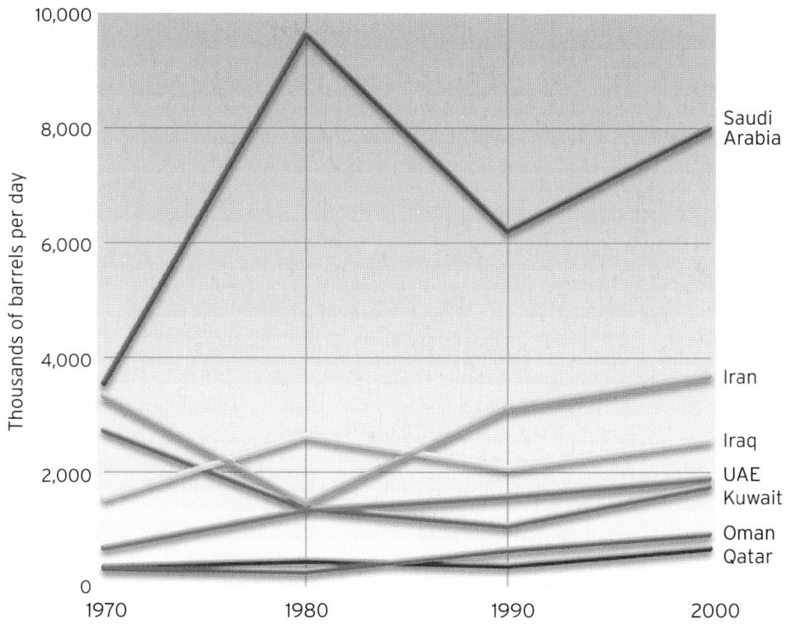

MIDDLE EAST EXPORTS AND GLOBAL OIL CONSUMPTION

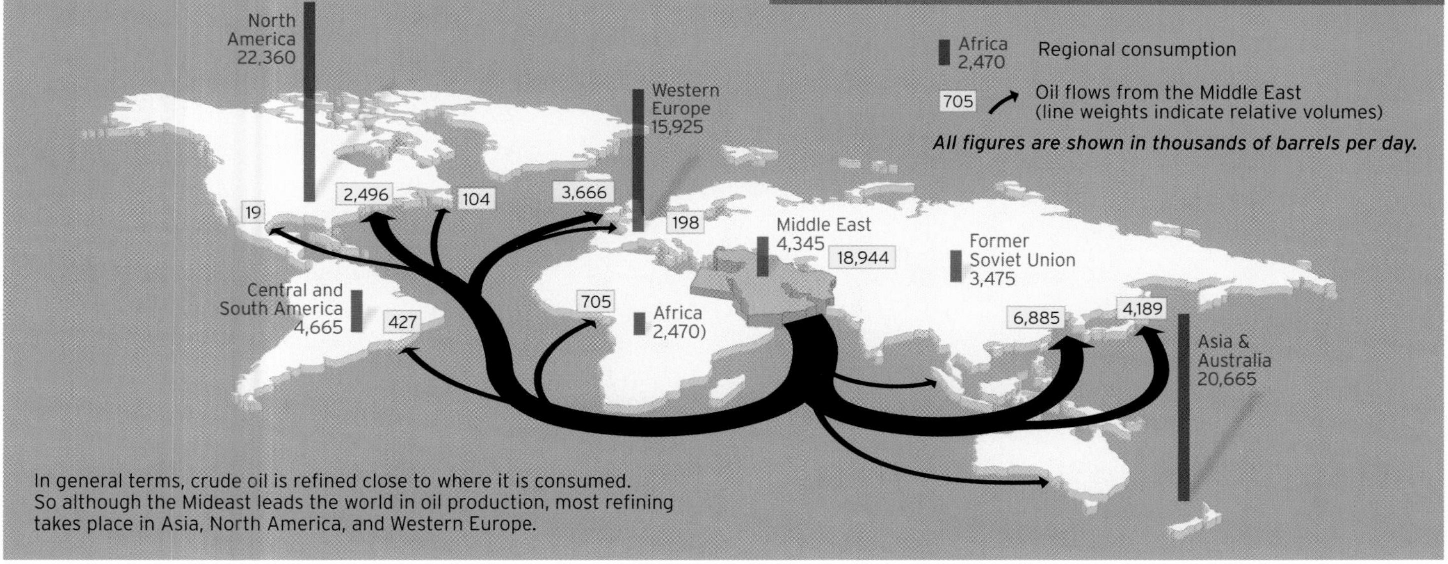
Africa
2,470
Regional consumption
705
Oil flows from the Middle East
(line weights indicate relative volumes)
All figures are shown in thousands of barrels per day.
North
America
22,360
Western
Europe
15,925
Middle East
4,345
Former
Soviet Union
3,475
Central and
South America
4,665
Africa
2,470)
Asia &
Australia
20,665
19
2,496
104
3,666
198
18,944
705
427
6,885
4,189
In general terms, crude oil is refined close to where it is consumed.
So although the Mideast leads the world in oil production, most refining
takes place in Asia, North America, and Western Europe.

TOP CRUDE OIL PRODUCERS, WORLDWIDE

2000 data. Figures listed in thousands of barrels per day.

Saudi Arabia	8,404	United Kingdom	2,275
Russia	6,479	Nigeria	2,144
United States	5,822	Kuwait	2,126
Iran	3,696	Canada	1,977
China	3,249	Indonesia	1,423
Norway	3,197	Libya	1,410
Mexico	3,012	Brazil	1,269
Venezuela	2,949	Algeria	1,244
Iraq	2,571	Oman	940
UAE	2,368	Argentina	761

TOP OIL CONSUMERS, WORLDWIDE

2000 data. Figures listed in thousands of barrels per day.

United States	19,701	Mexico	1,992
Japan	5,528	India	1,990
China	4,780	Italy	1,867
Germany	2,770	United Kingdom	1,721
Russia	2,500	Spain	1,461
Africa	2,440	Saudi Arabia	1,300
Brazil	2,155	Iran	1,080
Korea, South	2,146	Indonesia	1,035
Canada	2,073	Australia	859
France	2,021	Netherlands	852

Water

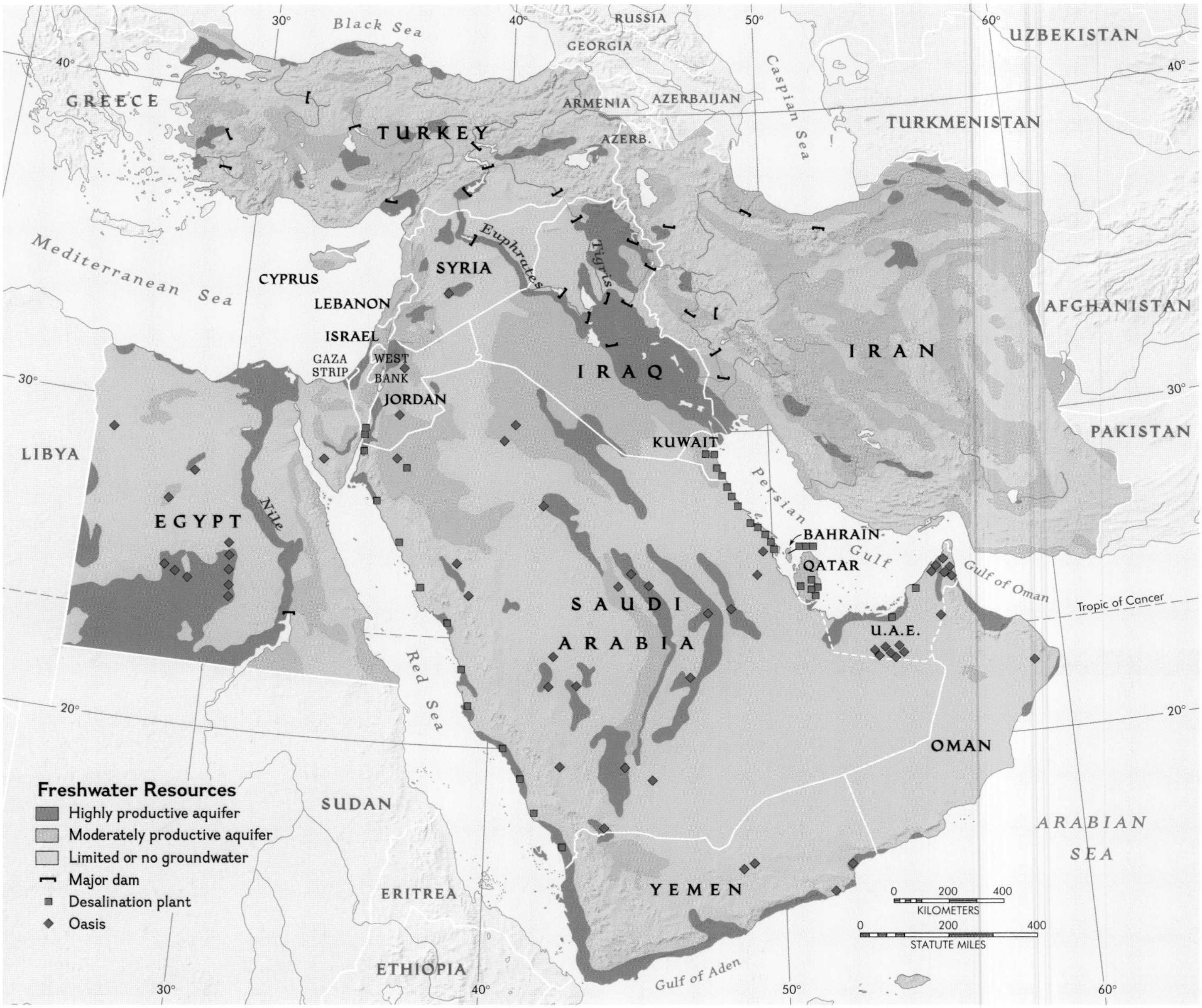

RENEWABLE FRESHWATER IN THE MIDDLE EAST

Renewable water supply figures shown in km³ per year.

Turkey	227	Oman	0.98
Iran	129	Cyprus	0.78
Iraq	35	Israel	0.75
Syria	7.0	Jordan	0.68
Lebanon	4.8	UAE	0.15
Yemen	4.1	Qatar	0.05
Saudi Arabia	2.4	Bahrain	0
Egypt	1.8	Kuwait	0

FRESHWATER WITHDRAWALS IN THE MIDDLE EAST

Year of data in parentheses. Freshwater withdrawal figures shown in km³ per year.

Iran	(1993)	70	Israel	(1997)	1.6
Egypt	(1996)	66	Lebanon	(1996)	1.3
Iraq	(1990)	43	Oman	(1991)	1.2
Turkey	(1997)	36	Jordan	(1993)	0.98
Saudi Arabia	(1992)	17	Kuwait	(1994)	0.54
Syria	(1995)	12	Cyprus	(1998)	0.30
Yemen	(1990)	2.9	Qatar	(1994)	0.28
UAE	(1995)	2.1	Bahrain	(1991)	0.24

RENEWABLE WATER SUPPLY AND PER CAPITA USE BY SECTOR

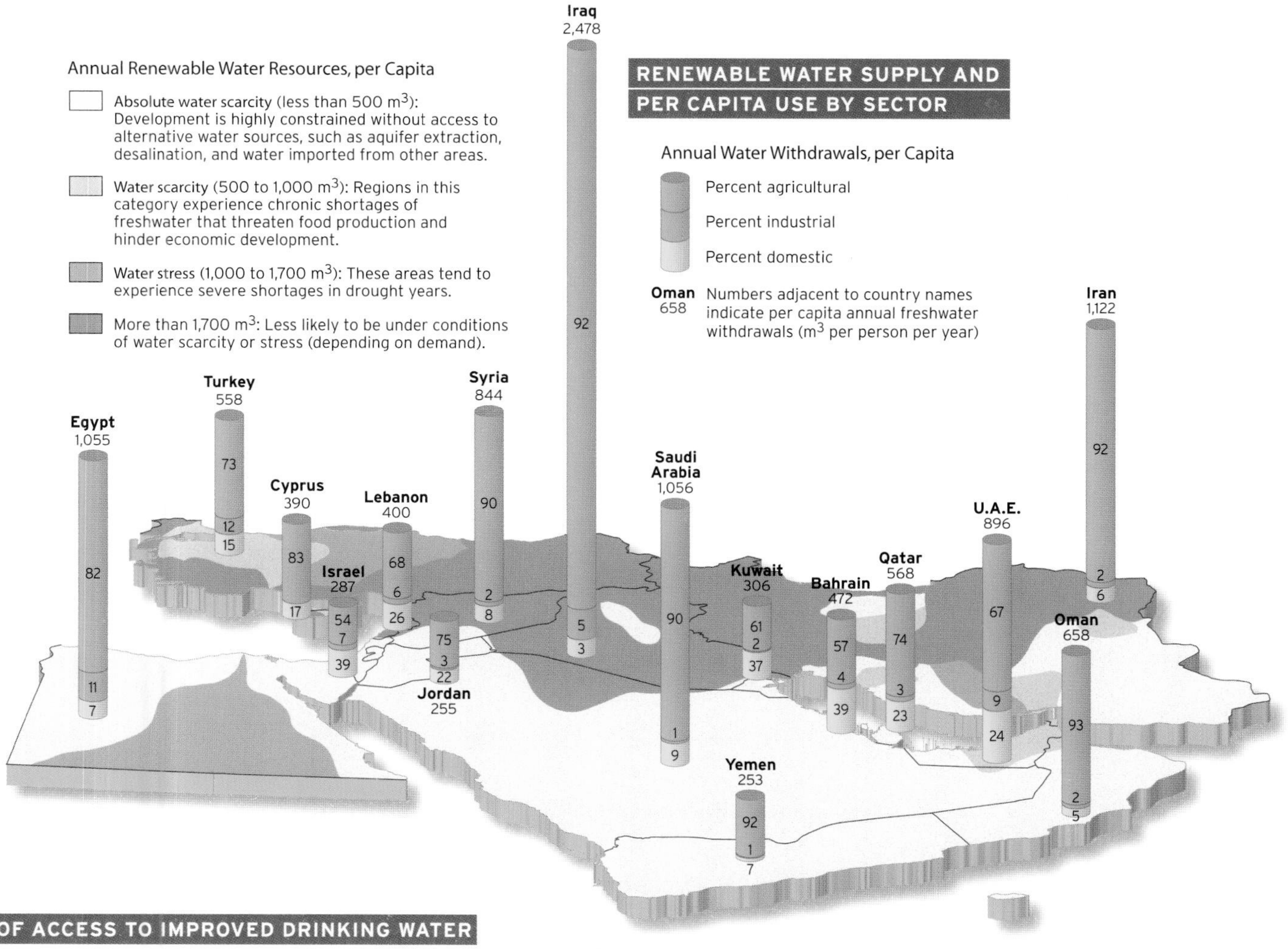
Annual Renewable Water Resources, per Capita
Absolute water scarcity (less than 500 m^3): Development is highly constrained without access to alternative water sources, such as aquifer extraction, desalination, and water imported from other areas.
Water scarcity (500 to 1,000 m^3): Regions in this category experience chronic shortages of freshwater that threaten food production and hinder economic development.
Water stress (1,000 to 1,700 m^3): These areas tend to experience severe shortages in drought years.
More than 1,700 m^3: Less likely to be under conditions of water scarcity or stress (depending on demand).
Annual Water Withdrawals, per Capita
Percent agricultural
Percent industrial
Percent domestic
Oman 658 Numbers adjacent to country names indicate per capita annual freshwater withdrawals (m^3 per person per year)
Egypt 1,055: 82, 11, 7
Turkey 558: 73, 12, 15
Cyprus 390: 83, 17
Lebanon 400: 68, 6, 26
Israel 287: 54, 7, 39
Jordan 255: 75, 3, 22
Syria 844: 90, 2, 8
Iraq 2,478: 92, 5, 3
Saudi Arabia 1,056: 90, 1, 9
Kuwait 306: 61, 2, 37
Bahrain 472: 57, 4, 39
Qatar 568: 74, 3, 23
U.A.E. 896: 67, 9, 24
Iran 1,122: 92, 2, 6
Oman 658: 93, 2, 5
Yemen 253: 92, 1, 7

LACK OF ACCESS TO IMPROVED DRINKING WATER

Water supply technologies considered to be "improved" include household connections, public standpipes, boreholes, protected dug wells and springs, and rainwater collection. Middle Eastern countries in which a portion of the population is known to lack access to improved water are shown below.

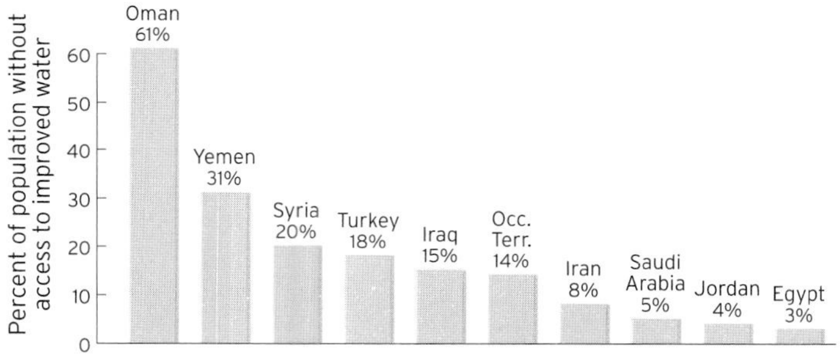
Percent of population without access to improved water
0
10
20
30
40
50
60
Oman 61%
Yemen 31%
Syria 20%
Turkey 18%
Iraq 15%
Occ. Terr. 14%
Iran 8%
Saudi Arabia 5%
Jordan 4%
Egypt 3%

SEVERE WATER STRESS: WATER USE AS % OF SUPPLY

When a country's total water use exceeds 40% of available renewable resources, it is likely to be under severe water stress, and often must turn to other water sources such as aquifer extraction, desalination, or external supplies (such as bottled water). Middle Eastern countries whose water use exceeds 40% of supply are listed below.

Bahrain	5,981%	Egypt	127%
Kuwait	3,097%	Yemen	123%
UAE	1,614%	Israel	108%
Saudi Arabia	955%	Iraq	80%
Qatar	570%	Iran	59%
Oman	181%	Syria	55%
Jordan	151%		

FRESHWATER WITHDRAWALS, WORLDWIDE (TOP 16)

Year of data in parentheses. Freshwater withdrawal figures shown in km³ per year.

China	(1993)	525	Iran	(1993)	70
India	(1990)	500	Egypt	(1996)	66
US	(1990)	467	Uzbekistan	(1994)	58
Pakistan	(1991)	156	Philippines	(1995)	55
Japan	(1992)	91	Brazil	(1992)	55
Mexico	(1998)	78	Vietnam	(1990)	54
Russia	(1994)	77	Germany	(1990)	46
Indonesia	(1990)	74	Canada	(1991)	45

DESALINATION CAPACITY, WORLDWIDE (TOP 16)

Capacity figures shown in m³ per day.

Saudi Arabia	5,006,194	Italy	483,668
United States	2,799,000	Iran	423,427
UAE	2,134,233	Iraq	324,476
Kuwait	1,284,327	Bahrain	282,955
Libya	638,377	Korea	265,957
Japan	637,900	Netherlands Antilles	210,905
Qatar	560,764	Algeria	190,837
Spain	492,824	Hong Kong	183,079

Development Indicators

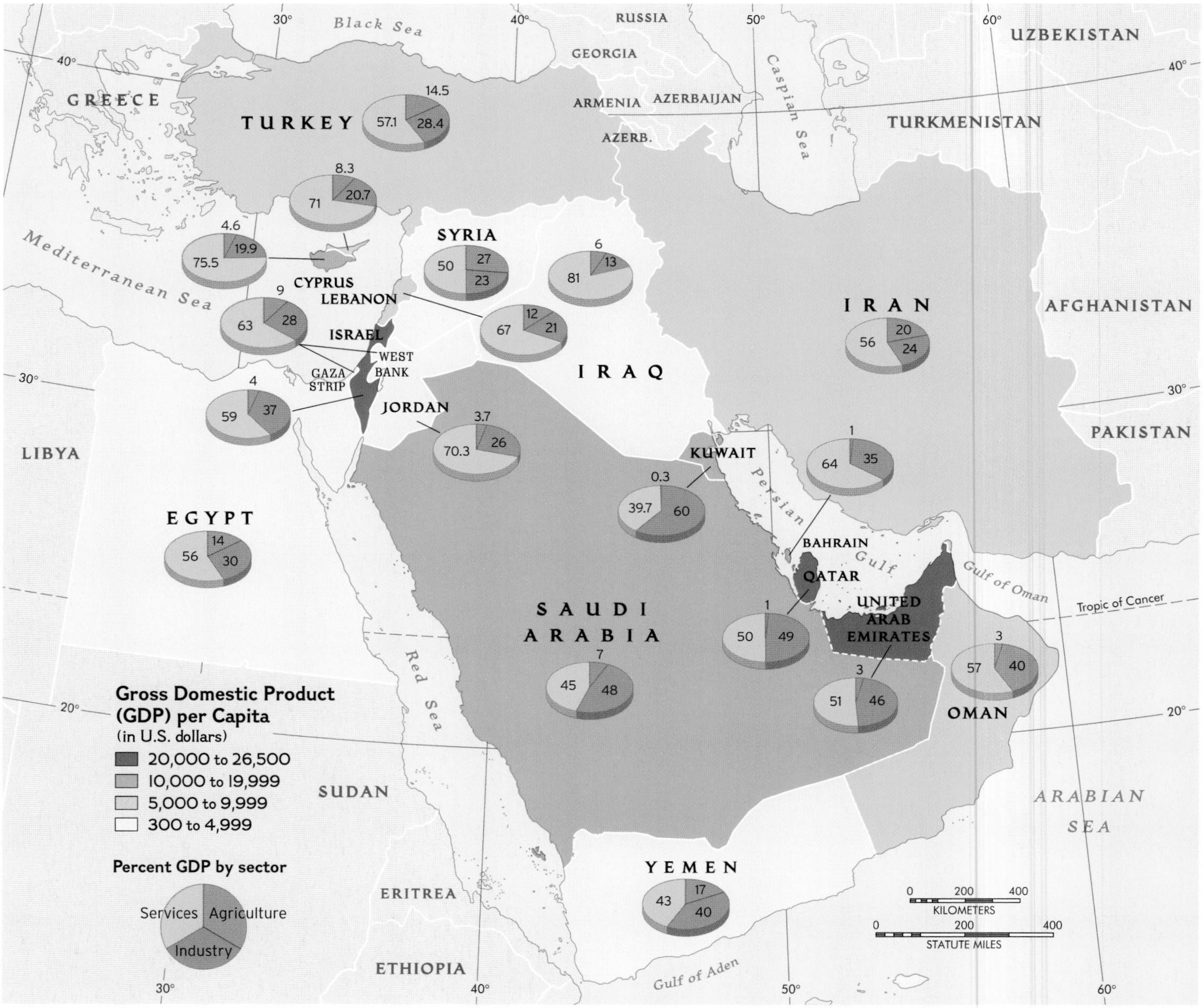

IMPORTS

Ranked by total value (billions of U.S. dollars), latest available year

Turkey	55.7	Oman	4.5
Israel	35.1	Bahrain	4.2
UAE	34.0	Jordan	4.0
Saudi Arabia	30.1	Qatar	3.8
Egypt	17.0	Cyprus, Greek	3.6
Iran	15.0	Syria	3.5
Iraq	13.8	Yemen	2.7
Kuwait	7.6	Cyprus, Turkish	0.4
Lebanon	6.2		

EXPORTS

Ranked by total value (billions of U.S. dollars), latest available year

Saudi Arabia	66.9	Egypt	7.1
UAE	47.6	Bahrain	5.5
Turkey	33.8	Syria	5.0
Iran	27.4	Yemen	3.9
Israel	26.5	Jordan	2.2
Kuwait	16.2	Cyprus, Greek	0.85
Iraq	15.8	Lebanon	0.7
Qatar	11.0	Cyprus, Turkish	0.05
Oman	10.9		

FOREIGN AID TO THE MIDDLE EAST

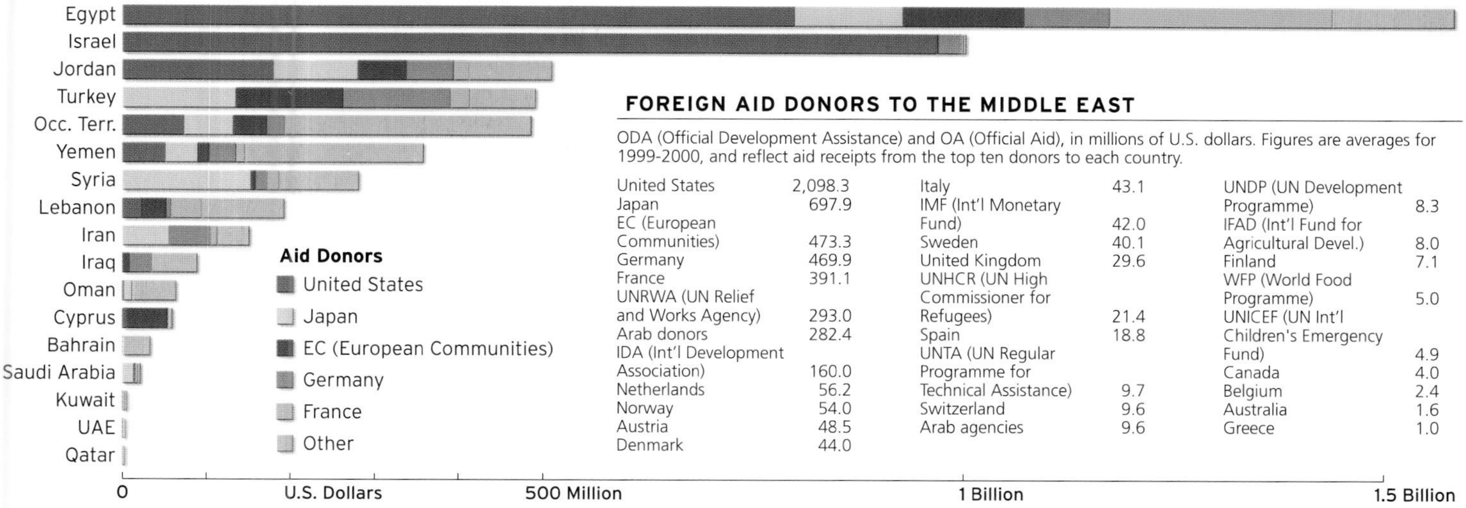

FOREIGN AID DONORS TO THE MIDDLE EAST

ODA (Official Development Assistance) and OA (Official Aid), in millions of U.S. dollars. Figures are averages for 1999-2000, and reflect aid receipts from the top ten donors to each country.

United States	2,098.3
Japan	697.9
EC (European Communities)	473.3
Germany	469.9
France	391.1
UNRWA (UN Relief and Works Agency)	293.0
Arab donors	282.4
IDA (Int'l Development Association)	160.0
Netherlands	56.2
Norway	54.0
Austria	48.5
Denmark	44.0
Italy	43.1
IMF (Int'l Monetary Fund)	42.0
Sweden	40.1
United Kingdom	29.6
UNHCR (UN High Commissioner for Refugees)	21.4
Spain	18.8
UNTA (UN Regular Programme for Technical Assistance)	9.7
Switzerland	9.6
Arab agencies	9.6
UNDP (UN Development Programme)	8.3
IFAD (Int'l Fund for Agricultural Devel.)	8.0
Finland	7.1
WFP (World Food Programme)	5.0
UNICEF (UN Int'l Children's Emergency Fund)	4.9
Canada	4.0
Belgium	2.4
Australia	1.6
Greece	1.0

LITERACY RATES

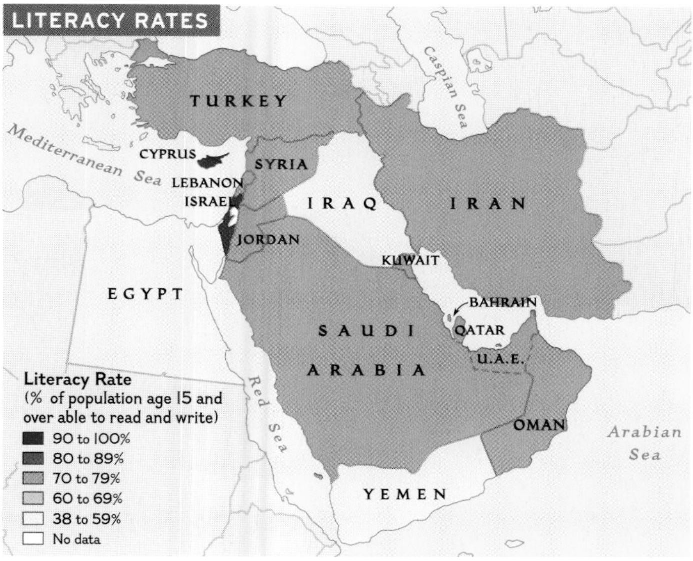

SCHOOL ENROLLMENT RATIOS

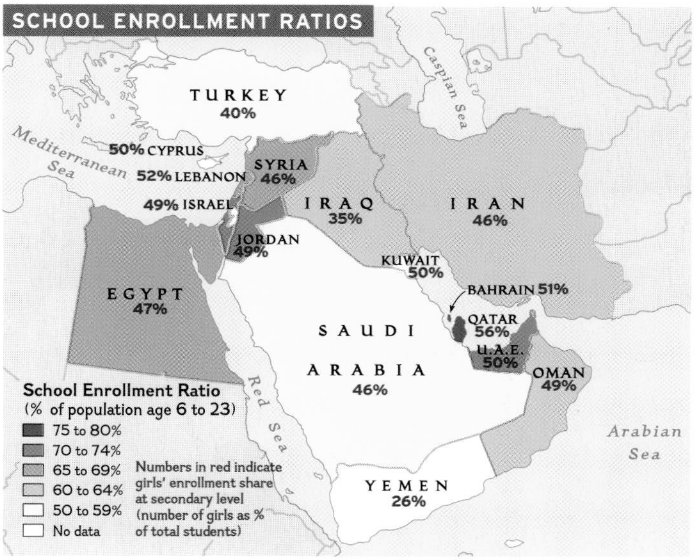

INFANT MORTALITY

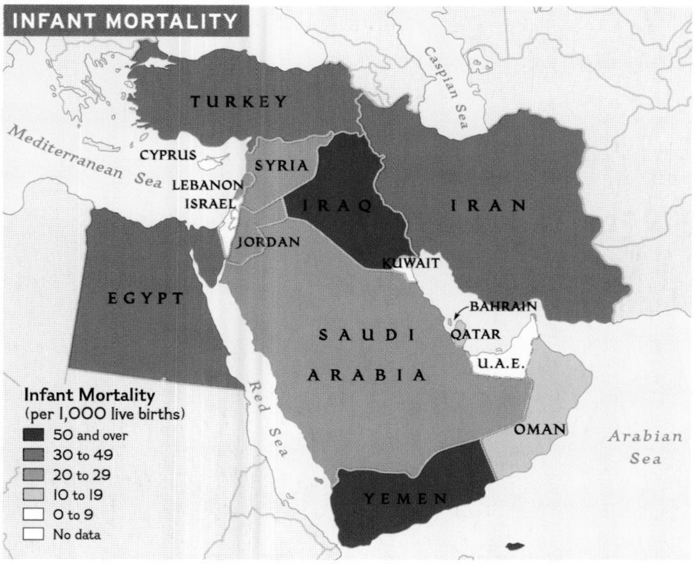

ACCESS TO SANITATION SERVICES

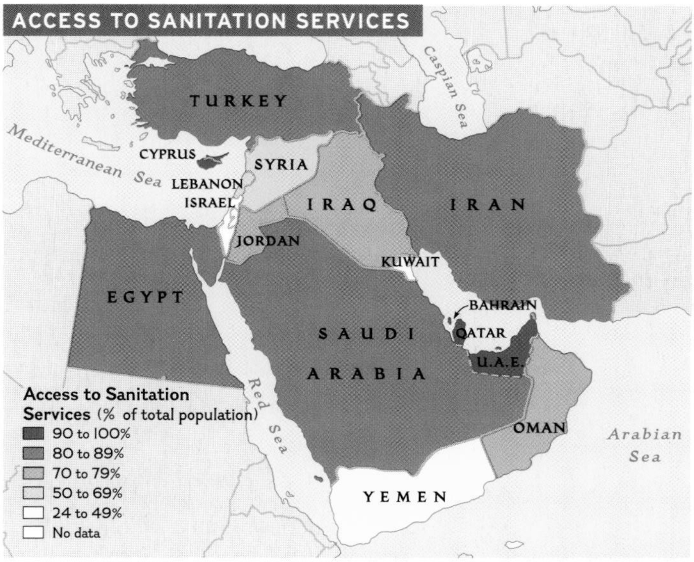

HISTORY

LEFT TO RIGHT: Schoolchildren wave flags at a rally following the proclamation of the independence of the newly formed state of Israel on May 14, 1948; Israeli troops in training prior to the 1956 Suez Crisis; Iranian women holding portraits of religious leader Ayatollah Khomeini during the 21st anniversary celebration of the 1979 Iranian Islamic Revolution; President Anwar Sadat of Egypt saluting at a military review parade shortly before he was assassinated on October 6, 1981; Camels search for untainted shrubs in the burning oil fields of Kuwait in 1991; A Palestinian boy in the Gaza Strip throws rocks during the second *intifada*, or uprising, which began in the fall of 2000.

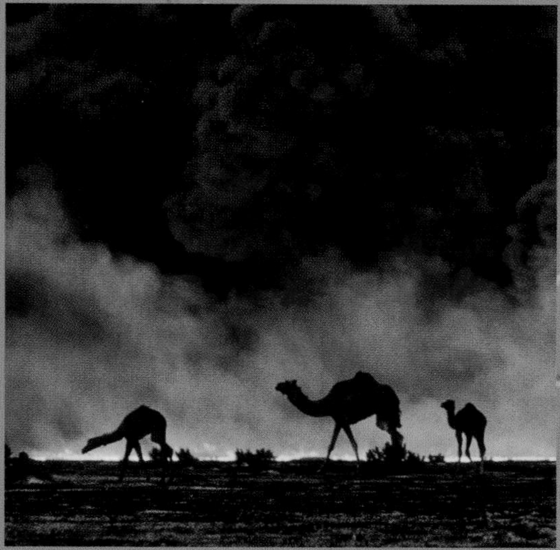

WORLD HERITAGE SITES

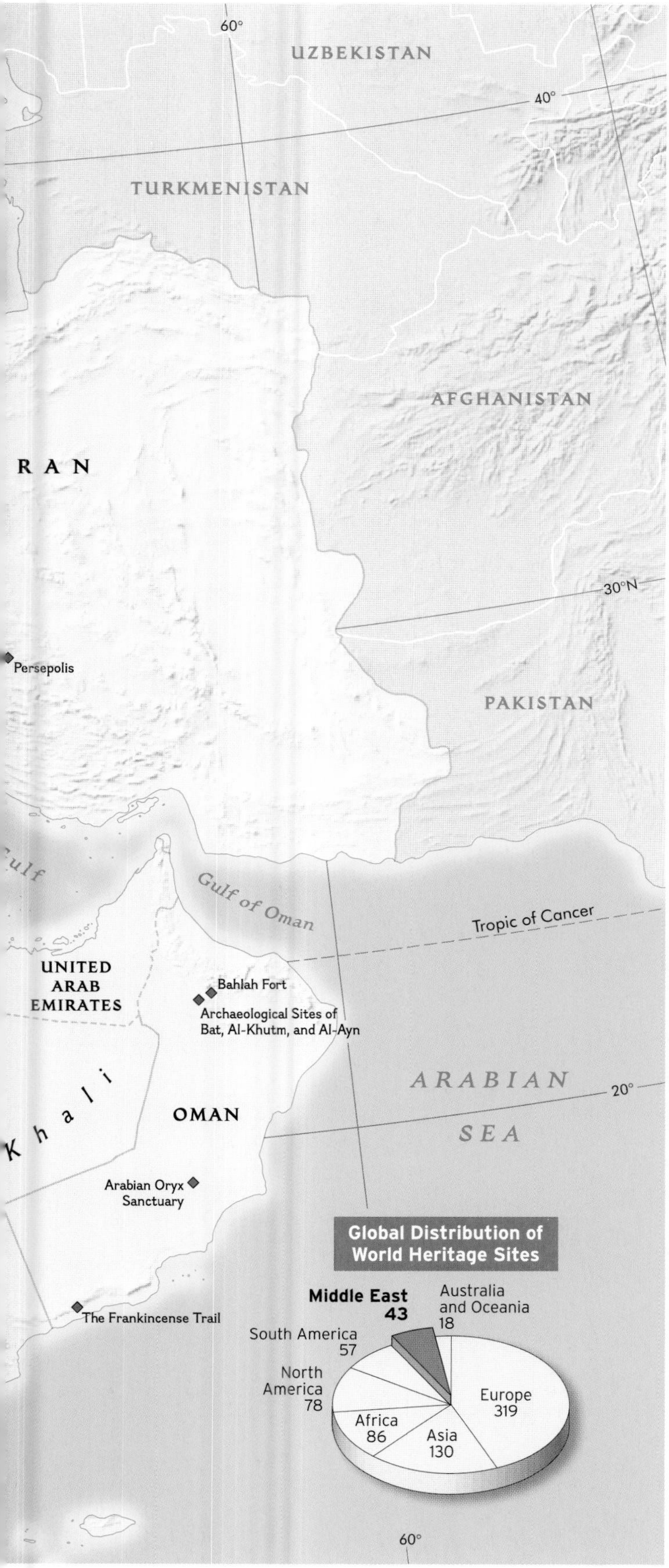
60°
UZBEKISTAN
40°
TURKMENISTAN
AFGHANISTAN
RAN
30°N
Persepolis
PAKISTAN
Gulf of Oman
Tropic of Cancer
UNITED ARAB EMIRATES
Bahlah Fort
Archaeological Sites of Bat, Al-Khutm, and Al-Ayn
ARABIAN SEA
20°
Khali
OMAN
Arabian Oryx Sanctuary
The Frankincense Trail
60°
Global Distribution of World Heritage Sites
Middle East 43
Australia and Oceania 18
South America 57
North America 78
Europe 319
Africa 86
Asia 130

ANCIENT EGYPT

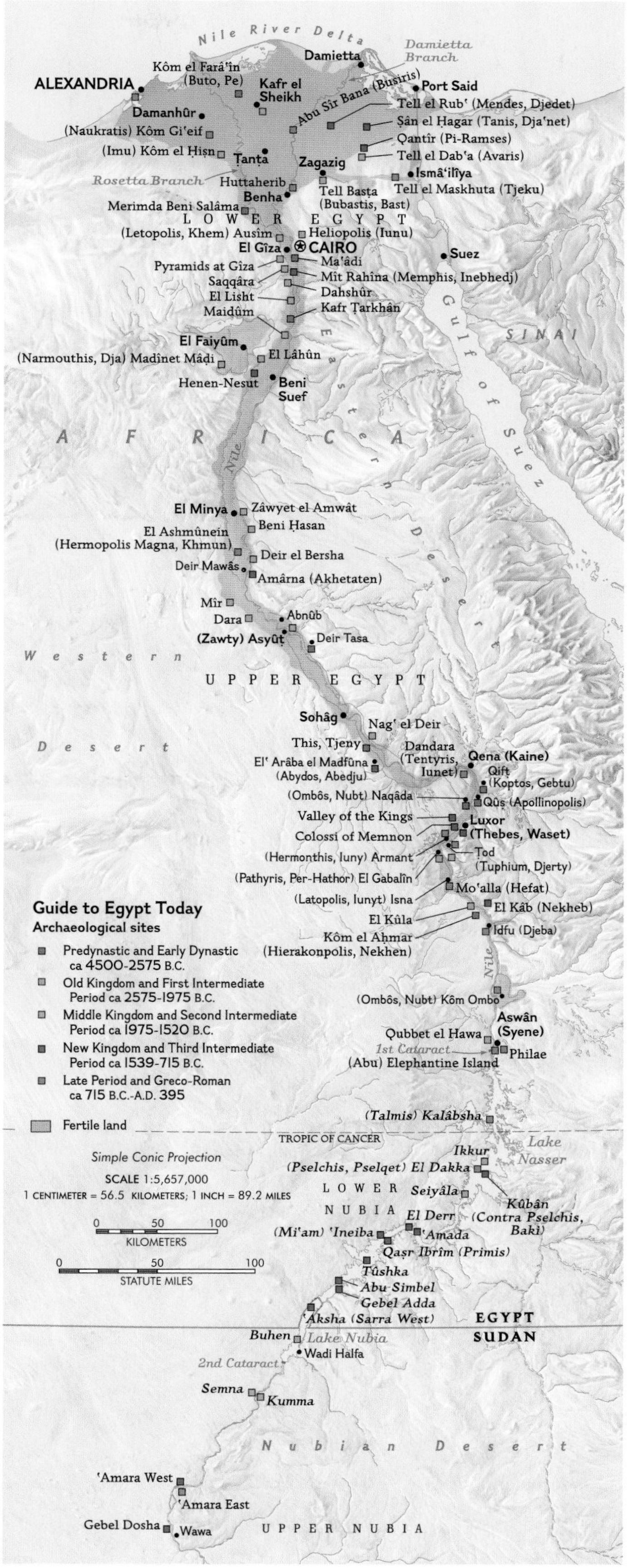
Nile River Delta
Damietta Branch
Damietta
ALEXANDRIA
Kôm el Farâ'in (Buto, Pe)
Kafr el Sheikh
Abu Sîr Bana (Busiris)
Port Said
Damanhûr
Tell el Rub' (Mendes, Djedet)
Şân el Ḥagar (Tanis, Dja'net)
(Naukratis) Kôm Gi'eif
Qantîr (Pi-Ramses)
(Imu) Kôm el Ḥiṣn
Ṭanṭa
Zagazig
Tell el Dab'a (Avaris)
Ismâ'ilîya
Rosetta Branch
Huttaherib
Benha
Tell Basṭa (Bubastis, Bast)
Tell el Maskhuta (Tjeku)
Merimda Beni Salâma
LOWER EGYPT
(Letopolis, Khem) Ausîm
Heliopolis (Iunu)
El Gîza
CAIRO
Suez
Pyramids at Gîza
Ma'âdi
Saqqâra
Mît Rahîna (Memphis, Inebhedj)
Dahshûr
El Lisht
Kafr Ṭarkhân
Maidûm
Gulf of Suez
SINAI
El Faiyûm
(Narmouthis, Dja) Madînet Mâdi
El Lâhûn
Henen-Nesut
Beni Suef
AFRICA
Eastern Desert
Nile
El Minya
Zâwyet el Amwât
Beni Ḥasan
El Ashmûnein (Hermopolis Magna, Khmun)
Deir el Bersha
Deir Mawâs
Amârna (Akhetaten)
Mîr
Dara
Abnûb
(Zawty) Asyûṭ
Deir Tasa
Western Desert
UPPER EGYPT
Sohâg
Nag' el Deir
This, Tjeny
Dandara (Tentyris, Iunet)
Qena (Kaine)
El' Arâba el Madfûna (Abydos, Abedju)
Qift (Koptos, Gebtu)
(Ombôs, Nubt) Naqâda
Qûṣ (Apollinopolis)
Valley of the Kings
Luxor (Thebes, Waset)
Colossi of Memnon
(Hermonthis, Iuny) Armant
Tod (Tuphium, Djerty)
(Pathyris, Per-Hathor) El Gabalîn
Mo'alla (Hefat)
(Latopolis, Iunyt) Isna
El Kâb (Nekheb)
El Kûla
Kôm el Aḥmar (Hierakonpolis, Nekhen)
Idfu (Djeba)
(Ombôs, Nubt) Kôm Ombo
Aswân (Syene)
Qubbet el Hawa
1st Cataract
Philae
(Abu) Elephantine Island
(Talmis) Kalâbsha
TROPIC OF CANCER
Lake Nasser
Ikkur
(Pselchis, Pselqet) El Dakka
LOWER NUBIA
Seiyâla
Kûbân (Contra Pselchis, Baki)
El Derr
(Mi'am) 'Ineiba
'Amada
Qaṣr Ibrîm (Primis)
Tûshka
Abu Simbel
Gebel Adda
'Aksha (Sarra West)
EGYPT
SUDAN
Buhen
Lake Nubia
Wadi Halfa
2nd Cataract
Semna
Kumma
Nubian Desert
'Amara West
'Amara East
Gebel Dosha
Wawa
UPPER NUBIA
Guide to Egypt Today
Archaeological sites
Predynastic and Early Dynastic ca 4500-2575 B.C.
Old Kingdom and First Intermediate Period ca 2575-1975 B.C.
Middle Kingdom and Second Intermediate Period ca 1975-1520 B.C.
New Kingdom and Third Intermediate Period ca 1539-715 B.C.
Late Period and Greco-Roman ca 715 B.C.-A.D. 395
Fertile land
Simple Conic Projection
SCALE 1:5,657,000
1 CENTIMETER = 56.5 KILOMETERS; 1 INCH = 89.2 MILES
0 50 100
KILOMETERS
0 50 100
STATUTE MILES

1914: ON THE EVE OF WAR

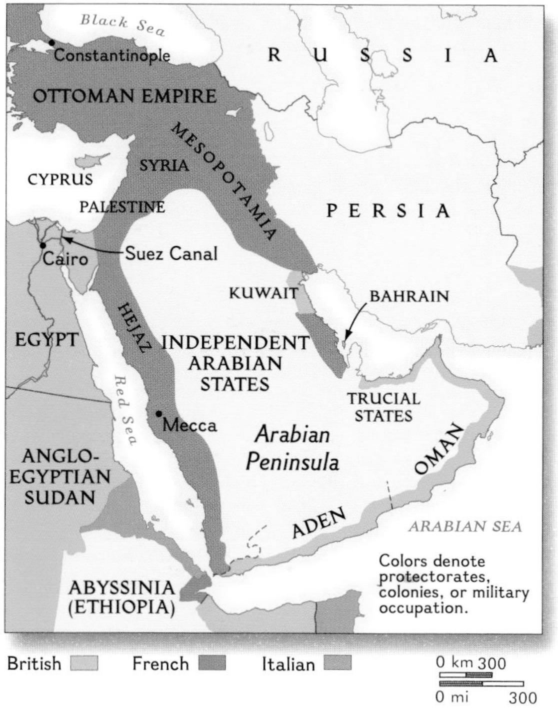

Black Sea
Constantinople
R U S S I A
OTTOMAN EMPIRE
MESOPOTAMIA
SYRIA
CYPRUS
PALESTINE
P E R S I A
Cairo
Suez Canal
KUWAIT
BAHRAIN
EGYPT
HEJAZ
INDEPENDENT ARABIAN STATES
TRUCIAL STATES
Red Sea
Mecca
Arabian Peninsula
OMAN
ANGLO-EGYPTIAN SUDAN
ADEN
ARABIAN SEA
ABYSSINIA (ETHIOPIA)
Colors denote protectorates, colonies, or military occupation.
British
French
Italian
0 km 300
0 mi 300

POST WORLD WAR I

Black Sea
Constantinople
GEORGIA
ARMENIA
AZERBAIJAN
R U S S I A
T U R K E Y
SYRIA AND LEBANON
CYPRUS
PALESTINE
I R A Q
P E R S I A
Cairo
TRANSJORDAN
KUWAIT
BAHRAIN
EGYPT
HEJAZ
Indefinite Boundary
QATAR
ARABIA OF IBN SAUD
TRUCIAL STATES
Red Sea
Mecca
Arabian Peninsula
ANGLO-EGYPTIAN SUDAN
ASIR
OMAN
YEMEN
ADEN
ARABIAN SEA
ETHIOPIA
Diagonal lines show mandates or military occupation.
British
French
Italian
0 km 300
0 mi 300

THE RISE OF NATIONALISM

Black Sea
Istanbul (Constantinople)
UNION OF SOVIET SOCIALIST REPUBLICS
LEBANON (1943)
TURKEY
CYPRUS
SYRIA (1946)
ISRAEL (1948)
IRAQ (1932)
I R A N
Cairo
KUWAIT
JORDAN (1946)
BAHRAIN
EGYPT (1922)
Neutral Zones
QATAR
SAUDI ARABIA (1932)
TRUCIAL STATES
Red Sea
Mecca
Arabian Peninsula
ANGLO-EGYPTIAN SUDAN
OMAN
YEMEN (1918)
ADEN
ARABIAN SEA
ETHIOPIA
Dates show year of independence.
British
French
0 km 300
0 mi 300

DEFENSE SPENDING, 2001

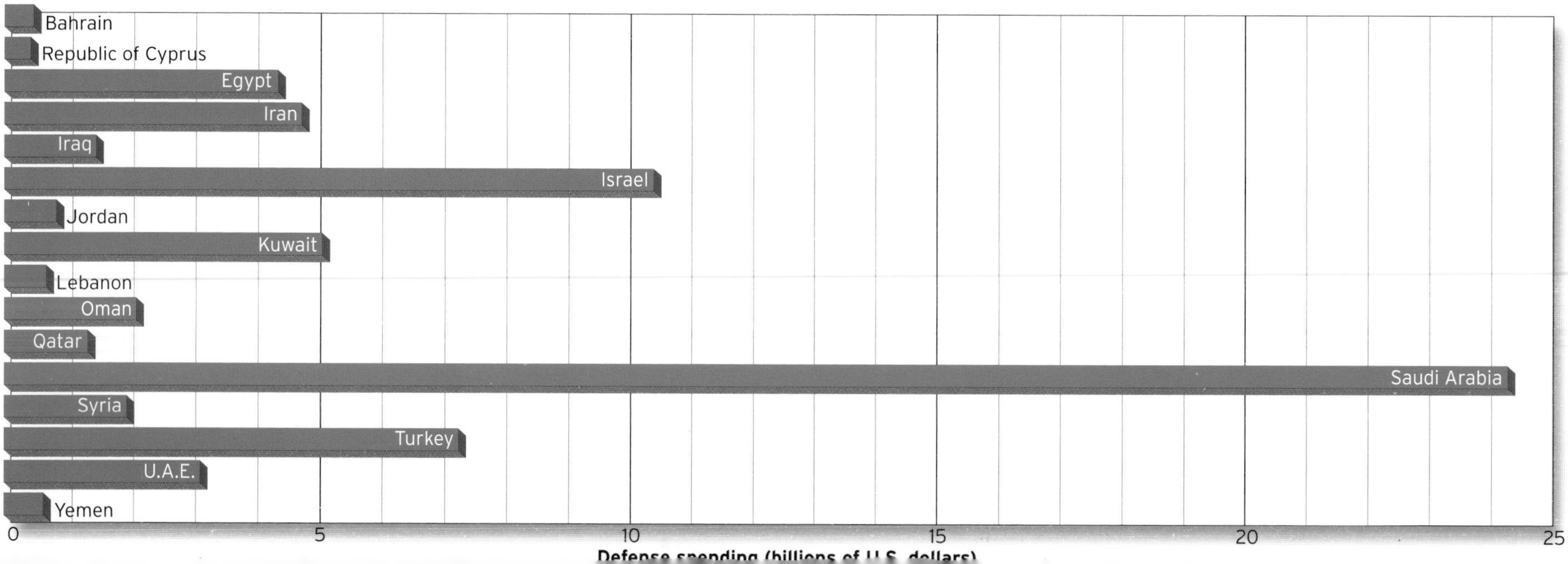

Bahrain
Republic of Cyprus
Egypt
Iran
Iraq
Israel
Jordan
Kuwait
Lebanon
Oman
Qatar
Saudi Arabia
Syria
Turkey
U.A.E.
Yemen
0
5
10
15
20
25
Defense spending (billions of U.S. dollars)

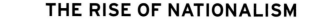

REGIONAL CONFLICTS, 1945-2002

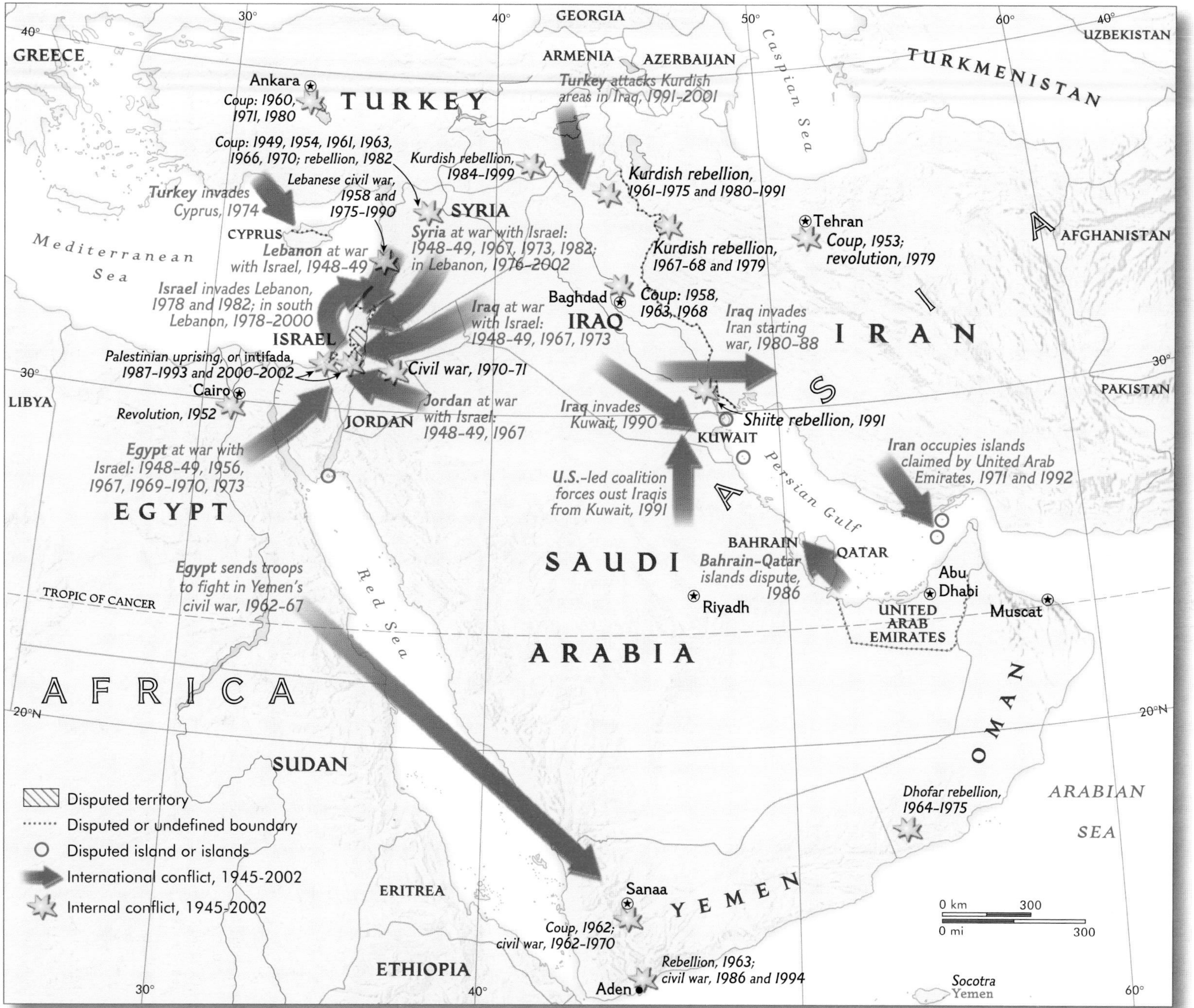
GREECE
TURKEY
Ankara
Coup: 1960, 1971, 1980
Coup: 1949, 1954, 1961, 1963, 1966, 1970; rebellion, 1982
Lebanese civil war, 1958 and 1975-1990
Turkey invades Cyprus, 1974
CYPRUS
Mediterranean Sea
Lebanon at war with Israel, 1948-49
Israel invades Lebanon, 1978 and 1982; in south Lebanon, 1978-2000
ISRAEL
Palestinian uprising, or intifada, 1987-1993 and 2000-2002
Cairo
Revolution, 1952
LIBYA
Egypt at war with Israel: 1948-49, 1956, 1967, 1969-1970, 1973
EGYPT
GEORGIA
ARMENIA
AZERBAIJAN
Turkey attacks Kurdish areas in Iraq, 1991-2001
Kurdish rebellion, 1984-1999
SYRIA
Syria at war with Israel: 1948-49, 1967, 1973, 1982; in Lebanon, 1976-2002
Kurdish rebellion, 1961-1975 and 1980-1991
Kurdish rebellion, 1967-68 and 1979
Baghdad
Coup: 1958, 1963, 1968
IRAQ
Iraq at war with Israel: 1948-49, 1967, 1973
Civil war, 1970-71
Jordan at war with Israel: 1948-49, 1967
JORDAN
Iraq invades Kuwait, 1990
Iraq invades Iran starting war, 1980-88
Shiite rebellion, 1991
KUWAIT
U.S.-led coalition forces oust Iraqis from Kuwait, 1991
Caspian Sea
TURKMENISTAN
UZBEKISTAN
AFGHANISTAN
PAKISTAN
Tehran
Coup, 1953; revolution, 1979
IRAN
ASIA
Persian Gulf
Iran occupies islands claimed by United Arab Emirates, 1971 and 1992
BAHRAIN
QATAR
Bahrain-Qatar islands dispute, 1986
Riyadh
SAUDI ARABIA
Abu Dhabi
Muscat
UNITED ARAB EMIRATES
OMAN
TROPIC OF CANCER
Egypt sends troops to fight in Yemen's civil war, 1962-67
Red Sea
AFRICA
SUDAN
ERITREA
ETHIOPIA
YEMEN
Sanaa
Coup, 1962; civil war, 1962-1970
Aden
Rebellion, 1963; civil war, 1986 and 1994
Dhofar rebellion, 1964-1975
ARABIAN SEA
Socotra Yemen
0 km 300
0 mi 300
40°
30°
20°N
50°
60°
Disputed territory
Disputed or undefined boundary
Disputed island or islands
International conflict, 1945-2002
Internal conflict, 1945-2002

Construction of the original oil pipeline in Persia, 1909

1900
Germany and the Ottoman Empire begin construction of Pan-Islamic Hejaz Railway.

1901
May 28 – Shah Muzaffar al-Din of Persia grants a concession to British investor William Knox D'Arcy to drill for oil.

1902
Abdulaziz ibn Saud captures the city of Riyadh from the rival House of Rashid.

1903-05
An Anglo-Turkish Commission partially demarcates the boundary between Yemen (then part of the Ottoman Empire) and the British protectorate of Aden.

1904
Apr. 8 – Entente Cordiale: Agreement between Great Britain and France includes acknowledgment of British preeminence in Egypt.

Theodor Herzl dies; he founded the Zionist Organization at the First Zionist Congress in Basel, Switzerland, in 1897.

1906
Aug. 5 – Constitutional Revolution (1905-1911) in Persia forces the shah to allow a constitution and a *Majlis*, or representative assembly.

1907
Aug. 31 – Great Britain and Russia sign an agreement that creates their respective spheres of influence in Persia.

1908
May 26 – First major oil strike occurs in the Middle East in southwest Persia at D'Arcy's drilling site at Masjid-i Suleiman.

Hejaz Railway is completed between Damascus and Medina.

July 24 – The Young Turk Revolution in the Ottoman Empire forces Sultan Abdul Hamid II to restore the Constitution of 1876.

1909
Tel Aviv founded by Zionist settlers as a suburb of the ancient city of Jaffa.

1912-13
Balkan Wars result in the loss of most of the Ottoman Empire's remaining European territories.

1913
June 21 – First Arab National Congress, held in Paris, demands recognition of the Arabs as a nation within the Ottoman Empire.

Boundary between Iraq and Kuwait defined by Anglo-Turkish Convention.

Enver Pasha

1914
Aug. – World War I (1914-1918) begins.

Oct. 29 – Ottoman Empire enters war on the side of Germany by an alliance engineered by Enver Pasha, Ottoman War Minister.

Dec. 16 – Egypt, under British military occupation since 1882, becomes a British protectorate. Cyprus is annexed by Great Britain.

1915
Apr. 24 – Ottoman Empire launches genocide against the Armenians.

Apr. 25 – British Gallipoli Campaign begins, ending disastrously by Jan. 8, 1916.

T.E. Lawrence

1916
May 16 – Sykes-Picot Agreement: Secret treaty is made by France, Great Britain, and Russia to partition the Ottoman Empire.

June – Grand Sharif Hussein of Mecca launches Arab Revolt against Ottomans in the Hejaz. Military campaign is led by his son Feisal (later first king of Iraq) with British Army advisor T.E. Lawrence, known as Lawrence of Arabia.

Nov. – Ruler of Qatar signs treaty of protection with Great Britain.

1917
Nov. 2 – Balfour Declaration asserts British government's support for the establishment of a national home for the Jewish people in Palestine.

1918
Oct. 3 – Feisal sets up an Arab government in Damascus.

Oct. 30 – Ottoman Empire signs armistice at Mudros.

Nov. – Imamate of Yemen gains independence.

Nov. 11 – Germany signs armistice.

1919
Jan. 18 – Opening of Paris Peace Conference. The Treaty of Versailles is signed on June 28.

1920
Jan. 16 – League of Nations holds first meeting.

Apr. 26 – At San Remo Conference, Allied Powers endorse British mandates in Palestine and Iraq, and French mandate in Syria, a portion from which the French created Lebanon.

July 24 – French oust Feisal from Damascus.

Aug. 10 – Treaty of Sèvres reduces the Ottoman Empire to a small area of northern Anatolia.

1921
Feb. 21 – Reza Khan, an officer in the Persian Cossack Brigade, leads a successful coup in Persia.

Apr. 1 – Great Britain splits Palestine mandate to create Emirate of Transjordan and names Abdullah, son of Sharif Hussein, its ruler.

Aug. 23 – Hashemite monarchy is established in Iraq under King Feisal I, whose Arab government was forced out of Damascus in July 1920.

1922
Feb. 28 – Great Britain declares Egypt an independent monarchy.

The Kingdom of Najd (Saudi Arabia) reaches boundary agreements with both Iraq and Kuwait.

Mustafa Kemal Atatürk

1923
July 24 – Treaty of Lausanne establishes modern Turkey's borders.

Oct. 29 – Republic of Turkey is established. Mustafa Kemal Atatürk is named President; the capital is moved from Constantinople to Ankara.

1924
Abdulaziz ibn Saud captures Mecca, ousting Sharif Hussein. His conquest of the Hejaz is complete by 1926.

1925
May 1 – Cyprus becomes a British Crown Colony.

Dec. 12 – Pahlavi Dynasty in Persia is established when Reza Khan is crowned Reza Shah Pahlavi.

1926
Boundary between Turkey and Iraq is settled by League of Nations initiative.

1927
Large oil deposits are discovered north of Kirkuk in Iraq.

1930
The collapse of the world pearl market following the Japanese introduction of cultured pearls leaves Qatar's economy in ruins.

1932
Sept. 18 – Kingdom of Saudi Arabia is proclaimed.

Oct. 3 – Iraq is recognized as an independent monarchy following end of British mandate.

1933
May 29 – King Abdalaziz ibn Saud allows Standard Oil to prospect in Saudi Arabia.

1934
Dec. 23 – Oil exploitation concession in Kuwait is granted to British-American-owned Kuwait Oil Company.

Abdulaziz ibn Saud, 1945

1900 1910 1920 1930

1935
eza Shah Pahlavi changes
ersia's name to Iran.

936
ug. 26 – Anglo-Egyptian
reaty of Alliance is signed.
ormal British occupation
nds, though British troops
emain in the Sinai and Suez
anal zone for 20 years.
arouk becomes king
ollowing death of his father
ing Fuad.

1937
uly 7 – British Peel
Commission recommends
hat Palestine be partitioned.
he Woodhead Commission,
he following year, rejects
artition as impracticable.

1938
Oil is discovered in Kuwait and Saudi Arabia.

Nov. 10 – Mustafa Kemal Atatürk dies.

1939
ept. 1 – World War II (1939-
945) begins when Nazi
ermany invades Poland.

1941
May – British troops invade Iraq to prevent coup by pro-Axis nationalist movement.

June – Invasion of Syria and Lebanon by British and Free French troops to remove pro-Vichy France governments.

Aug. 25 – British and Soviet troops occupy Iran to counter threat of expanding German influence. Reza Shah Pahlavi abdicates in favor of his son, Mohammad Reza Pahlavi.

1942
Oct. 23-Nov. 4 – British check German advance into Egypt at the Battle of El Alamein.

1943
Nov. 22 – Lebanon declares independence from France.

1945
Mar. 22 – Arab League forms.

World War II ends: Germany surrenders May 7; Japan surrenders Aug. 14.

June 26 - United Nations is founded.

1946
Apr. 17 – Syria achieves complete independence.

May 15 – Britain formally recognizes Transjordan as an independent state. Emir Abdullah becomes king.

1947
UN Partition Plan proposes that, upon termination of the British mandate on May 15, 1948, Palestine be partitioned into separate Jewish and Arab states, with the city of Jerusalem under UN control. Jews accept the plan. Arabs throughout the Middle East reject it.

Truman Doctrine results in large-scale U.S. military and economic aid to Turkey.

avid Ben-Gurion proclaims the birth of the State of
srael to the National Jewish Congress on May 14, 1948.

1948
May 14 – State of Israel is proclaimed following end of British mandate in Palestine.

May 15 – Israel's War of Independence: Arab forces from Egypt, Syria, Transjordan, Lebanon, and Iraq attack Israel, which defeats the invading armies. Many uprooted by war, including 750,000 Palestinian refugees.

1949
Qatar begins to produce and export oil ten years after discovering it.

Feb. 24 – Armistice agreement is signed between Israel and Egypt, followed by armistices with other Arab countries later in the year.

1950
Apr. 24 – The West Bank is annexed by Transjordan, and the country's name is changed to Jordan.

1951
Apr. 30 – Mohammad Mossadegh becomes Prime Minister of Iran. He nationalizes British-owned oil industry.

July 20 – King Abdullah of Jordan is assassinated.

1952
Feb. 18 – Turkey is admitted as a member of NATO.

July 23 – Gamal Abdel Nasser leads a coup by the Free Officers' Movement in Egypt. King Farouk is forced to abdicate.

1953
June – Egypt is declared a republic.

Aug. 16-19 – Prime Minister Mossadegh of Iran is overthrown by British-U.S. sponsored coup.

1955
Feb. 24 – Baghdad Pact: Iraq allies itself with Turkey and Britain to contain Soviet expansionism.

1956
Oct. 31-Nov. 7 – Suez Crisis: In secret pact with Britain and France, Israel invades Sinai, reaching the Suez Canal. France and Britain land troops to "retake" canal. Pressure from U.S. and Soviet Union force withdrawal of invading forces.

British recover hidden weapons in Suez Canal, 1956.

1958
Feb. 22 – Syria and Egypt form the United Arab Republic (U.A.R.)

July 14 – King Feisal II of Iraq is assassinated in coup by the army. General Qasim takes power.

July 15 – U.S. Marines land in Lebanon to quiet Muslim-Christian civil strife.

Nasser in Damascus, 1960

1960
Aug. 15 – Cyprus becomes an independent republic.

Sept. 10-14 – OPEC (Organization of Petroleum Exporting Countries) is founded in Baghdad by Iran, Iraq, Kuwait, Saudi Arabia, and Venezuela.

1961
June 19 – Kuwait, under Al Sabah family and British protectorate since 1899, gains independence. British troops sent in July to thwart an Iraqi attempt to annex Kuwait are later replaced by Arab League troops who remain there for two years.

Sept. 28 – Syria withdraws from the United Arab Republic. Egypt retains name until 1971.

1962
Sept. 28 – North Yemen becomes the Yemen Arab Republic. Civil war begins.

1963
Jan. 18 – Former British colony of Aden joins Federation of South Arabia.

Feb. 8 – In Iraq General Qasim is overthrown by Baath Party coup. Nine months later pro-Nasser military officers retake power from the Baath Party.

1964
June 1 – Palestinian Liberation Organization (PLO) is established.

Aug. 9 – A cease-fire ends eight months of warfare between Greek and Turkish factions on Cyprus.

Nov. 2 – King Saud is deposed. Faisal, his brother, succeeds him as King of Saudi Arabia.

Israeli tank in action during the Six Day War

1967
June 5-10 – Six Day War: Following buildup of Arab troops on its borders and the closure of the Strait of Tiran, Israel launches a preemptive attack on the surrounding Arab states. Israel occupies the West Bank, including East Jerusalem, the Golan Heights, Gaza Strip, and the Sinai Peninsula.

Nov. 30 – Independent People's Democratic Republic of South Yemen forms.

1968
July 30 – Baath Party returns to power in Iraq when a military coup led by President Ahmad Hasan al-Bakr ousts non-Baathist allies.

1969
Feb. 3 – Yasser Arafat is elected head of the PLO.

Mar. 17 – Golda Meir becomes Prime Minister of Israel.

Sept. 1 – Monarchy in Libya is overthrown by military coup led by Muammar Qaddafi.

1970
Sept. – King Hussein of Jordan sends army against PLO-controlled areas in Jordan. Defeated PLO retreats to Lebanon.

Sept. 28 – Egyptian President Nasser dies of a heart attack. He is succeeded by Vice President Anwar Sadat.

Nov. 13 – Hafez al Assad seizes power in Syria as leader of a Baath Party military coup. Baath Party in Syria is a rival faction of Iraqi Baath Party.

Nov. 30 – South Yemen is renamed People's Democratic Republic of Yemen.

Dec. – Eight-year civil war in the Yemen Arab Republic (North Yemen) ends.

1940 1950 1960 1970

1971
Aug. 15 – Bahrain declares independence.

Sept. 3 – Qatar declares its independence from Great Britain.

Dec. 2 – Six of the Trucial States form the United Arab Emirates. The seventh joins the following year.

1972
Nov. 21 – Israel and Syria clash in heaviest fighting since 1967 war.

July 18 – Sadat expels Egypt's 15,000 Soviet military advisers and experts.

Israeli artillery engaged during Yom Kippur War

1973
Oct. 6 – Yom Kippur War: Egypt and Syria launch surprise attack against Israel. After initial Arab victories Israel recaptures Golan Heights, pushes six miles into Syria, and crosses the Suez Canal. Diplomatic interventions by the United States and Soviet Union lead to a cease-fire.

Oct. 20 – Organization of Arab Petroleum Exporting Countries (OAPEC) imposes an oil embargo on the United States.

1974
Mar. 4 – Israel returns Suez Canal to Egypt.

Mar. 18 – OAPEC ends oil embargo.

July 15 – Greece engineers coup in Cyprus.

July 20 – Turkey invades Cyprus, occupying the northern one-third of the island.

Nov. 13 – UN General Assembly affirms Palestinians' right to sovereignty and grants PLO observer status.

1975
Mar. 25 – Saudi King Faisal is assassinated; his half brother, Crown Prince Khalid, succeeds him.

Apr. – Political and religious conflict between Christian and Muslim factions in Lebanon escalates into civil war.

1976
Apr.-May – Syrian troops intervene in Lebanon to restore peace but also to curb the Palestinians.

Oct. – Following Arab summit meetings in Riyadh and Cairo, a cease-fire in Lebanon is arranged and a predominantly Syrian Arab Deterrent Force (ADF) is established to maintain it.

1977
May 17 – Menachem Begin becomes prime minister of Israel.

Nov. 19-21 – Egyptian President Anwar Sadat becomes the first Arab leader to visit Israel.

Sadat, Carter, and Begin at White House 9/17/78

1978
Mar. 14 – In reprisal for PLO attacks on its territory, Israel invades southern Lebanon.

Apr. 6 – United Nations Interim Force in Lebanon (UNIFIL) moves into southern Lebanon to enforce Security Council resolution calling on Israel to withdraw from Lebanon.

Sept. 17– Camp David Accords are signed in Washington by Egyptian President Anwar Sadat and Israeli Prime Minister Menachem Begin with U.S. President Jimmy Carter as intermediary.

Khomeini's supporters on the streets of Tehran

1979
Jan. 16 – Mohammed Reza Shah Pahlavi leaves Iran due to mounting protests.

Feb. 1– Religious leader Ayatollah Ruhollah Khomeini returns from 15-year exile to establish an Islamic Republic in Iran.

Mar. 26 – Egypt and Israel sign peace accords.

July 16 – Saddam Hussein assumes Iraqi presidency.

Nov. 4 – Militant Iranian students overrun U.S. Embassy in Tehran, taking 52 hostages.

Dec. 27 – Soviet Union invades Afghanistan.

1980

1980
Apr. 24 – U.S. commandos' attempt to rescue hostages in Iran ends in failure.

June – Israel completes withdrawal to security zone in southern Lebanon.

Sept. 22 – Iraq invades Iran, beginning a war that lasts eight years.

Iraqi soldiers at the front during the Iran-Iraq War

1981
Jan. 20 – Iran releases all the American hostages.

June 7 – Israel bombs non-operational Iraqi nuclear reactor on the outskirts of Baghdad.

Oct. 6 – Sadat is assassinated by Islamic fundamentalists in Egypt. Hosni Mubarak succeeds him as President.

Dec. 14 – Israel annexes the Golan Heights.

1982
Apr. 25 – Israel completes withdrawal from Sinai.

June 6 – Israel invades Lebanon on "Operation Peace for Galilee."

Aug. 21-Sept. 4 – PLO evacuates Beirut during Israeli siege of the city.

Sept. 18 – Phalangist militia kill Palestinians in the Sabra and Shatila refugee camps.

Sept. 24 – The first contingent of a mainly U.S., French, and Italian peacekeeping force, requested by Lebanon, arrives in Beirut.

1983
Apr. 18 – Bomb blast destroys U.S. Embassy in Beirut.

Oct. 23 – Shiite suicide bombers attack U.S. Marine barracks at Beirut Airport.

Nov. 15 – Turkish Republic of Northern Cyprus is declared. UN Security Council condemns the move.

1984
Feb. 26 – U. S. Marines withdraw from Lebanon.

May 20 – Arab League condemns Iranian attacks on Persian Gulf shipping.

June 5 – Saudi jets down two Iranian planes over Persian Gulf.

Aug. 6 – U. S. and British ships are sent to Gulf to clear mines. Russian, French, and Italian ships arrive within two weeks to keep shipping lanes open.

1985
May-June – Israel withdraws from most of southern Lebanon to narrow security zone along the Israeli-Lebanese border.

Oct. 1 – Israeli jets attack PLO headquarters in Tunis, Tunisia.

1986
Mar. 24 – U. S. Navy exercises in the Gulf of Sidra draw attacks from Libyan jets and patrol boats.

Apr. 14 – U. S. bombers attack military installation near Tripoli, Libya.

1987
Feb. 26 – Palestinian uprising or *intifada*, protesting Israeli occupation, breaks out in Gaza Strip and spreads to the West Bank.

1988
Mar. 11 – Iraqi planes drop mustard gas and cyanide bombs on Iraqi town of Halabja in territory occupied by Iran. Nearly 5,000 Iraqi Kurds are killed.

July 20 – Iran accepts UN-drafted cease-fire plan to end eight-year war with Iraq.

July 31 – King Hussein relinquishes Jordan's claim to the West Bank.

Sept. 3 – Kurds flee to Turkey as rebellion is crushed in northern Iraq.

Nov. 15 – Palestinian National Council (P. N. C.) proclaims an independent Palestinian state.

1989
Feb. 15 – Last Soviet troops leave Afghanistan.

July 3 – Ayatollah Ruhollah Khomeini dies.

1990

1990
May 22 – The Republic of Yemen is created.

Aug. 2 – Iraq invades Kuwait. UN Security Council condemns attack.

Aug. 7 – Start of Operation Desert Shield; U.S.-led multinational coalition sends troops and supplies to Saudi Arabia to deter Iraqi attack.

Nov. 29 – UN Security Council authorizes use of force against Iraq unless it withdraws from Kuwait by Jan. 15, 1991.

Saddam Hussein

1991
Jan. 17 – Operation Desert Storm begins with a massive allied air attack against strategic targets in Baghdad and throughout Iraq.

Feb. 24 – Allied coalition forces launch ground offensive into Iraq and occupied Kuwait.

Feb. 27 – Kuwait is liberated. A cease-fire takes effect the next day. Retreating Iraqi troops set hundreds of oil wells on fire, causing an environmental disaster.

Apr. 3 – UN Security Council resolution requires Iraq to give up all chemical and biological weapons and materials for developing nuclear weapons. Iraq is required to provide arms inspection body UNSCOM complete access to all sites to monitor Iraqi disarmament.

American soldier stands on destroyed Iraqi tank while Kuwaiti oil wells, ignited by Saddam's retreating forces, burn in the distance.

1992
Aug. 27 – Allied forces begin enforcing "no-fly zone" in southern Iraq, preventing Iraqi air attacks against the Shiite population.

1993
Aug. – During secret talks in Oslo, Norway, between Israel and the PLO, the Declaration of Principles (Oslo Accords) is announced. This agreement provides for Palestinian self-rule to be phased in over several years in the West Bank and Gaza Strip.

Sept. 13 – Historic handshake between Israeli Prime Minister Rabin and PLO Chairman Arafat occurs at Oslo Accords signing ceremony hosted by U.S. President Bill Clinton on the White House Lawn.

1994
May 4 – PLO assumes authority in the Gaza Strip and town of Jericho. Israeli withdrawal begins two weeks later.

Oct. 13 – Iraq deploys two divisions near border with Kuwait. Rapid deployment of U.S. forces in the area causes Iraq to withdraw troops.

Oct. 26 – Jordanian King Hussein and Israeli Prime Minister Rabin sign formal peace treaty.

Yasser Arafat returns to Gaza Strip on July 1, 1994.

1995
Sept. 21 – PLO and Israel sign Oslo II agreement.

Nov. 16 – Israeli Prime Minister Yitzhak Rabin is assassinated by a Jewish religious extremist. His successor, Shimon Peres, vows to continue peace efforts.

1996
Jan. 20 – Yasser Arafat is elected president of the Palestinian Authority.

May 22 – Saddam Hussein accepts UN "oil for food" program.

Nov. 29 – Benjamin Netanyahu is elected Prime Minister of Israel.

1997
Jan. 16 – Israeli troops withdraw from West Bank town of Hebron the day after Israel signs Hebron Protocol with the Palestinian Authority.

1998
Oct. 23 – Wye River Memorandum: Israel agrees to further troop withdrawals; the PLO to eliminate clauses from the PLO Covenant calling for Israel's destruction.

Dec. 17-20 – U.S. and British warplanes bomb Iraq to force compliance with UNSCOM agreements. Following the attack Iraq refuses to readmit the UN weapons inspectors.

1999
Feb. 7 – King Hussein of Jordan dies. He is succeeded by his son Abdullah II.

July 6 – Ehud Barak of the Labor Party replaces Netanyahu as Israeli Prime Minister.

2000

Palestinians flee after throwing stones at Israeli army jeep during clashes in the West Bank city of Ramallah.

2000
May – Israel completes withdrawal from security zone in southern Lebanon.

June – President Assad of Syria dies. He is succeeded by his son Bashar.

July 11-25 – At Camp David II summit, Palestinian Authority leader Arafat and Israeli Prime Minister Barak fail to reach final peace settlement.

Sept. 28 – Second Palestinian uprising, the al Aqsa Intifada, begins in the Occupied Territories.

Oct. 12 – USS *Cole* is bombed in Yemen by Islamic fundamentalists controlled by Osama bin Laden.

2001
Feb. 6 – Ariel Sharon becomes Israeli Prime Minister.

Sept. 11 – Islamic terrorists hijack U.S. commercial jets and crash them into the World Trade Center in New York, and the Pentagon in Washington, D.C.

Oct. 7 – U.S.-led military action starts in Afghanistan to remove the Taliban regime from power.

Terrorists attack the World Trade Center on 9/11/01.

2002
Jan. 29 – U.S. President George W. Bush declares Iran, Iraq, and North Korea "constitute an axis of evil."

Mar. – Trying to stop a wave of suicide bombings, Israel has reoccupied land it previously relinquished in the Occupied Territories.

Nov. 8 – UN Security Council Resolution 1441 calls on Iraq to disarm.

Nov. 21 – UN weapons inspection team UNMOVIC resumes inspections in Iraq.

2003
Jan. 27 – UNMOVIC and the IAEA report to the UN Security Council.

OTHER FLAGS OF THE MIDDLE EAST

ARAB LEAGUE The color green and the crescent are often symbols in member countries of the League of Arab States, founded in 1945.

GULF COOPERATION COUNCIL The Arabian peninsula appears within the inscription "In the Name of Allah the All-Merciful." The Council, created in 1981, works for regional development.

ISLAM "There Is No God But Allah and Muhammad Is the Prophet of Allah" is written on this widely used but unofficial flag.

KURDISTAN After the '91 Gulf War, Kurds in northern Iraq established de facto self-rule. Their traditional ethnic flag was recognized in '99 by the Kurdish Regional Government.

MULTINATIONAL FORCE AND OBSERVERS The MFO has monitored the border between Egypt and Israel since 1982. The dove and olive branch stand for peace; orange was chosen as a neutral color.

ORGANIZATION OF THE ISLAMIC CONFERENCE The traditional green flag of Islam with a red crescent, "God Is Almighty" motto, and stylized globe symbolizes this worldwide Muslim organization.

PALESTINIANS Since 1922 Palestinians have used this flag, with traditional Arab dynastic colors, as a symbol of the statehood they desire.

RED CRESCENT In Muslim nations, Geneva Convention organizations rejected the red cross in favor of a red crescent, officially recognized in 1906.

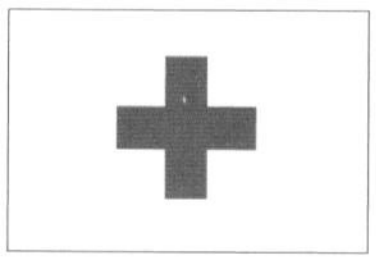

RED CROSS The Geneva Convention chose its symbol and flag in 1864 to identify people, vehicles, and buildings protected during wartime.

RED SHIELD OF DAVID SOCIETY Although not officially recognized by the Geneva Conventions, the "Magen David Adom" has provided medical services in Israel since 1948.

TURKISH REP. OF NORTHERN CYPRUS In 1983 part of Cyprus unilaterally proclaimed independence as the Turkish Republic of Northern Cyprus. Its flag is based on the one used by Turkey.

SOVEREIGN BASE AREAS Since 1960 the United Kingdom, by treaty exercising sovereignty over certain parts of the Republic of Cyprus, has flown the Union Jack.

UNITED NATIONS Olive branches of peace and a world map form the symbol adopted by the United Nations in 1946. The flag dates from 1947.

GEOGRAPHIC EQUIVALENTS

'Ain	*spring, well*
Arḑ	*area*
Aylagy	*bay, gulf*
Bāb	*gate, strait*
Bahr	*river*
Baḩr, Baḩra	*lake*
Bandar	*anchorage, bay, bight, port*
Barajı	*dam, reservoir*
Baţn	*depression, wadi*
Be'er	*well*
Bi'r	*spring*
Birket	*lake, pool, swamp*
Boğazi	*strait*
Buḩayrat	*lake, reservoir*
Burnu, Burun	*cape, point*
Dağ, Dağı	*hill, mountain*
Dağları	*mountains*
Darya	*river*
Daryācheh	*lake*
Dasht	*desert*
Dawḩat	*bay, cove, inlet, channel*
Denizi	*sea*
'Emeq	*valley*
Garagum	*desert*
Gardaneh	*pass*
Gebel	*mountain-s, range*
Geçidi	*mountain pass*
Gezîret, Gezâir	*island-s*
Ghubbat	*bay, gulf*
Gölü	*lake*
Gowd	*depression*
Haḑabat	*plateau*
Ḩadd	*spit*
Ḩālat	*island*
Har	*hill, mountain*
Hawr	*lake, marsh*
Ḥolot	*dunes*
Jabal	*hill-s, mountain-s*
Jazīrat, Jazā'ir	*island, islands*
Jībal	*hill-s, mountain-s*
Jūn	*bay*
Juzur	*islands*
Kavīr	*salt desert*
Kawr	*mountain*
Khabrat	*depression*
Khalîg, Khalīj	*bay, gulf*
Khawr	*channel*
Khirbat	*ancient site, ruins*
Köl, Kul	*lake*
Körfezi	*bay, gulf*
Kūh	*mountain-s*
Lac	*lake*
Masabb	*mouth of river*
Mīnā'	*harbor*
Nafūd	*area of dunes, desert*
Qā'	*depression, mud flat*
Qal'at	*fort*
Qarn	*hill*
Qaşr	*castle, fort*
Qiryat	*settlement, suburb*
Qulbān	*well-s*
Qurayyāt	*hills*
Ra's, Râs, Ras	*cape, point*
Ramlat	*dune, area*
Rhiy	*point*
Sabkhat	*salt lake*
Shaggat, Shiqqat	*elongated depression*
Sha'īb	*ravine, watercourse*
Shatt	*large river*
Tall	*hill, mound*
Tepe	*mountain*
Tur'at	*channel*
Ţuwayyir	*hill*
'Urqūb	*hill, plateau*
'Urūq	*dune area*
Wādī, Wâdi	*valley, watercourse*
Wâḩât	*oasis*

ABBREVIATIONS

A.D.	*In the year of the Lord*
Af.	*Africa*
AGR	*Agriculture*
Arm.	*Armenia*
Ave.	*Avenue*
Avg.	*Average*
Azerb.	*Azerbaijan*
B.C.	*Before Christ*
Blvd.	*Boulevard*
°C	*degrees Celsius (centigrade)*
ca	*circa*
Dr.	*Drive*
EXP	*Exports*
°F	*degrees Fahrenheit*
GDP	*Gross Domestic Product*
Gez.	*Gerzîret*
Gezr.	*Gezâir*
GMT	*Greenwich Mean Time*
IAEA	*International Atomic Energy Agency*
IND	*Industry*
Leb.	*Lebanon*
Mt.-s	*Mount-ain-s*
Occ. Terr.	*Occupied Territories*
Org.	*Organization*
PLO	*Palestine Liberation Organization*
Ra.	*Range*
Rep.	*Republic*
St.	*Street*
Str.	*Strait*
Syr.	*Syria*
Terr.	*Territories*
Turk.	*Turkey*
U.A.E.	*United Arab Emirates*
U.K.	*United Kingdom*
U.N.	*United Nations*
UNMOVIC	*United Nations Monitoring, Verification, and Inspection Commission*
UNSCOM	*United Nations Special Commission*
U.S.	*United States*
W.	*Wādī, Wâdi*

CONVERSIONS

CONVERSION TO METRIC

	multiply by	
in	2.54	cm
ft	.30	m
mi	1.61	km
in^2	6.45	cm^2
ft^2	.09	m^2
mi^2	2.59	km^2
°F	5/9 after subtracting 32	°C

CONVERSION FROM METRIC

	multiply by	
cm	.39	in
m	3.28	ft
km	.62	mi
cm^2	.16	in^2
m^2	10.76	ft^2
km^2	.39	mi^2
°C	9/5 then add 32	°F

PLACE-NAME INDEX

The following system is used to locate a place on a map in the National Geographic Atlas of the Middle East. The boldface type after an entry refers to the plate on which the map is found. The letter-number combination refers to the grid on which the particular place-name is located. The edge of each map is marked horizontally with numbers and vertically with letters. In between, at equally spaced intervals, are index ticks (▲). If these ticks were connected with lines, each page would be divided into a grid. Take Alanya, Turkey, for example. The index entry reads "Alanya, *Turk.* **44** H6." On page 44, Alanya is located within the grid square where row H and column 6 intersect.

A place-name may appear on several maps, but the index lists only the best presentation. Usually, this means that a feature is indexed to the largest-scale map on which it appears in its entirety. (Note: Rivers are often labeled multiple times even on a single map. In such cases, the rivers are indexed to labels that are closest to their mouths.) The name of the country or continent in which a feature lies is shown in italic type and is sometimes abbreviated.

The index lists more than proper names. Some entries include a description, as in "Forūr, *island, Iran* **24** L7." In languages other than English, the description of a physical feature may be part of the name; e.g., the "Ţuwayyir" in "Ţuwayyir al Ḩamīr, *Qatar* **38** K5," means "hill." The Geographic Equivalents list on page 86 translates such terms into English. When a feature or place can be referred to by more than one name, both names appear in the index with cross-references.

Aalma ech Chaab, *Leb.* **34** M1
Abā as Sa'ūd, *Saudi Arabia* **40** L6
Ābādān, *Iran* **24** H3
Ābādeh, *Iran* **24** H5
Abâr el Kanâyis, *well, Egypt* **22** C3
Abarkūh, *Iran* **24** H6
Abasān, *Gaza Strip* **50** L2
'Abda (Eboda), *ruin, Israel* **29** M3
'Abd al 'Azīz, Jabal, *Syr.* **42** C9
'Abdalī, *customs post, Kuwait* **33** A7
'Abd al Kūrī, *island, Yemen* **49** H15
'Abdd Khān-e Pā'īn, *Iran* **27** H12
Abhā, *Saudi Arabia* **40** L5
Abnûb, *Egypt* **23** G7
Abrād, Wādī, *Yemen* **48** E7
Abraq al Ḩabārī, *escarpment, Kuwait* **32** F3
Abraq Khayţān, *Kuwait* **33** G9
Abrūq, Ra's, *Qatar* **38** E4
Abū aḑ Ḑuhūr, *Syr.* **42** D3
Abū 'Ajram, *Saudi Arabia* **40** C3
Abū al Abyaḑ, *island, U.A.E.* **47** G6
Abū al 'Awsaj, *area, Bahrain* **19** F7
Abū 'Alī, *island, Saudi Arabia* **40** E9
Abū al Khaşīb, *Iraq* **27** K11
Abū al Lasan, *Jordan* **30** K3
Abū 'Arīsh, *Saudi Arabia* **48** C3
Abu 'Aweiḑ, Râs, *Egypt* **23** H10
Abu 'Aweigîla, *Egypt* **29** M1
Abū aẓ Ẓulūf, *Qatar* **38** B5
Abū Baḩr, *plain, Saudi Arabia* **40** H8
Abu Ballâṣ, *peak, Egypt* **22** J3
Abū Daghmah, *Syr.* **42** C5
Abū Dālī, *Syr.* **42** G3
Abu Dhabi *see* Abū Ẓaby, *U.A.E.* **47** F8
Abu Dukhân, Gebel, *Egypt* **23** G9
Abu Durba, *Egypt* **23** E9
Abu el Ḩuṣein, Bîr, *Egypt* **23** L6
Abu Gharâdiq, Bîr, *Egypt* **23** D4
Abū Hāmūr, *Qatar* **38** G7
Abu Ḩarba, Gebel, *Egypt* **23** F9
Abu Hashaifa, Khalîg, *Egypt* **23** C4
Abū Jarjūr, Ra's, *Bahrain* **19** D8
Abū Kamāl, *Syr.* **43** G10
Abū Madd, Ra's, *Saudi Arabia* **40** F2
Abu Mareiwât, Bîr, *Egypt* **23** G9
Abu Minqâr, Bîr, *Egypt* **22** G3
Abū Mūsá, *island, Iran* **47** B9
Abū Qumayyiş, Raḩs, *Saudi Arabia* **38** L7
Ābūr, *Jordan* **30** H4
Abu Rudeis, *Egypt* **23** E8
Abū Samrah, *Qatar* **38** K4
Abū Sidrah, *Qatar* **38** D4
Abu Simbel, *site, Egypt* **23** L7
Abu Sôma, Râs, *Egypt* **23** G9
Abū Şukhayr, *Iraq* **27** H7
Abu Tîg, *Egypt* **23** G7
Abū Urayqiţ, Ra's, *Saudi Arabia* **18** E2
Abū Ẓaby (Abu Dhabi), *U.A.E.* **47** F8
Abu Zenîma, *Egypt* **23** E8
Abyek, *Iran* **24** D4
Achna, *Cyprus* **20** G6
Acıgöl, *lake, Turk.* **44** F4
Acıpayam, *Turk.* **44** F4
Acre *see* 'Akko, *Israel* **28** C4
Adam, *Oman* **37** F8
'Adan (Aden), *Yemen* **48** H6
Adana, *Turk.* **44** G9
Adapazarı *see* Sakarya, *Turk.* **44** B5
Aḑ Ḑafrah, *region, U.A.E.* **46** J3
Ad Daghghārah, *Iraq* **27** H8
Ad Dahnā', *desert, Saudi Arabia* **40** E7
Aḑ Ḑāli', *Yemen* **48** G6
Ad Dammām, *Saudi Arabia* **40** E9
Ad Dār al Ḩamrā', *Saudi Arabia* **40** D2
Ad Darb, *Saudi Arabia* **40** L5
Ad Dawādimī, *Saudi Arabia* **40** F6
Ad Dawḩah (Doha), *Kuwait* **33** F8
Ad Dawḩah (Doha), *Qatar* **38** G7
Ad Dawr, *Iraq* **27** E7
Ad Dayr, *Bahrain* **19** A8
Ad Dibdibah, *region, Iraq-Kuwait-Saudi Arabia* **32** F3
Aḑ Ḑiffah *see* Libyan Plateau, *Egypt* **22** C2
Ad Dilam, *Saudi Arabia* **40** G7
Ad Dirāz, *Bahrain* **19** B6
Ad Dīwānīyah, *Iraq* **27** H8
Aḑ Ḑubā'īyah, *Kuwait* **33** J10
Ad Dujayl, *Iraq* **27** F7
Ad Dūr, *Bahrain* **19** F8
Ad Durra, *Jordan* **30** M2
Ad Duwayd, *Saudi Arabia* **40** C5
Aden *see* 'Adan, *Yemen* **48** H6
Aden, Gulf of, *Af.-Asia* **17** M11
Adhanah, Wādī, *Yemen* **48** F5
Adh Dhakhīrah, *Qatar* **38** D7
Adh Dhayd, *U.A.E.* **47** D11
'Adiyah, Jabal, *Yemen* **48** E5
Adıyaman, *Turk.* **45** F12
Adrianople *see* Edirne, *Turk.* **44** A2
Aegean Sea, *Europe* **16** C6
'Afak, *Iraq* **27** H8
'Afīf, *Saudi Arabia* **40** G5
Afiq, *Israel* **28** D6
Afqā, *Leb.* **34** E5
'Afrīn, *Syr.* **42** C3
Afşin, *Turk.* **45** E11
'Afula, *Israel* **28** D4
Afyon, *Turk.* **44** E5
Aghbar, Jabal al, *Yemen* **48** H4
Agh Bolāgh, *Iran* **27** A8
Aghûrmi, *Egypt* **22** E2
Agia Napa, *Cyprus* **20** H6
Agios Amvrosios, *Cyprus* **20** F5
Agios Sergios, *Cyprus* **20** G6
Agios Theodoros, *Cyprus* **20** F6
Ağrı *see* Karaköse, *Turk.* **45** C16
Ağrı Dağı (Mount Ararat), *Turk.* **45** C17
Ahar, *Iran* **24** B2
Ahlat, *Turk.* **45** E16
Ahlatlıbel, *ruin, Turk.* **44** D7
Ahram, *Iran* **24** J5
Āhū, *Iran* **24** H3
Ahvāz, *Iran* **24** G3
Aḩwar, *Yemen* **48** G8
Aigialousa, *Cyprus* **20** E7
'Ajaltūn, *Leb.* **34** F4
Ajban, *U.A.E.* **47** F9
'Ajīrah, Jazīrat, *Bahrain* **19** J11
'Ajlūn, *Jordan* **30** D4
'Ajmān, *U.A.E.* **47** D10
'Ajūzah, Ra's, *Kuwait* **33** F9
Akaki, *Cyprus* **20** G4
Akanthou, *Cyprus* **20** F6
Akarsu, *Turk.* **43** A10
'Akāshāt, *Iraq* **26** F2
Akçaabat, *Turk.* **45** B13
Akçadağ, *Turk.* **45** E12
Akçakale, *Turk.* **45** G13
Akçakışla, *Turk.* **45** D10
Akçakoca, *Turk.* **44** B6
Akçay, *Turk.* **44** D2
Akçay, *Turk.* **44** G4
Akdağ, *peak, Turk.* **44** E1
Ak Dağlar, *Turk.* **44** G4
Akdağmadeni, *Turk.* **45** D10
Akdoğan, *Turk.* **42** A9
Akhḑar, Al Jabal al, *Oman* **37** E8
Akhisar, *Turk.* **44** D3
Akhmîm, *Egypt* **23** G7
Akhtarīn, *Syr.* **42** C4
Akıncı Burnu, *Turk.* **21** B12
'Akko (Acre), *Israel* **28** C4
Akkuş, *Turk.* **45** B11
Akra, *peak, Turk.* **21** C12
Akrotiri, *Cyprus* **20** J3
Akrotiri Bay, *Cyprus* **20** J3
Akrūm, *ruin, Leb.* **34** B8
Aksaray, *Turk.* **44** E8
Akşehir, *Turk.* **44** E6
Akşehir Gölü, *Turk.* **44** E6
Akseki, *Turk.* **44** G6
'Aksha, *ruin, Egypt* **23** M7
Aksu, *river, Turk.* **44** G5
Aktepe (Güvenç), *Turk.* **42** B2
Akyaka, *Turk.* **45** B17
Akyazı, *Turk.* **44** C5
Al 'Abdalīyah, *Kuwait* **33** H7
Alaca, *Turk.* **44** C9
Alaca Dağ, *Turk.* **44** F7
Alacahöyük, *ruin, Turk.* **44** C9
Alaçam, *Turk.* **45** A10
Aladağ, *peak, Turk.* **44** F6
Aladağ, *peak, Turk.* **44** F9
Al 'Adā'im, *ruin, Bahrain* **19** F6
Al 'Adhbah, *Qatar* **38** B6
Al Aflāj, *region, Saudi Arabia* **40** H7
Al Aḩmadī, *Kuwait* **33** H9
Al 'Ajā'iz, *Oman* **37** J7
Al Akhḑar, *Saudi Arabia* **40** D2
Alalakh, *ruin, Turk.* **45** H10
Al 'Amādīyah, *Iraq* **27** A6
Al 'Amar, *Bahrain* **19** F7
Al 'Amārah, *Iraq* **27** H10
'Alam el Rûm, Râs, *Egypt* **22** C3
Al 'Āmirīyah, *Qatar* **38** K5
Al 'Ānāt, *Syr.* **42** M3
Alanya, *Turk.* **44** H6
Al 'Aqabah (Aqaba), *Jordan* **30** L2
Al 'Aqīq, *Saudi Arabia* **40** J4
Al 'Āqūrah, *Leb.* **34** E5
Al 'Arīḑah, *Leb.* **34** A6
Al 'Arīsh, *Qatar* **38** B5
Al 'Armah, *plateau, Saudi Arabia* **40** F7
Al Arţāwīyah, *Saudi Arabia* **40** E7
Al 'Āṣ (Orontes), *river, Syr.* **42** E2
Al As'ad, *Saudi Arabia* **40** D2
Alaşehir, *Turk.* **44** E3
Al 'Ashārah, *Syr.* **42** F9
Al Ashkharah, *Oman* **37** F9
Al Atārib, *Syr.* **42** D3
'Alawīyīn, Jabal al, *Syr.* **42** E2
Alāyat Samā'il, *Oman* **37** E8
Al 'Ayn, *U.A.E.* **47** G11
Al 'Ayzarīyah (Bethany), *W. Bank* **51** H8
Al 'Azīzīyah, *Saudi Arabia* **19** B3
Al Bāb, *Syr.* **42** C4
Al Bad', *Saudi Arabia* **40** D1
Al Badī', *Saudi Arabia* **40** H7
Al Badī, *Iraq* **27** C4
Al Bāḩah, *Saudi Arabia* **40** J4
Al Başrah (Basra), *Iraq* **27** K11
Al Baţḩā', *Iraq* **27** J9
Al Bayāḑ, *plain, Saudi Arabia* **40** H8
Al Bayḑā, *Yemen* **48** G7
Al Bazm al Gharbā, *island, U.A.E.* **47** G5
Al Bi'āj, *Iraq* **27** B4
'Al Biqā' (Bekaa Valley), *Leb.* **34** G5
Al Bi'r, *Saudi Arabia* **40** C2
Al Bīrah, *W. Bank* **51** F7
Al Birk, *Saudi Arabia* **40** L4
Al Budayyi', *Bahrain* **19** B6
Al Burayj, *Gaza Strip* **50** K2
Al Buraymī, *Oman* **37** D6
Ālbū Şāliḩ, *Iraq* **27** J10
Al Busayţā', *plain, Saudi Arabia* **40** C3
Al Busaytīn, *Bahrain* **19** A8
Al Buşayyir, *Qatar* **38** D5
Al Chabaish, *Iraq* **27** K10
Aleppo *see* Ḩalab, *Syr.* **42** C3
Alexandria *see* El Iskandarîya, *Egypt* **23** C6
Alexandrium, *ruin, W. Bank* **51** E9
Aley, *Leb.* **34** G4
Al Fallūjah, *Iraq* **27** F7
Al Faqū, *U.A.E.* **47** E10
Al Fatḩah, *Iraq* **27** D6
Al Fāw, *Iraq* **27** L12
Al Fintās, *Kuwait* **33** G10
Al Fīyay, *island, U.A.E.* **47** G5
Al Fuḩayḩīl, *Kuwait* **33** H10
Al Fujayrah, *U.A.E.* **47** D12
Al Furāt (Euphrates), *river, Iraq* **27** J9
Al Ghābah, *Oman* **37** G7
Al Ghammās, *Iraq* **27** J8
Al Ghāriyah, *Syr.* **42** M2
Al Gharīyah, *Qatar* **38** B6
Al Gharrāf, *Iraq* **27** J9
Al Ghashshāmīyah, *Qatar* **38** B6
Al Ghayḑah, *Yemen* **49** D15
Al Ghayḑah, *Yemen* **49** F12
Al Ghayl, *Saudi Arabia* **40** H7
Al Ghaynah, *dry salt lake, Bahrain* **19** F7
Al Ghazālah, *Saudi Arabia* **40** E4
Al Ghāzīyah, *Leb.* **34** J2
Al Ghuwayrīyah, *Qatar* **38** C6
Al Ḩabbānīyah, *Iraq* **27** F6
Al Habbārīyah, *Iraq* **27** H5
Al Habiyah, *U.A.E.* **47** E10
Al Ḩadd, *Bahrain* **19** B9
Al Ḩadīdah, *crater, Saudi Arabia* **40** H9
Al Ḩadithah, *Saudi Arabia* **30** F7
Al Ḩaḑr, *Iraq* **27** C5
Al Ḩaffah, *Syr.* **42** E1
Al Hā'ī, *Iran* **27** H12
Al Ḩājib, *Syr.* **42** D4
Al Ḩalfāyah, *Iraq* **27** H11
Al Ḩamād, *plain, Saudi Arabia* **40** B4
Al Hamalah, *Bahrain* **19** C6
Al Ḩamīdīyah, *Syr.* **42** G1
Al Ḩamrīyah, *U.A.E.* **47** C10
Al Ḩammār, *Iraq* **27** K10
Al Ḩamrā', *Saudi Arabia* **40** G3
Al Ḩamzah, *Iraq* **27** J8
Al Ḩanākīyah, *Saudi Arabia* **40** F4
Al Ḩanīyah, *hill, Iraq* **27** M9
Al Ḩarf, *Yemen* **48** D5
Al Ḩarīq, *Saudi Arabia* **40** G7
Al Hārithah, *Iraq* **27** K11
Al Ḩarrah, *lava field, Saudi Arabia* **40** B3
Al Ḩasakah, *Syr.* **43** C10
Al Hāshimīyah, *Iraq* **27** H8
Al Ḩawrah, *Yemen* **48** G9
Al Ḩayy, *Iraq* **27** H9
Al Ḩazm, *Yemen* **48** D6
Al Hījānah, *Syr.* **42** K2
Al Ḩijāz (Hejaz), *region, Saudi Arabia* **40** E2
Al Ḩillah, *Iraq* **27** G7
Al Ḩillah, *Saudi Arabia* **40** G7
Al Hindīyah, *Iraq* **27** G7
Al Ḩişn, *Jordan* **30** C4
Al Ḩudaydah, *Yemen* **48** F3
Al Hufūf (Hofuf), *Saudi Arabia* **40** F9
Al Ḩujayjah, *Kuwait* **33** D10
Al Ḩulaybah, *customs post, Kuwait* **33** A6
Al Ḩumayḑah, *Saudi Arabia* **30** M2
Al Ḩumrah, *area, U.A.E.* **47** K8
Al Ḩuqnah, *Iraq* **27** B5
Aliabad, *Iran* **24** K7
'Alī al Gharbī, *Iraq* **27** G10
'Alī ash Sharqī, *Iraq* **27** H10
Al Ikhwān (The Brothers), *islands, Yemen* **49** H16
Al 'Irqah, *Yemen* **48** G9
Alişar Hüyük, *ruin, Turk.* **44** D9
Al 'Īsāwīyah, *Saudi Arabia* **40** B3
Al Iskandarīyah, *Iraq* **27** G7
'Ālīyah, Jazīrat al, *Qatar* **38** F8
Al Jābirīyah, *Kuwait* **33** F9
Al Jafr, *Jordan* **30** J5
Al Jāfūrah, *desert, Saudi Arabia* **40** F9
Al Jahrā', *Kuwait* **33** F7
Al Jasrah, *Bahrain* **19** C6
Al Jawādīyah, *Syr.* **43** B12
Al Jib, *W. Bank* **51** G7
Al Jifārah, *Saudi Arabia* **40** G6
Al Jīzah, *Jordan* **30** E4
Al Jubayl, *Saudi Arabia* **40** E9
Al Judaydah, *Leb.* **34** G3
Al Judhay', *Qatar* **38** C6
Al Jufayr, *Bahrain* **19** B8
Al Jumaylīyah, *Qatar* **38** E5
Al Junaynah, *Saudi Arabia* **40** J5
Al Kahfah, *Saudi Arabia* **40** E5
Al Karak, *Jordan* **30** G4
Al Kawm, *Syr.* **42** F6
Al Kaẓimīyah, *Iraq* **27** F7
Al Khābūrah, *Oman* **37** D7
Al Khalīl (Hebron), *W. Bank* **51** K7
Al Khāliş, *Iraq* **27** F7
Al Kharfah, *Saudi Arabia* **40** H7
Al Kharj, *Saudi Arabia* **40** G8
Al Kharrārah, *Qatar* **38** J5
Al Khaşab, *Oman* **47** B12
Al Khāşirah, *Saudi Arabia* **40** G6
Al Khatam, *region, U.A.E.* **47** G9
Al Khatam, *U.A.E.* **47** G9
Al Khaţţīyah, *Qatar* **38** F3
Al Khawkhah, *Yemen* **48** G4
Al Khawr, *Qatar* **38** D7
Al Khiḑr, *Iraq* **27** J9
Al Khīrān, *Kuwait* **33** L11
Al Khīsah, *Qatar* **38** F7
Al Khiyām, *Leb.* **34** L4
Al Khubar, *Saudi Arabia* **40** E9
Al Khufayfīyah, *Saudi Arabia* **40** F6
Al Khunn, *Saudi Arabia* **40** G9
Al Khurayb, *Qatar* **38** F6
Al Khuraybah, *Syr.* **42** G2
Al Khuraybah, *Yemen* **49** E10
Al Khurayţīyāt, *Qatar* **38** F7
Al Khurmah, *Saudi Arabia* **40** H5
Al Khuwayr, *Qatar* **38** B5
Al Kifl, *Iraq* **27** H7
Al Kir'ānah, *Qatar* **38** H5
Al Kiswah, *Syr.* **34** K7
Al Kūfah, *Iraq* **27** H7
Al Kūt, *Iraq* **27** G9
Al Kuwayr, *Iraq* **27** C6
Al Kuwayt (Kuwait), *Kuwait* **33** F9
Al La'bān, *Jordan* **30** G4
Al Labwah, *Leb.* **34** D8
Al Lādhiqīyah (Latakia), *Syr.* **42** E1
Allahüekber Tepe, *Turk.* **45** C16
Al Lajā, *lava field, Syr.* **42** L2
'Allāk, Ra's al, *Qatar* **38** J8
'Allâqi, Wâdi el, *Egypt* **23** L9
Allenby Bridge, *W. Bank* **51** G10
Al Lidām, *Saudi Arabia* **40** J6
Al Līth, *Saudi Arabia* **40** J4
Al Luḩayyah, *Yemen* **48** E3
Al Luwaymī, *Saudi Arabia* **40** D5
Al Ma'āmīr, *Bahrain* **19** C8
Al Madīnah (Medina), *Saudi Arabia* **40** F3
Al Madwar, *Jordan* **30** D4
Al Mafjar, *Qatar* **38** B6
Al Mafraq, *U.A.E.* **47** G8
Al Mafraq, *Jordan* **30** C5
Al Maḩāwīl, *Iraq* **27** G7
Al Maḩfid, *Yemen* **48** G8
Al Maḩmūdīyah, *Iraq* **27** G7
Al Mahrah, *area, Yemen* **49** D14
Al Maḩwīt, *Yemen* **48** E4
Al Majma'ah, *Saudi Arabia* **40** F6
Al Makhrūq, *ruin, Bahrain* **19** E7
Al Mālikīyah, *Bahrain* **19** D6
Al Mālikīyah, *Syr.* **43** A12
Al Mamţalah, *Bahrain* **19** G7
Al Manāmah (Manama), *Bahrain* **19** B8
Al Manāşif, *area, Syr.* **43** F10
Al Manqaf, *Kuwait* **33** H10
Al Manşūrah, *Syr.* **42** D6
Al Manşūrīyah, *Leb.* **34** G3
Al Ma'qil, *Iraq* **27** K11
Al Maqwa', *Kuwait* **33** G9
Al Marāwi'ah, *Yemen* **48** F4
Al Marj, *Leb.* **34** G5
Al Markūz, *Saudi Arabia* **40** C5
Al Marrawnah, *Qatar* **38** B7
Al Mashrafah, *Syr.* **42** F3
Al Ma'shūqah, *Saudi Arabia* **40** J4
Al Mawşil (Mosul), *Iraq* **27** B6
Al Mayādīn, *Syr.* **42** F9
Al Maymūnah, *Iraq* **27** H10
Al Mayyāh, *Saudi Arabia* **40** D5
Al Mazra'ah, *Jordan* **30** F3
Al Mintirib, *Oman* **37** F9
Al Minyah, *Leb.* **34** B5
Al Miqdādīyah, *Iraq* **27** E8
Al Mismīyah, *Syr.* **42** K2
Al Mubarraz, *Saudi Arabia* **40** F9
Al Mudawwarah, *Jordan* **30** M4
Al Mughayrā', *U.A.E.* **47** G6
Al Muḩammadīyah, *island, Bahrain* **19** B6
Al Muḩarraq, *Bahrain* **19** A8
Al Mukallā, *Yemen* **49** F11
Al Mukhā (Mocha), *Yemen* **48** G4
Almus, *Turk.* **45** C11
Al Muşallá, *Bahrain* **19** B7
Al Musayyib, *Iraq* **27** G7
Almus Barajı, *Turk.* **45** C11
Al Mushannaf, *Syr.* **42** L3
Al Mu'tariḑ, *islands, Bahrain* **19** J9
Al Muwaqqar, *ruin, Jordan* **30** E5
Al Muwassam, *Saudi Arabia* **40** M5
Al Muwayh, *Saudi Arabia* **40** H4
Al Na'āyim, *hills, Kuwait* **33** F4
Al Na'man, *Qatar* **38** C5
Al Qābil, *Oman* **37** D6
Al Qaḑīmah, *Saudi Arabia* **40** H3
Al Qadmūs, *Syr.* **42** F2
Al Qaffāy, *island, U.A.E.* **46** F2
Al Qā'im, *Iraq* **27** E4
Al Qa'īyah, *Saudi Arabia* **40** G5
Al Qā'īyah, *Qatar* **38** D5
Al Qāmishlī, *Syr.* **43** A11
Al Qārah, *Saudi Arabia* **26** L2
Al Qaryah, *Bahrain* **19** C8
Al Qaryatayn, *Syr.* **42** H3
Al Qaşīm, *region, Saudi Arabia* **40** E6
Al Qaşr, *Jordan* **30** F4
Al Qaţīf, *Saudi Arabia* **40** E9
Al Qatn, *Yemen* **49** E10
Al Qaţrānah, *Jordan* **30** G4
Al Qayşūmah, *Saudi Arabia* **40** D7
Al Qayyārah, *Iraq* **27** C6
Al Qua'a, *U.A.E.* **47** J10
Al Qu'ayţī, *area, Yemen* **49** F11
Al Qudayr, *Syr.* **42** F6
Al Qunayţirah (El Quneitra), *Syr.* **42** K1
Al Qunfudhah, *Saudi Arabia* **40** K4

Gal-Kem

Nil-Shi

Shi–Zyg

CONSULTANTS

PHYSICAL AND POLITICAL MAPS

Central Intelligence Agency (CIA)

National Geographic Maps

National Imagery and Mapping Agency (NIMA)

Office of the Geographer, U.S. Department of State

U.S. Board on Geographic Names (BGN)

NATIONS

CARL HAUB
Population Reference Bureau

WHITNEY SMITH
Flag Research Center

KENNETH W. STEIN
Emory University

REGIONAL THEMES

Climate

ROLAND GEERKEN, JASON EVANS
Yale University

NILI HARNIK
Lamont-Doherty Earth Observatory, Columbia University

Development Indicators

RICHARD FIX
Development Data Group, World Bank

Oil

MICHAEL J. GRILLOT
Energy Information Administration, U.S. Dept. of Energy

Population

CARL HAUB
Population Reference Bureau

GREGORY YETMAN
Center for International Earth Science Information Network (CIESIN)

Religion

HARVEY COX
Harvard Divinity School

REUVEN KIMELMAN
Brandeis University

NEGUIN YEVARI
Columbia University

Water

AMY CASSARA, YUMIKO KURA, DAN TUNSTALL
World Resources Institute

HISTORY

World Heritage Sites/Other Archaeological Sites

CHARLES E. JONES
Oriental Institute, University of Chicago

PAUL MICHAEL TAYLOR
Smithsonian Institution

PRINCIPAL REFERENCE SOURCES

Alcamo, Joseph, Thomas Henrichs, and Thomas Rösch. *World Water in 2025: Global modeling and scenario analysis for the World Commission on Water for the 21st Century.* Center for Environmental Systems Research, University of Kassel, 2000.

Atlas of the Middle East. Washington, D.C.: Central Intelligence Agency, 1993.

Blake, Gerald, John Dewdney, and Jonathan Mitchell. *The Cambridge Atlas of the Middle East and North Africa.* Cambridge: Cambridge University Press, 1987.

Britannica Yearbook, 2002. Chicago: Encyclopaedia Britannica, Inc.

Cohen, Saul B., ed. *Columbia Gazetteer of the World.* New York: Columbia University Press, 1998.

Earthtrends: The Environmental Information Portal. Washington, D.C.: World Resources Institute. Available at http://earthtrends.wri.org.

EdStats. World Bank's Education Group of the Human Development Network (HDNED) and the Development Economics Data Group in collaboration with the UNESCO Institute for Statistics (UIS), OECD, and other agencies. Available at http://www1.worldbank.org/education/edstats/index.html.

Gridded Population of the World (GPW), Version 2. Palisades, New York: Center for International Earth Science Information Network (CIESIN), Columbia University; International Food Policy Research Institute (IFPRI); and World Resources Institute (WRI). Available at http://sedac.ciesin.columbia.edu/plue/gpw.

International Energy Annual 2001. Washington, D.C.: U.S. Department of Energy.

International Migration 2002. New York: Population Division of the U.N.

International Petroleum Encyclopedia 2002. Tulsa, Okla.: PennWell Corp.

Merriam Webster's Geographical Dictionary, 3rd ed. Springfield, Ma.: Merriam-Webster, Incorporated, 1997.

Middle East Patterns: Places, Peoples, and Politics. Boulder, Westview Press, 2000.

The Military Balance: 2002-2003, International Institute for Strategic Studies. Oxford University Press, 2003.

Millennium Energy Atlas. London, U.K.: Petroleum Economist, Ltd., 1999.

Millennium Indicators. United Nations Statistics Division, 2003.

National Geographic Atlas of the World, 7th ed. Washington, D.C.: The National Geographic Society, 1999.

National Geographic Family Reference Atlas of the World. Washington, D.C.: The National Geographic Society, 2002.

National Geographic Maps. *"In Focus: Middle East, Crossroads of Faith and Conflict"* (map supplement). *National Geographic,* October 2002.

Population Data Sheet, 2002. Washington, D.C.: Population Reference Bureau.

Revenga, Carmen, et al. *Pilot Analysis of Global Ecosystems: Freshwater Systems.* Washington, D.C.: World Resources Institute, 2000.

Roaf, Michael. *Cultural Atlas of Mesopotamia and the Ancient Near East.* Oxford: Facts on File, 1990.

Turner, Barry, ed. *The Statesman's Yearbook,* 138th ed. New York, New York: Palgrave, 2002.

WMO Global Climate Normals, 1961-1990, Version 1.0. NOAA/National Climatic Data Center, November 1998.

World Development Indicators, 2002. Washington, D.C.: World Bank.

The World Factbook 2002. Washington, D.C.: Central Intelligence Agency.

World Urbanization Prospects: The 2001 Revision. Population Division of the Dept. of Economic and Social Affairs of the U.N. Secretariat. New York: United Nations.

PRINCIPAL ONLINE SOURCES

Central Intelligence Agency
www.cia.gov

Center for International Earth Science Information Network (CIESIN)
www.ciesin.org

Energy Information Administration, U.S. Department of Energy
www.eia.doe.gov

Ethnologue
www.ethnologue.com

Lamont-Doherty Earth Observatory, Columbia University
www.ldeo.columbia.edu

Organisation for Economic Co-operation and Development
www.oecd.org

National Geographic Maps
www.nationalgeographic.com/maps

NIMA Geographic Names Database
www.nima.mil

NOAA/National Climatic Data Center
www.ncdc.noaa.gov

Pacific Institute
www.worldwater.org

Population Reference Bureau
www.prb.org

UNESCO World Heritage Center
www.wch.unesco.org

United Nations Statistics Division
www.unstats.un.org

World Bank
www.worldbank.org

World Resources Institute
www.wri.org

PHOTOS AND IMAGERY

FRONT JACKET
Globe: WorldSat International. Images (left to right): Richard Nowitz/NGS Image Collection; National Geographic map; Joanna B. Pinneo; James L. Stanfield; Hans Christian Heap/Getty Images.

FRONT MATTER
PAGES 2-3: WorldSat International. PAGE 4: Laurence Dutton/Getty Images. PAGE 6: Bill Ellzey/NGS Image Collection. PAGE 7: Wayne Eastep/Getty Images. PAGE 9: Mohamed Amin/Camerapix.

NATIONS
PAGES 14-15 (left to right): David Turnley/CORBIS; Richard List/CORBIS; Richard Ellis/ CORBIS Sygma; Annie Griffiths Belt; Reza; AFP Photo/Thomas Coëx.

REGIONAL THEMES
PAGES 58-59 (left to right): Antoine Gyori/CORBIS Sygma; Nevada Wier/Getty Images; Peter Turnley/CORBIS; Hans Christian Heap/Getty Images; AFP Photo/Menaham Kahana; Ed Kashi.

HISTORY
PAGES 76-77 (left to right): Bettmann/CORBIS; Hulton-Deutsch Collection/ CORBIS; AFP/Behrouz Mehri/CORBIS; Keving Fleming/CORBIS; Steve McCurry; Chris Anderson/AURORA.

TIME LINE
PAGE 82: (upper three), Hulton|Archive by Getty Images; (lower left), Courtesy Imperial War Museum, London, Neg. #I46094; (lower right), CORBIS. PAGE 83: (upper left), Hulton|Archive by Getty Images; (upper right), Vittoriano Rastelli/CORBIS; (lower left), AFP Photo; (lower right), Hulton-Deutsch Collection/CORBIS. PAGE 84 (upper left), Bettmann/CORBIS; (upper right), Hulton|Archive by Getty Images; (lower left), CORBIS; (lower right), Bettmann/CORBIS. PAGE 85 (upper left), Peter Turnley/CORBIS; (upper right), AFP/CORBIS; (lower left), Reuters NewMedia, Inc./CORBIS; (lower middle), AFP Photo/Manoocher Deghati; (lower right), AFP/Seth McAllister/CORBIS.

END PAGE
PAGE 96 : Globe: Gene C. Feldman, Norman Kuring NASA/Goddard Space Flight Center, SeaWiFS.

KEY TO COUNTRY FACTS

The National Geographic Society, whose cartographic policy is to recognize de facto countries, counted 192 independent nations in early 2003. Within the "Nations" section of *The Atlas of the Middle East,* the 16 independent nations in this region plus the Occupied Territories are featured on political maps. Accompanying each map is a table that includes some important statistical data, providing highlights of geography, demography, and economy. These details offer a brief overview of each political entity; they present general characteristics and are not intended to be comprehensive studies. The structured nature of the text results in some generic collective or umbrella terms. The industry category, for instance, includes services in addition to traditional manufacturing sectors. Space limitations dictate the amount of information included. For example, only the most widely spoken languages in each country are listed. The flag of each independent nation is shown. The conventional or official long form of the country's names appears besides the flag; if no long form exists, the short form is repeated.

AREA accounts for the total area of a country, which includes all land and inland water delimited by international boundaries, intranational boundaries, or coastlines. The figures are from *The World Factbook 2002,* Central Intelligence Agency, Washington, D.C. Its website is www.cia.gov/cia/publications/factbook/index.html.

POPULATION figures for countries are mid-2002 estimates from the 2002 World Population Data Sheet of the Population Reference Bureau, Washington, D.C. Their website is www.prb.org. The numbers are rounded to the nearest hundred thousand. Two issues of note: the population of Cyprus shows the number of persons living on the entire island—within both the Republic of Cyprus, and the Turkish Cypriot area in the north. Separate population figures for the West Bank and the Gaza Strip are shown; these are from the October 2001 issue of the National Geographic Magazine.

CAPITAL gives the name of the seat of government, followed by the city's population, which is from the United Nations Population Division's *World Urbanization Prospects: The 2001 Revision*: Table A.13, Population of capital cities in 2001. The UN Population Division's web site is: www.un.org/esa/population/unpop.htm. These capital city population figures are rounded to the nearest thousand.

RELIGION gives the percent of the population who are adherents of the faiths practiced there. Muslims, who are adherents of Islam, make up the greatest percentage for all political entities except for Israel, where a large majority of the population is Jewish followers of Judaism, and Cyprus which has a Greek Orthodox majority. The predominant Muslim sects are shown in rank order in parentheses following the Muslim listing.

Under LANGUAGE, the official language is listed first. It is labeled (official) if space allows, and when there are more than one official languages in a country or a language is official in a particular area of a country, this is noted also.

LITERACY generally indicates the percentage of the population above the age of 15 who can read and write. There are no universal standards of literacy, so these estimates (from the CIA's *World Factbook*) are based on the most common definition available for a nation.

LIFE EXPECTANCY represents the average number of years a newborn infant can expect to live under *current* mortality levels as defined in the 2002 World Population Data Sheet of the Population Reference Bureau (PRB).

TROOPS list both active and reserves. Most recent figures are from *The Military Balance: 2002-2003,* International Institute for Strategic Studies.

GDP PER CAPITA is Gross Domestic Product divided by midyear population estimates. GDP estimates are from the CIA World Factbook 2002. They use the purchasing power parity (PPP) conversion factor designed to equalize the purchasing powers of different currencies. GDP methodology can be found on their website. Individual income estimates such as GDP PER CAPITA are some of the many indicators used to assess a nation's well-being. But as statistical averages, they hide extremes of poverty and wealth. Furthermore, they take no account of factors that affect quality of life, such as environmental degradation, educational opportunities, and health care.

CRUDE OIL RESERVES show in billions of barrels the quantity of crude oil indicated by geological and engineering studies that can be recovered in the future from known underground oil deposits under existing economic and operating conditions. Primary data comes from the U.S. Department of Energy's *International Energy Annual*: Table 8.1, World Crude Oil and Natural Gas Reserves, January 1, 2001, at www.eia.doe.gov/emeu/iea/table81.html.

ECONOMY is divided into three general categories: Industry, Agriculture, and Exports. Because of structural limitations, only the primary industries (IND), agricultural commodities (AGR), and exports (EXP) are reported. Agriculture serves as an umbrella term for not only crops but also livestock, products, and fish. In the interest of conciseness, agriculture for the independent nations presents, when applicable but not limited to, two major crops, followed respectively by leading entries for livestock, products, and fish.

AREA COMPARISON: The area of each country is divided by the area of the 48 contiguous United States, which is 8,018,000 square kilometers (3,095,765 square miles). The country shape superimposed over the map of the 48 contiguous U.S. presents a visual comparison of the respective areas of the two countries.

NA indicates that data are not available.

PUBLISHED BY THE NATIONAL GEOGRAPHIC SOCIETY

John M. Fahey, Jr. *President and Chief Executive Officer*
Gilbert M. Grosvenor *Chairman of the Board*
Nina D. Hoffman *Executive Vice President*

PREPARED BY THE BOOK DIVISION

Kevin Mulroy *Vice President and Editor-in-Chief*
Charles Kogod *Illustrations Director*
Marianne R. Koszorus *Design Director*

STAFF FOR THIS ATLAS

Carl Mehler *Project Editor and Director of Maps*

Laura Exner, Thomas L. Gray, Joseph F. Ochlak, Nicholas P. Rosenbach *Map Editors*

Sven M. Dolling, Thomas L. Gray, Joseph F. Ochlak, Nicholas P. Rosenbach, The M Factory, XNR Productions *Map Research and Compilation*

Matt Chwastyk, Gregory Ugiansky *Map Production Managers*

James Huckenpahler, The M Factory, Mapping Specialists, Martin S. Walz, XNR Productions *Map Production*

NATIONAL GEOGRAPHIC MAPS

Kevin Allen *Director of Map Services*

David B. Miller *Principal Geographer*

Jan D. Morris *Project Manager, Geographic Information System (GIS) Support*

Mary Kate Cannistra, Windy A. Robertson *GIS Support*

Michael Horner, Eric Lindstrom, Bey Wesley *Contributing Geographers*

David Griffin *Book Design*

Sadie Quarrier *Photo Editor*

Carolinda E. Averitt, K. M. Kostyal, Rebecca Lescaze, Alex Novak *Text Editors*

Meredith Wilcox *Photo Assistant*

R. Gary Colbert *Production Director*

MANUFACTURING AND QUALITY CONTROL

Christopher A. Leidel *Chief Financial Officer*
Phillip L. Schlosser *Managing Director*
John T. Dunn *Technical Director*
Vincent P. Ryan *Manager*

One of the world's largest nonprofit scientific and educational organizations, the National Geographic Society was founded in 1888 "for the increase and diffusion of geographic knowledge." Fulfilling this mission, the Society educates and inspires millions every day through its magazines, books, television programs, videos, maps and atlases, research grants, the National Geographic Bee, teacher workshops, and innovative classroom materials. The Society is supported through membership dues, charitable gifts, and income from the sale of its educational products. This support is vital to National Geographic's mission to increase global understanding and promote conservation of our planet through exploration, research, and education.

For more information, please call 1-800-NGS LINE (647-5463) or write to the following address:

National Geographic Society
1145 17th Street N.W.
Washington, D.C. 20036-4688 U.S.A.

Visit the Society's Web site at
www.nationalgeographic.com.

Reproduction by Quad Graphics, Alexandria, Virginia
Printed and bound by R. R. Donnelley & Sons, Roanoke, Virginia

Printed in the U.S.A.

Library of Congress Cataloging in Publication data is available upon request.

TP: ISBN 0-7922-5066-4
HC: ISBN 0-7922-6460-6

Cover (L to R): "Wailing Wall" foreground, Dome of the Rock, Jerusalem; map of Iraq; Palestinian in Amman; Ultra-Orthodox Jew at the "Wailing Wall"; Saudi Arabia

Below: SeaWiFS satellite composite image collected during the boreal spring